Presence

PRESENCE

*Philosophy, History, and Cultural Theory
for the Twenty-First Century*

Edited by
RANJAN GHOSH AND ETHAN KLEINBERG

CORNELL UNIVERSITY PRESS
ITHACA AND LONDON

Copyright © 2013 by Cornell University

All rights reserved. Except for brief quotations in a review, this book, or parts thereof, must not be reproduced in any form without permission in writing from the publisher. For information, address Cornell University Press, Sage House, 512 East State Street, Ithaca, New York 14850.

First published 2013 by Cornell University Press
Printed in the United States of America

Library of Congress Cataloging-in-Publication Data
Presence (Ithaca, N.Y.)
   Presence : philosophy, history and cultural theory for the twenty-first century / edited by Ranjan Ghosh and Ethan Kleinberg.
       pages cm
   Includes bibliographical references.
   ISBN 978-0-8014-5220-8 (cloth : alk. paper)
   1. Presence (Philosophy) 2. Representation (Philosophy) 3. Philosophy and civilization. I. Ghosh, Ranjan, editor of compilation. II. Kleinberg, Ethan, 1967- editor of compilation. III. Kleinberg, Ethan, 1967- Presence in absentia. IV. Title.

BD355.P74 2013
901—dc23
                                    2013015491

Cornell University Press strives to use environmentally responsible suppliers and materials to the fullest extent possible in the publishing of its books. Such materials include vegetable-based, low-VOC inks and acid-free papers that are recycled, totally chlorine-free, or partly composed of nonwood fibers. For further information, visit our website at www.cornellpress.cornell.edu.

Cloth printing   10 9 8 7 6 5 4 3 2 1

All chapters except 4 and 9 were previously published in Ranjan Ghosh, ed., "Making Sense of Presence: Philosophy, History and Politics," *Storia della Storiographia* 55 (2009), and are reprinted by permission of the Freiburg Institute for Advanced Studies.

In memory of Roger I. Simon

Contents

Prologue   1
Ethan Kleinberg

1. Presence *in Absentia*   8
   Ethan Kleinberg

2. Be Here Now: Mimesis and the History of Representation   26
   Vincent P. Pecora

3. Meaning, Truth, and Phenomenology   45
   Mark Bevir

4. Of Photographs, Puns, and Presence   62
   Susan A. Crane

5. The Public Rendition of *Images Médusées*: Exhibiting Souvenir Photographs Taken at Lynchings in America   79
   Roger I. Simon

6. The Presence of Immigrants, or Why Mexicans and
   Arabs Look Alike   103
   John Michael

7. Transcultural Presence   122
   Bill Ashcroft

8. "It Disturbs Me with a Presence": Hindu History and
   What Meaning Cannot Convey   144
   Ranjan Ghosh

9. The Presence and Conceptualization of Contemporary
   Protesting Crowds   160
   Suman Gupta

   Epilogue: Presence Continuous   186
   Ranjan Ghosh

   Notes   199

   Contributors   221

Presence

Prologue

Ethan Kleinberg

This volume seeks to investigate the theoretical paradigm known as "presence." The odd and wonderful thing about the philosophy of "presence" is that it attempts to understand, or at least convey, the ways that the past is literally with us in the present in significant and material ways. It is a turn away from the seemingly endless interpretations manufactured by "theory" and a return to a relationship with the past predicated on our unmediated access to actual things that we can feel and touch and that bring us into contact with the past. There are differing ideas at play as to how the past presses into the present and the scope of the "presence effect": that is, the nonproximate presence of persons, of moods, of environment. In short, things that we cannot touch but which nonetheless touch us. As a result, in all variants there is an emphasis on the "real" and the "material." This makes "presence" a postlinguistic or postdiscursive theory that seeks to challenge current understandings of "meaning" or "interpretation," or both, and for many this entails a rejection of constructivism and textualism via a mode of academic engagement that reestablishes contact with material reality.

But while "presence" is a movement away from the notion of constructed meaning and toward an engagement with things (the past included) that actually exist, it would be a mistake to assume that it is a return to the positivism or realism that characterized much academic discourse before the "linguistic turn." Frank Ankersmit puts it this way: "It is certainly distressing that the liberation of philosophy from the narrow straits of transcendentalism that we may find in their [Jacques Derrida, Hans-Georg Gadamer, Richard Rorty] writings did change so desperately little that it left the world of history, of representation, of our experience of art, music, and of the more existential aspects of the *condition humaine* as unexplained and devoid of philosophical interest as had been the case in the heyday of logical positivism."[1] Indeed, in some ways it is the failures of these earlier movements that allowed for the ascendancy of the later ones. But this is because "we have long been led astray by the phenomenon of 'meaning'—first by pursuing it, then by forswearing it."[2] So while on one level "presence" is presented as a counter to traditional understandings of "meaning," it is also presented as a response to the attack on meaning (Whitean representationalism, Derridean deconstruction, Gadamerian hermeneutics, Rortian contructivism) that conserves the category as essential for understanding and communication but demotes its status in terms of our relation to the past and other non-proximate, though nevertheless present, conditions.

Over the past five years, "presence" has developed into one of the most important trends (and theoretical lenses) in the philosophy of history and the humanities. Much of this development has taken place in the pages of the journal *History and Theory* through numerous articles engaging "presence" as well as a special forum on the subject featuring Frank Ankersmit, Michael Bentley, Ewa Domanska, Hans Gumbrecht, and Eelco Runia. In Ankersmit's magisterial and provocative work *Sublime Historical Experience* he presents the movement as a shift "away from language toward experience" in the attempt to reclaim "meaning" from the clutches of language and representationalism.[3] But interest in, and the possibilities for, this theoretical paradigm has moved well beyond the specialized field of the philosophy of history. Although the movement's philosophical origins can be traced to earlier thinkers such as Martin Heidegger and Gadamer it came to a fuller articulation in Jean-Luc Nancy's work from 1993, *The Birth to Presence*.[4] More recently, Hans Gumbrecht's book, *Production of Presence: What Meaning Cannot Convey*, situated "presence" in a dialogue about the role and place of the humanities in the twenty-first century and now the immanent, material, and actual implications of the "presence" model continue to stir great interest from scholars in cultural studies, political theory, and media studies.

This book expands on this trend by providing the first multidisciplinary set of chapters on "presence." While maintaining sensitivity to, and awareness of, the connection between the "presence" model and its philosophical origins, this book extrapolates fresh templates of ideas drawing on history, sociology, literature, cultural theory, media studies, photography, memory, and political theory. Such treatment provides a wider and more eclectic scope to the possible applications of the "presence" paradigm that opens the model to scholars in a wider range of fields and disciplines. Beyond the multidisciplinary approach, this book is also the first venture to provide a serious critique of "presence" in its attempt to foster genuine intellectual debate and discussion that we hope will propel and refine the theoretical model and disciplinary possibilities of "presence." In what follows I hope to situate the contributions to the book so as to provide the reader with a roadmap of the ways that the chapters compiled engage and expand upon the presence paradigm.

The book is loosely divided into three groups. The first section provides a critical overview of the "presence" paradigm that informs the reader of its origins and basic precepts while offering original innovations as to where this movement might go. Thus we begin with three critical engagements, one from the perspective of intellectual history, one from that of literary criticism, and one from the philosophy of history (though all blur the lines between traditional disciplinary scholarship). In my chapter, "*Presence* in Absentia" I follow the ghosts of Jacob Marley and Christmas Present in Charles Dickens's *A Christmas Carol* to provide the reader with an intellectual history of the current incarnation of the "presence" paradigm that explores and articulates some of its key claims in the work of thinkers such as Ankersmit, Gumbrecht, Domanska, and Runia. I then trace the claims back to some of the earliest articulations of the model in the work of Runia and, in so doing, I parse out the role of thinkers such as Giambattista Vico and Sigmund Freud in the service of "presence." In the end I return to Dickens to offer some critiques and counters to the movement. In Vincent Pecora's contribution, "Be Here Now: Mimesis and the History of Representation,"

Pecora focuses on the work of art, poetry, and the place of aesthetics in understanding the relation of presence and representation. By engaging with the works of Gumbrecht and Elaine Scarry, Pecora considers whether the turn to presence is a return to the modernist agon of mimesis versus representation in which the "discovery" of the viability of concepts such as beauty and "presence" are primarily a rediscovery of the lure of a redemptive mimesis in the face of a fallen world of representation. Mark Bevir's "Meaning, Truth, and Phenomenology" provides a deep philosophical investigation that draws the work of Derrida into our discussion in Bevir's attempt to reconstitute phenomenology after deconstruction and "presence." Here we see that Bevir shares the critique of Derrida and other "postmodern" theorists such as Hayden White offered by thinkers such as Ankersmit, Gumbrecht, and Runia but not the alternatives. When Bevir turns to "presence" it is from a postfoundationalist perspective.

The second section allows the reader to build on the exposition and critique offered in the first by offering three original case studies that utilize "presence" to investigate the role and place of photographs in our relation with the past, with memory, and with the "other." In "Of Photographs, Puns, and Presence," Susan A. Crane's playful approach belies her serious investigation into the ways that historians use photographs as she questions how photographs both establish and overcome categorical definitions of history through "presence." Crane engages with the theorists of "presence" but also casts her gaze back to the work of Wilhelm Dilthey to provide a philosophy of history that supports appreciation for a "mind-constructed" world of presence. In this way she endeavors to move photographs from the category of self-evident historical object and into a more metaphysically risky realm of historical knowledge. Roger Simon's contribution, "The Public Rendition of *Images Médusée*: Exhibiting Souvenir Photographs Taken at Lynchings in America," explores the question of how might the "presence" encountered in the display and viewer reception of a series of lynching (or other atrocity) photographs be understood as a force to thought and action. This then provokes the subsequent question as to the ways these displays can be either progressive, in leading the viewer to overcome ethical lapses of the past, or debilitating by, distracting the viewer's gaze away from atrocities committed in the present (or both). As Simon works through these questions he also examines the way that the exhibition logic organizing the public presentation of these photos is implicated in the viewer's response.

John Michael, by contrast, looks to one specific photograph to approach the "Presence of Immigrants, or Why Mexicans and Arabs Look Alike." In his chapter, Michael marshals the focus on aesthetics as an embrace of "presence" and a rejection of meaning that Gumbrecht champions as a program for literary studies to ask about the role aesthetics plays in the geopolitical world. Swiveling between his reading of a photograph of a family in front of the Gaza-Egypt border and that of Harriet Beecher Stowe's *Uncles Tom's Cabin*, Michael challenges the reader to consider a genealogy that associates ethics and aesthetics via the presence of others. In so doing Michael argues that at least since David Hume and Adam Smith, the presence of others implied in the question of ethics has entailed aesthetics in a way closely akin to what Gumbrecht means by "presence."

The final section segues naturally from Michael's discussion of the "presence" of others by exploring the ways that the "presence" paradigm can provide an opening to the other in the realm of literary studies, postcolonial history, and cultural studies. The overall focus of this section can perhaps best be summed up by the title of Ashcroft's chapter, "Transcultural Presence." Ashcroft seeks to discuss a production of "presence" that is not so much a moment of aesthetic intensity as it is a moment of cultural transformation. To do so he looks to postcolonial poetry in translation to demonstrate how the construct of "transcultural presence," developed through analysis of reading, proposes a more constructive dialogue, a zone of contact that produces a new cultural space based on the possibility of meaning beyond interpretation. The payoff for such an approach, Ashcroft demonstrates, is that "otherness" is encouraged but not captured in the act of interpretative writing. In coeditor Ranjan Ghosh's contribution, "'It Disturbs Me with a Presence': Hindu History and What Meaning Cannot Convey," Ghosh argues that "presence" is complicit in the understanding of Hindu history and the unfolding ramifications of the contemporary essentialist and sectarian Hindu attitude toward the "other." By placing the concept of "presence" into dialogue with the Indian concept of history, or *itihasa*, Ghosh demonstrates some areas in our understanding of religion, tradition, and historiography where presence manages to convey what "meaning" under the Western principles of historical understanding has failed to comprehend. Suman Gupta's "The Presence and Conceptualization of Contemporary Protesting Crowds" completes this section as Gupta brings the category of presence to bear on recent and current political events. Gupta argues that contemporary crowd formations, especially those that gather to express political protests, often fracture the unity of conventional ontological assumptions about what a "crowd" is or may be. Beginning with early sociological accounts of crowds by Gustave le Bon and Georg Simmel, Gupta reevaluates the definition and use of "crowd" by pressing into the ways that "transnational massings" in 2003 and the gatherings of crowds that characterized the Arab Spring of 2010 have made manifest the discontinuities between mainstream media representations of the crowd as an identifiable "mass" and the self-understanding of social media groupings as transnational presence.

Finally, Ranjan Ghosh's epilogue reflects on the poetics of "presence" and the promise of the movement for scholarship to come.

Thus, whereas some chapters, such as Mark Bevir's, are deeply philosophical in nature, others, like those of Vincent Pecora, Ethan Kleinberg, and Bill Ashcroft, work in the interstices of literature, history, and philosophy. Where Ranjan Ghosh's chapter deals with the infusion of "presence" in our understanding of Indian history, the work of John Michael brings concepts of foreignness and otherness "home" to reflect on American social practices. In the work of Susan A. Crane and that of Roger Simon we see strikingly different notions of the place and utility of photographs for understanding and working through our relation with the past. And Suman Gupta's contribution points the way toward analyses of the future as one could imagine his engagement with the "presence" of the (virtual) crowd applied to the netizens of China or Occupy Wall Street.

It should also be noted that the aim of this collection is *not* to construct some sort of orthodox methodology or definition of presence but rather to ask scholars from differing disciplines and approaches to see what they can do with this paradigm. For some of the contributors, such as myself, this involves a critical engagement with previous articulations of the presence paradigm. For others, it involves a reimagination of how this real and immediate engagement with the nonproximate object that is the past might be applied to our relationship and understanding of other nonproximate objects or conditions. Finally, for some it involves an attempt to construct a synthesis between the discursive strategies of theorists such as Derrida and the desire to reconnect with the material and the real as announced in "presence." What these diverse but overlapping chapters have in common is a shared commitment to investigate this postlinguistic or postdiscursive attempt to return to the real, to material objects and conditions, and to push the paradigm of "presence" beyond its current uses and incarnations in pursuit of new philosophies, histories, and cultural theories for the twenty-first century.

1

Presence *in Absentia*

Ethan Kleinberg

> The past is never dead. It's not even past.
> WILLIAM FAULKNER, *Requiem for a Nun*

> If we were not perfectly convinced that Hamlet's Father died before the play began, there would be nothing more remarkable in his taking a stroll at night, in an easterly wind, upon his own ramparts, than there would be in any other middle-age gentleman rashly turning out after dark in a breezy spot—say Saint Paul's Churchyard for instance—literally to astonish his son's weak mind.
> CHARLES DICKENS, *A Christmas Carol*

"Marley was dead: to begin with."[1] So opens Dickens's classic tale of Christmas redemption, and it is with the ghost of Jacob Marley that I want to begin this exploration of the concept of "presence" in relation to the project of history. Dickens's point is that if time were not out of joint, if Marley was not dead and we were not absolutely sure of his ghostly, spectral, and immaterial nature, then "nothing wonderful" could come of the story. To be sure, Marley is not the only ghost in Dickens's *A Christmas Carol* but the other three have a strikingly different nature. For Dickens, Marley is the only ghost whose death concerns us because he is the only ghost who is out of time. This is to say that unlike the ghost of Marley, the Ghosts of Christmas Past, Present, and Future appear to be well jointed in terms of our classic understanding of temporality. The past precedes the present, which is followed by the future, and each is announced by the ordered sounding of the clock. But while these three Ghosts are bound by this temporal structure they too are each distinct. Not unlike the past itself, the Ghost of Christmas Past is a figure that "fluctuated in its distinctness: being now a thing with one arm, now with one leg, now with twenty legs, now a pair of legs without a head, now a head without a body: of which dissolving parts, no outline would be visible in the dense gloom wherein they melted away. And in the very wonder of this, it would be itself again; distinct and clear as ever." In the gloom the Ghost of Christmas Past emits a "bright clear jet of light" from the crown of its head though it also possesses a "great extinguisher of a cap."[2] The futural Ghost of Christmas Yet to Come is a figure shrouded in a "deep black garment which concealed its head, its face, its form" and whose "mysterious presence filled him [Scrooge] with a solemn dread."[3] By contrast, the Ghost of Christmas Present is a gregarious fellow, a "jolly Giant, glorious to see" seated before a "mighty blaze that roared up the chimney" upon a "kind of throne" made up of "turkeys, geese, game, poultry, brawn, great joints of meat, sucking-pigs, long wreaths of sausages, mince pies, plum puddings, barrels of oysters, red-hot chestnuts, cherry cheeked apples, juicy oranges, immense twelfth-cakes, and seething bowls of punch, that made the chamber dim with their delicious steam."[4] And here we should think about the way Hans Gumbrecht differentiates "presence effects" from "meaning effects" in that "presence effects appeal exclusively to the senses."[5] A more sensuous or welcoming figure could not be imagined: "'Come in!' exclaimed the Ghost. 'Come in! and know me better, man!'"

Thus even beyond the material comfort one receives in his presence, there seems more to be gained from the Ghost of Christmas Present than from the others. The past is gone and the future is yet to come. It is only in the present that one can actually do things; that one can change in ways that of course cannot rectify the past but that can serve the future. This is precisely what happens to Scrooge and in this light one can certainly see the attraction of a focus on presence and the present: on a philosophy of history that eschews the endless turning over of the past or fruitless speculation on the future in favor of an emphasis on actual things that are present here and now. In the words of Eelco Runia, "'Presence,' in my view, is 'being in touch'—either literally or figuratively—with people, things, events, and feelings that made you into the person you are."[6] Thus "before" and "after" meet in the very real place of the present, safe from the brackish ontological waters of the past and the uncertainty and anxiety of the future.[7] One might say that the present "is what it is" and in this respect the present distinguishes itself from the past and the future because it positions itself as a category of space and not time.⁸ As such the interpretive paradigm of "presence" takes priority over the other temporal modes because it investigates the place where a "whisper of life" is "breathed into what has become routine and clichéd—it is fully realizing things instead of just taking them for granted."⁹ It is a place of change and a place of redemption or so it appears.¹⁰ This certainly seems to be the case for Scrooge who "fully realized things" that he had previously "taken for granted" that fine Christmas morning. For Scrooge as for thinkers such as Frank Ankersmit, Michael Bentley, Ewa Domanska, Hans Gumbrecht, and Eelco Runia the present is where they want to be and the present of "presence" is a place of experience and unmediated contact with material things freed from the ambivalence and multiplicity of recollection, interpretation, and narration embodied in the shape shifting Ghost of Christmas Past and protected from the deathly specter (or specter of inevitable death) of the future embodied in the Ghost of Christmas Yet to Come. Thus one can understand Scrooge's compulsion to retreat to the inviting chamber of the present and away from the specters of death and absence that haunt both his past and future, but on what is our current compulsion for "presence" predicated?¹¹

The Return of the Real

For Eelco Runia, the publication of Hayden White's *Metahistory* was a watershed moment that led to a "process in which the philosophy of history was emptied of reflection on what had actually happened in the past . . . and inaugurated the heyday of 'metahistoriography.'"¹² Runia laments the ways that the historical profession became obsessed with the construction of narratives about the past at the expense of losing touch with the past itself. Gumbrecht and Ankersmit expand this critique by enlarging the field to include other figures and movements of the "linguistic turn." Gumbrecht tells us that he has

> grown weary of this intellectual one-way traffic as it has been based on and upheld by a certain narrow and yet totalizing understanding of hermeneutics. I also have long experienced the absolutism of all post-linguistic turn varieties of philosophy as intellectually limiting, and I have not found much consolation in what I want to characterize as the "linguistic existentialism"

of deconstruction, that is the sustained complaint and melancholia (in its endless variations) about the alleged incapacity of language to refer to the things of the world.[13]

Thus, Gumbrecht believes that the current emphasis on the production of meaning via language that dominates higher academia, the "culture of interpretation" as he calls it, has led to "intellectual relativism" and our estrangement from the past.[14] This is to say that the quest to understand how historical "meaning" is constructed led to a subsequent assault on meaning that has rendered it virtually meaningless. "In the last three or four decades—philosophers of history have tried to purge their discipline of attempts to establish meaning."[15] Runia, Gumbrecht, and Ankersmit all seek to move beyond this climate of constructivism and to return to what is real. Ankersmit describes a shift "away from language toward experience" and attempts to reclaim "meaning" from the clutches of language and representationalism.[16] To Ankersmit's mind, "philosophy of history, in the last half century, has predominantly been an attempt to translate the success of philosophy of language to historical writing" but "'Theory' and meaning no longer travel in the same direction; meaning has now found a new and more promising traveling companion in experience."[17] All three call for a turn away from the seemingly endless interpretations manufactured by "theory" and a return to a relationship with the past predicated on our unmediated access to actual things that we can feel and touch and that bring us into contact with the past. "Rather than having to think, always and endlessly, what else there could be, we sometimes seem to connect with a layer in our existence that simply wants the things of the world close to our skin."[18] In the same vein, Domanska states: "I am trying to rethink the material aspects of traces of the past in a context other than semiotics, discourse theory, or representation theory, and to focus the analysis of those traces on an aspect that is marginalized or neglected by traditional notions of the source. That is, I mean to focus on the materiality or thingness of the trace rather than on its textuality and content."[19] In this sense, the paradigm of presence is an explicit rejection of discursive theory and can be seen as part of a larger backlash against postmodernism and the perceived dominance of language.[20] It is an attempt to reconnect "meaning" with something "real."

The most obvious targets are thinkers such as Jacques Derrida, Richard Rorty, Hayden White, and those historical theorists who have advocated a constructivist or deconstructive approach to the study of history via the investigation into language ("textuality and content").[21] But it is also indicative of a larger social unease about secularism, proceduralism, and a social contract that is no longer guaranteed by either God or a fixed "human nature." If all there is "language all the way down," then there is nothing to assure the validity of the contract. I have argued elsewhere that as "we grow less and less confident in humankind's ability to provide a moral or ethical scaffold to guide us, we are left searching for a new authority to validate that which humankind has surveyed and measured."[22] This desire for stability has become all the more acute in the wake of September 11, 2001.[23] The rise of "presence" as a category of historical reflection in its more and less sublime incarnations is a direct response to this growing unease that seeks to grab the past and hold it in the present to help us divine guidance for the future. This is what Runia describes as his "focus not on the past but on the present, not on history *as what is irremediably gone*, but on *history as an ongoing process*" and the basis for his claim that "the concept of presence is a convenient way to put an edge on the issue of how exactly the past can be said to exist."[24]

"Presence" is a movement away from a constructed past and toward a past that actually exists. But it would be a mistake to assume that it is a return to the positivism or realism that characterized the philosophy of history before the "linguistic turn." Ankersmit puts it this way: "It is certainly distressing that the liberation of philosophy from the narrow straights of transcendentalism that we may find in their [Derrida, Hans-Georg Gadamer, Rorty] writings did change so desperately little that it left the world of history, of representation, of our experience of art, music, and of the more existential aspects of the *condition humaine* as unexplained and devoid of philosophical interest as had been the case in the heyday of logical positivism."[25] Indeed, in some ways it is the failures of these earlier movements that allowed for the ascendancy of the later ones. But this is because "in the philosophy of history we have long been led astray by the phenomenon of 'meaning'—first by pursuing it, then by forswearing it."[26] "Presence" is presented as a counter to meaning but also as a response to the attack on meaning exemplified in Whitean representationalism, Derridean deconstruction, Gadamerian hermeneutics, and Rortian contructivism wherein meaning is conserved as a category that is essential for understanding and communication, but demotes its status in terms of our relation to the past. Runia states:

I take the position that, on consideration, it is not meaning we want, but something else, something that is just as fundamental, something that outside the philosophy of history, in society at large, is pursued with a vehemence quite like the vehemence with which we—within the discipline—believe only meaning can be pursued. For it is, I think, not a need for meaning that manifests itself in the enthusiasm for remembrance, in the desire for monuments, in the fascination for memory. My thesis is that what is pursued in the Vietnam Veterans Memorial, in having a diamond made "from the carbon of your loved one as a memorial to their unique life," in the reading of names on that anniversary of the attack on the World Trade Center, in the craze for reunions, and in a host of comparable phenomena, is *not* "meaning" but "presence."[27]

For Runia, "presence—being in touch with reality—is just as basic as meaning" but our quest for "meaning" has been misguided because it is actually a response to our desire for "presence."[28] So presence offers a return to the real that can in turn help us rehabilitate our belief in meaning, and it does so by literally bringing the past into the present. But what is the transhistorical mechanism by which one can do this? What brings the past into the present?

The Storehouse of Presence

Runia suggests that it can be gleaned in the way that presence allows the past to be both present and absent at once.[29] Investigations into "meaning," of both the epistemological and ontological order, focus on one or the other and thus miss out on the connection between the two. Runia presents this connection in terms of the "problem of continuity and discontinuity," which is in turn a "symptom of the determination to account for the fact that our past—though irremediably gone—may feel more real than the world we inhabit." So the trick is to establish a discourse of presence that does not "explain discontinuity away in some kind of 'meaning,' but gives it its due," and, for Runia, *metonymy* is a "surprisingly suitable tool to do so.... My thesis is, to put it somewhat paradoxically, that metonymy is a metaphor for discontinuity. Or rather, that metonymy is a metaphor for the entwinement of continuity and discontinuity."[30] Runia asserts that the trope of metonymy allows one to take account of the ways that the past is contiguous with the present; that is the way the past touches the present to affect both continuity and discontinuity. But "coming to grips with discontinuity requires an adjustment many philosophers of history will hesitate to make." As previously noted the adjustment is "to focus not on the past but on the present, not on history *as what is irremediably gone*, but on *history as an ongoing process*."³¹ Furthermore, Runia tells us that this adjustment is

> not unlike the momentous modification Freud came to make in his approach to the past of his patients. Somewhere around 1900 Freud stopped heading for that past *straight away*. Instead of delivering himself to the alluring stories his patients volunteered to tell him, he opted, not for a Rankean "turning to the sources," but for a radical (and counterintuitive) "presentism." By sticking to the present as steadfastly as he could, by exploring the symptoms and the transferences that made themselves *felt in the here and now* of the analytic encounter, Freud was able to come forward with much more "original," much more "convincing," much more "effective," versions of the past of his patients then they had entertained themselves.³²

This quote gives us some purchase on the transhistorical workings of presence and we will need to return to Freud, but for Runia what is important is that Freud recognized the ways that focusing exclusively on the past "never takes you anywhere but to places in sight of your departure, whereas exploring the present may have you somewhere, someplace, tumbling into depths you didn't suspect were there." Thus the historian of presence "walks the plane of time," as Runia calls it, scanning the surface of both "present day reality" and the "discipline of history" ("the assemblage of texts, codes, habits, topics, trends, and fashions") with an "evenly suspended attention" as in the therapeutic session advocated by Freud.³³ In doing so we come to see that both surfaces are "*at one and the same time*, a tightly knit, 'organic,' functioning whole as well as a jumble of things that are genetically, ontologically, and existentially separate." In other words, the Freudian attention to the surface of the present reveals a wonder of continuity and discontinuity:

> "Continuity" and "discontinuity," that is, *not* in a historical, temporal, vertical" sense, but in the *spatial* "horizontal" sense of "being thoroughly interwoven" and "radically contiguous." Trying to envision continuity and discontinuity

in its temporal sense is so hard as to be virtually impossible. To understand continuity and discontinuity requires being able "to walk around" the events in question—but as soon as we start to look backwards, the second dimension needed for approaching events from different angles somehow gets lost.[34]

Here, Runia asks us to cede temporal investigation in favor of a spatial one that will expose the ways that the past is contiguous with the present. Rather than focusing on an impossible object irretrievably lost in the past we should instead concentrate on things and places in the here and now even if these things are metonymical markers for other things or events that are temporally absent. "Consequently, a metonymy is a 'presence in absence' not just in the sense that it presents something that isn't there, but also in the sense that in the absence (or at least the radical inconspicuousness) that *is* there, the thing that isn't there is still present." It is this contiguous relation that the present has with the past that allows the past to affect the present in real ways through the experience of the individual. "Metonymical 'presence in absence,' in other words, works both ways: up *to* the present, and downward from *the* present." For Runia, these two ways correspond to two aspects of Giambattista Vico's "topics": invention and storage. "As *inventio*, metonymy transposes something to the present, or more correctly: as *inventio*, metonymy has *made* the surface as we know it; the present consists of metonymies that were once *Fremdkörper* [foreign substances] but are now taken for granted. As 'storage,' metonymy contains what was left behind. But what it stands for can still be found in—or, as Vico would say, 'invented' out of—what he may find on the plane of time."[35] Of course it is storage, what was left behind, that provides the material for invention that may be innovative and shocking at first but soon comes to be accepted as convention or forgotten and again filed away in storage. But invention never runs dry because there is always plenty of the past (all of it in fact) left in storage waiting to be unpacked. In both cases, however, this takes place in the here and now of the present through actual engagement with material things and places.

As the name suggests, the "plane of time" is a spatial category where the temporal past is accessed in the places of the present. These are common places "in the sense that anybody can visit them, that they lie open for examination ... But they are not 'commonplaces'—they are not empty but full, they are not shallow but deep, not dead but alive. They are repositories of time—or, perhaps even better, the places where history can get a hold of you. Places are, in short, storehouses of 'presence.' "[36] This has an enormous impact on the writing of history because, as Ankersmit notes, it broaches the question as to whether "the past can actually be carried into the present by historical representation, in much the same way that one may carry a souvenir from a foreign country into one's own." And to which he responds, "Under such conditions, the past would be made 'present' in the present in the most literal sense of the word."[37] It is not surprising that to support this claim Ankersmit turns to an earlier article by Runia and it is with this article that we will return to Freud in an attempt to understand the transhistorical workings of this storehouse and its relation to space and time.

Parallel Processes: Presence *in Absentia*

Ankersmit turns to Runia's article "'Forget about It': 'Parallel Processing' in the Srebrenica Report," which was published in *History and Theory* in October 2004.[38] The article itself is illuminating because it precedes Runia's fully formed articulation of "presence" and instead focuses on the phenomenon of "parallel processes."[39] In this piece, Runia sought to articulate one way that the past is literally present in the here and now by exploring the ways that historical accounts of past events parallel those very happenings. Specifically, Runia sought to show the ways that the NIOD Report, the Dutch report on the 1995 massacre in Srebrenica, parallels the event it describes. Runia presents the "way the NIOD researchers unwittingly replicated several key aspects of the events they studied, and discusses some instances in which paralleling highlights precisely those features of the events under consideration that are hard to come to terms with."[40] The starting point for Runia's analysis is Dominick LaCapra's assertion that "when you study something, at some level you always have a tendency to repeat the problems you are studying"; there is something ironic in this connection as LaCapra's work is regularly associated with the language-based construction/deconstruction of meaning that becomes a target of the presence movement in its return to the real.[41] Building on this assertion Runia tells us that "parallel processes are an important manifestation of this tendency." The concept of "parallel processes," in Runia's usage, originates in psychoanalytic supervision and refers to instances when "supervisees manifest toward their supervisors many psychic patterns which parallel processes that are prominent in their interactions with their patients."[42] In essence, the behavior of the patient is transferred to the analyst who then exhibits this same behavior toward the supervisor. But the key to this move in relation to the formation of "presence" does not lie in the issue of transference or countertransference but in the relation of two aspects of the parallel process articulated by Runia:

> When a parallel process is operative there is always a dual set of transferences and countertransferences involved—the one, the patient/therapist set, as it were *in absentia*, the other in the here and now of the supervision. Yet parallel processes are not reducible to transferences or countertransferences. Key to parallel processes is a 180 degree turn of the "middle man"—the therapist. Paralleling occurs when therapists, in the supervision setting, unconsciously identify with their patients, enact this identification, and elicit responses from the supervisors that replicate the difficulties they themselves have encountered—as *therapists*—in the therapy.[43]

In the Srebrenica article, the emphasis is on the ways that historians, like therapists, unconsciously identify with their objects of study and thus unwittingly replicate the difficulties present in the object of study. Thus aspects of the past that are not actively sought for smuggle themselves into the present through the historian. This then justifies the turn to Freudian surface analysis articulated in the "Presence" article but already announced in this earlier piece. "Instead of delving deep, one had better stay at the surface. The important thing, as Freud said, is to conceive of the illness 'not as something of the past but as a force that influences the present.'"[44] It is precisely these unconscious reenactments of the past that allow us access to what was actually there but only if we pay attention to the ways they surprise us in the present. This is one aspect of Runia's "plane of time."

There is another aspect of this statement in the Srebrenica article that is undeveloped but becomes the most important, and problematic, factor in the later articulations of "presence." In his move toward the, at the time, more important point of showing how therapists and historians unconsciously mirror their object of investigation, Runia quite casually tells us that the parallel process operates as a dual set of transferences and countertransferences, "the one, the patient/therapist set, as it were *in absentia*, the other in the here and now of the supervision." It is this move, uncoupled from explicit reference to the transferences and countertransferences of the individual, that is the basis for his presentation of the plane of time as "present day reality" and the "discipline of history." In effect, the *in absentia* of the patient/therapist set is the absence of the historical event and the here and now of supervision is the presence of present-day reality. This then becomes the embodiment of the entwining of continuity and discontinuity that is exposed by metonymy as "presence."

But the entire move is predicated on, tied to, the unconscious reenactment of the past event. Thus the transhistorical mechanism that allows the past to literally be present is a psychohistorical one as in Freud's *Totem and Taboo* and *Moses and Monotheism*. In this psychohistorical model it is an early trauma that is conserved and repeated not by the individuals but by their descendants. Here Freud asserts that there is a permanent psychic mechanism that is at play and given the correct conditions the archaic memory of the event can be triggered. Thus, in Freud's telling, the murder of the Egyptian Moses turns out to be the repetition of the primal killing of the father as enunciated in *Totem and Taboo*.[45] Richard Bernstein tells us this acting out is the result of a psychic memory but triggered by specific historical events: "The great deed and misdeed of primeval times, the murder of the father, was brought home to the Jews, for fate decreed that they should repeat it on the person of Moses, an eminent father substitute."[46] Freud goes on to show that, as with the first patricide, this crime is also repressed and the memory lies latent until such historical conditions occur as to bring it forth again with the arrival of a second Moses and the transformation of the Yahweh religion. Freud's analysis of Moses is not based on any hard evidence of what happened in the past but is predicated on the discoveries of psychoanalysis in the present. As in Runia's presence paradigm, the analysis of the historic event (Moses's role in founding Judaism) *in absentia* is predicated on a psychoanalytic investigation of the here and now (the current condition of Judaism in Freud's present). Freud is a perfect touchstone for Runia and the other thinkers of presence because he advocates a scientific, secular, and material methodology for investigating the past based on the immanent condition of the present. This is to say that he advocates a means by which one can literally access the past but that denies the possibility of transcendent meaning. This transhistorical mechanism is modified by Runia and appropriated to greater and lesser degrees by Ankersmit, Domanska, and Gumbrecht. But, as I have argued elsewhere, the belief in the transhistorical nature of these models (Freudian or presence based) requires the same sort of "leap of faith" that is necessary in religious belief but now applied to the infallibility of scientific or material (modern secular) thought. Thus the seemingly neutral term "transhistorical" assumes that the model itself is able to transcend time and place to be universally applicable.[47] Even though Gumbrecht is surprised by "the suspicion (or was it rather meant to sound like praise?) that [he] had turned into a religious 'thinker'" and counters that his "desire to reconnect with the things of the world" is as strictly immanentist as "one could possibly imagine," I would argue that "presence" as conceived by these thinkers is really a postsecular articulation of transcendence that conceals its temporal leap of faith by keeping the emphasis on the material and spatial focus on what is present in the here and now.[48] In this way it is always presence that defines absence and never the converse.[49]

The *Wunderblock*

Here I would like to turn to a different piece by Freud, his "Note Upon the 'Mystic Writing-Pad'" in an effort to discern what is going on in "presence" both in relation to the "meaning based" construction/deconstruction of history and to the issue of immanence and transcendence in relation to presence and absence.[50] The note on the mystic writing-pad, the *Wunderblock*, is a meditation on the nature and limits of perception in relation to memory. The *Wunderblock* itself is a device composed of a "dark slab of brown resin or wax; over the slab is laid a thin transparent sheet, the top end of which is firmly secured to the slab while its bottom end rests on it without being fixed. This transparent sheet . . . consists of two layers, which can be detached from each other except at their two ends. The upper layer is a transparent piece of celluloid; the lower layer is made of thin translucent wax paper."[51] The trick is that one can write on the *Wunderblock* as much as one likes and then lift the two sheets to make the writing disappear. "The close contact between the waxed paper and the wax slab at the places which have been scratched (upon which the visibility depended) is thus brought to an end and it does not recur when the two surfaces come together once more."[52] Freud finds that the *Wunderblock*'s "construction shows a remarkable agreement with my hypothetical structure of our perceptual apparatus" in that it can provide "both an ever ready receptive surface and permanent traces of the notes that have been made upon it" just as our mental apparatus has an "unlimited receptive capacity for new perceptions and nevertheless lays down permanent—even though not unalterable—memory traces of them."[53] On first glance, the *Wunderblock* seems to affirm the mechanism presented by the thinkers of presence in that it demonstrates the way that the past is always available to the present via the imperceptible but undeniably present etchings on the wax slab below the two sheets. Indeed, "it is easy to discover that the permanent trace of what was written is retained upon the wax slab itself and is legible in suitable lights."[54] On this reading, the wax slab represents the past and the two sheets represent present-day reality. We can extend the analogy and say that what the theorists of presence consider problematic in meaning-based models is that they either focus on the means of writing on the top of the pad or ceaselessly lift the two sheets together to erase the writing and expose the limits of meaning.

But here too the mechanism warrants a closer look. At the end of his note, Freud asserts that the parallel between the *Wunderblock* and the perceptual apparatus of our mind reveals more than the way that the system perception-consciousness is infiltrated by the unconscious:

> It is as though the unconscious stretches out feelers, through the medium of the system *Pcpt.-Cs.* [perception-consciousness], towards the external world and hastily withdraws them as soon as they have sampled the excitations coming from it. Thus the interruptions, which in the case of the Mystic Pad have an external origin, were attributed by my hypothesis to the discontinuity in the current of innervation; and the actual breaking of contact which occurs in the Mystic Pad was replaced in my theory by the periodic nonexcitability of the perceptual system. *I further had a suspicion that this discontinuous method of functioning of the system* Pcpt.-Cs. *lies at the bottom of the origin of the concept of time.*[55]

Freud had previously articulated this claim in *Beyond the Pleasure Principle*:

> We have learnt that unconscious mental processes are in themselves "timeless." This means in the first place they are not ordered temporarily, that time does not change them in any way and that the idea of time cannot be applied to them. These are negative characteristics which can only be understood if a comparison is made with *conscious* mental processes. On the other

hand, our abstract idea of time seems to be wholly derived from the method of working of the system *Pcpt.-Cs.* and to correspond to a perception on its own part of the working method.[56]

So while the unconscious is permanently timeless and thus not susceptible to any temporal ordering, our abstract idea of time is based on the functioning of the system Pcpt.-Cs. that necessarily orders our perceptions so that consciousness can make sense of them. But we can only think the timelessness of the unconscious based on the abstract or vulgar idea of time.[57]

Runia and the thinkers of presence claim that the past is made present not in the temporal sense but in the "spatial 'horizontal' sense of 'being thoroughly interwoven' and 'radically contiguous,'" and thus they manage to avoid what is most uncanny and unsettling about the wax block, the unconscious, and the past: its radical alterity in relation to time.[58] In this light, we see that "presence" only appears to bring the traces on the wax block to the surface of the two sheets of our present and at best it lifts the protective sheet to reveal what was written below.[59] This is all the more so when one moves beyond the psychoanalytic investigation of the individual mind and to the psychohistorical investigation of the past because of its character *in absentia* that eschews the spatial component that "presence" demands. Runia is certainly aware of this when he states: "Trying to envision continuity and discontinuity in its temporal sense is so hard as to be virtually impossible. To understand continuity and discontinuity requires being able 'to walk around' the events in question—but as soon as we start to look backwards, the second dimension needed for approaching events from different angles somehow gets lost."[60] Clearly, Runia wants to make sense of the past in some fashion but this assertion leads us to another possible reading of the parallel process that is especially illuminating. What if the parallel process is not about accessing the past, but about recognizing the forces in the past that press upon us but that are not accessible. What if what is at stake is not the ability to "walk around the events in question," to make them understandable, but to recognize our relation to continuity and discontinuity in a "temporal sense," a recognition that "is so hard as to be virtually impossible." It is in this sense that one can speak of the parallel process as "uncanny."[61] On this reading, it is precisely "when the therapist does *not understand* the meaning of a patient's enacted communication, [that] he may convey the meaning to his supervisor by parallel enactment."[62] Despite the appeal to space, the thinkers of presence never get to the timeless place of the past because they remain in the most comforting moment in time: the here and now of the present.

So perhaps we can think more on the comfort "presence" affords in all of its material splendor by critically examining the comfort Scrooge finds in the Ghost of Christmas Present. After all, neither presence nor the Ghost of Christmas Present is exactly what it appears to be. To begin, the Ghost's encounter with Scrooge escapes the present by pressing into the future, the near future to be sure, but a near future far more definite than anything revealed by the Ghost of Christmas Yet to Come. And this near future is made all the more meaningful to us because of its relation to Scrooge's recent past. We see Christmas at the Cratchit household, then Christmas for Miners on a bleak and distant moor, and finally Christmas at Scrooge's nephew's house. The emphasis on space, on material things, and on experience conceals the way the Ghost moves in time much in the way that Ankersmit does when he tells us that "the past *itself* can be said to have survived the centuries and to be still present in objects that are given to us here and now.... Hence, the notion of historical experience does not necessarily require a sudden disappearance of time or some mystical union with the past, for the past can properly be said to be present in the artifacts that it has left us. They are protuberances, so to say, of the past in the present."[63] Similarly, Runia pushes the past through the present up into the future as in the ways that "in the cells and corridors of Abu Ghraib, Saddam Hussein's torture practices were so overwhelmingly present, and the sheer possibility of using them—though horrifying—loomed so large, that sooner or later the Americans *had* to repeat them."[64] The emphasis on space downplays the role of time. There is another troubling aspect of the Ghost of Christmas Present that initially went unnoticed. At the end of the evening we are told: "It was a long night if it were only a night; but Scrooge had his doubts of this, because the Christmas Holiday appeared to be condensed into the space of time they passed together. It was strange, too, that while Scrooge remained unaltered in outward form, the Ghost grew older, clearly older.... 'Are spirits' lives so short?' asked Scrooge. 'My life on this globe, is very brief,' replied the Ghost. 'It ends to-night.' "[65] Thus the spatial presence of the present is constricted and bound by a conventional or vulgar concept of time in ways that are not apparent when one focuses primarily on space.

But perhaps the strangest secret concealed by the Ghost of Christmas Present are the "two children: wretched, abject, frightful, hideous, miserable" hidden under his robes. "'They are Man's,' said the Spirit, looking down upon them. 'And they cling to me, appealing from their fathers. This boy is Ignorance. This girl is Want." Ignorance and want are both concealed by the present. "'Beware them both,' the Ghost continues, "and all of their degree, but most of all beware this boy, for on his brow I see that written which is Doom, unless the writing be erased. Deny it!'"[66] And it is in relation to the ignorance that the present conceals that I would like to return to Dickens's musings on Hamlet's Father. There is an odd way in which "presence" ignores what is most troubling about ghosts and about the past, and perhaps the future, by shifting the emphasis to place, thus privileging "presence" over "absence." Presence is comforting because it affords a place to posit oneself as self in time and in relation to real phenomena but in so doing it empties the category of its force and potency as it asserts the dominance and mastery of presence over absence. This is to say that what is uncanny about the ghost is effaced as metonymy makes absence present and in Runia's words "insinuates that there is an urgent *need* for meaning."[67] In this light the turn to presence is a return to meaning, the traveling partner of experience, and as such it is a retreat from the meaninglessness revealed in the parallel process. What is troubling and powerful about the ghost of Hamlet's Father is not that it is present (which it is) but the ways that its presence disturbs all the categories by which we make sense of the world around us. The ghost troubles both time and space and thus one cannot "walk around" it in the way that Runia suggests. We cannot actually say what the ghost means. Indeed, if one could, if Hamlet's Father was actually there, "there would be nothing more remarkable in his taking a stroll at night, in an easterly wind, upon his own ramparts, than there would be in any other middle-age gentleman rashly turning out after dark in a breezy spot."[68] In other words, if time were not out of joint there would be nothing dramatic, remarkable, or eventful (to use Gumbrecht's phrase) at all.[69]

Unlike the Ghosts of Christmas, who are all circumscribed by the temporal marker of Christmas day and who imbue their moment with an otherworldly authority, the ghost of Jacob Marley represents an existence without end and in this way evokes Emmanuel Levinas's category of the *il y a*, the "there is" of impersonal existence. For Levinas, the *il y a* is the recognition of being in all of its strangeness and alterity, as that which is beyond representation or localization and thus is completely beyond our control. It is this lack of control that makes the *il y a* so frightening because in it "the *private* existence of each term, mastered by a subject that is, loses this private character and returns to an undifferentiated background."[70] For Levinas, this anonymous and infinite being is in fact the opening to ethics because of the way it displaces the primacy of the subject as the original and proprietary owner of a position in place and time and instead asks one to consider the way that one's own presence compromises the existence of an other. For our purposes, what is important is the way that Levinas characterizes the present as a "situation in being where there is not only being in general, but there is a being, a subject."[71] Here, as in Freud's meditation on time, the timeless space of anonymous being is interrupted by the hypostasis of an individual subject that posits itself in time. All access to time and meaning now flows though the spatial position of this subject. In presence, this positing is presented as a transhistorical/transcendent portal through which meaning flows from the past to the present. What is not considered in this emphasis on space, secretly coupled to time, is the "spot trampled in a subject's taking position" and the way this spot/space serves "not only as a resistance, but also as a base, as a condition for the effort."[72]

There is a way in which the movement of "presence" actually forecloses the possibility of change and justifies the status quo through its claims to produce unmediated access to the past via a return to the real. Runia's discussion of the ways that Abu Ghraib's past conditioned the actions of individuals in the present absolves those actors of agency and in fact cedes agency and responsibility to a past that we are doomed to repeat. Hans Gumbrecht's emphasis on Heideggerian *Gelassenheit*, the patient waiting or letting things be, also describes a condition where one passively waits for something to appear and takes no action in the meantime.[73] For Ankersmit, too, the past is literally present and thus conditions the present, but in his presentation this relationship takes on a radically individualistic and seemingly incommunicable character through "sublime historical experience."[74] Thus despite the rhetorical move away from the endless game of interpretation and a return to things that really matter, there appears to be nothing to do but wait for sublime historical experience or presence to come to us. The desire for control, for a position, for real presence comes at the expense of others and it is in this sense that "nothing wonderful" can come from it. This is important for it is not the "presence" of the Ghost of Christmas Present and his heartening display of material goods or real material objects to engage every sense, nor the other two Ghosts of Christmas, important as they all may be, that is the catalyst for Scrooge's journey of redemption. No, it is the uncanny ghost of Jacob Marley that provokes the change in Scrooge and Marley was dead: to begin with.

2

BE HERE NOW

Mimesis and the History of Representation

Vincent P. Pecora

The idea that thinking about things—analyzing them, interpreting them, finding meaning in them, discovering whether they formed what G. E. Moore (following Aristotle and G. W. F. Hegel) named "organic [that is, complex and integrated] wholes" rather than just shapeless heaps, and generally looking for the relationship between "particulars" and "universals"—the idea that what we call "thinking" in such fashion should represent a signal failure of modernity is one of the grand motifs that defines modernity itself.[1] This idea also defines just about everything we might want to call the prerational (or what Martin Heidegger found in the pre-Socratics). In that sense modernity (and with this term, I mean largely what Heidegger meant, in his "Age of the World Picture," by that era between the scientific revolution, or the Renaissance, and Hiroshima, though this could obviously be extended fitfully back to the Stoics and forward to the present day) has been determined as much by the coming to fruition of rationality and social rationalization as by resistance to them.[2] Modernity in Heidegger's postmodern terms also gives us a clue to what Jacques Derrida meant by the history, but also possible closure, of Western philosophy from the Stoics to the present, the history of "onto-theology" in which the pursuit of "presence"—the fullness and permanence of the origin, the end or final purpose, speech, mind, and being, that is, of ἀρχή, τέλος, λόγος, νόος, and ἐόν—is revealed to be no more than a peculiarity of what Heidegger called "our Western languages": "languages of metaphysical thinking, each in its own way."[3] For Heidegger there remained an "open question," that is, "whether the nature of Western languages is in itself marked with the exclusive brand of metaphysics, and thus marked permanently by onto-theo-logic, or whether these languages offer other possibilities of utterance—and that means at the same time of a telling silence [*sagenden Nichtsagens*]."[4] This became the philosophical project of Derridean deconstruction, designed to produce both "other possibilities of utterance," beyond the demand for presence in the phonocentric, logocentric languages of Western metaphysics, as well as "a telling silence." But the view that there was something amiss, flawed, illusory, or destructive in the two-millennia trajectory of Western metaphysics, which was at the same time figured by Heidegger (and Derrida) as spawning the age of Western science, technology, morality, and authority, or what Derrida once called the "white mythology" of the West, predated the postmodern writings of Heidegger; it first came to philosophical prominence in the course of Nietzsche's powerful dismantling of both a Judeo-Christian moral tradition and a Greco-German metaphysical one.[5]

What is at stake here, as Heidegger and Derrida both made clear, is the historical fate of representation—or perhaps we should say, the fate of representability, for Heidegger, a Western obsession explicitly associated with the European Enlightenment, though nevertheless with origins in Homeric Greek. And it is by no means the case that this fate was put into question only by the Nietzsche-Heidegger axis of deconstruction. For a parallel line of concern about the distortions produced by the rise and dominance of the West's obsession with representation or representability emerged with the Hegelian Marxist critical theory of the Frankfurt School for Social Research in the first half of the twentieth century. For the Frankfurt School, dialectical reasoning, for all its worry over what was falsified or left out or contradictory in every act of representation, nevertheless wound up *by default* producing conceptual identities that justified, and were justified in turn by, a bad totality, a world so thoroughly but convincingly distorted that no one could any longer see the distortion, a world something like a discursive version of *The Matrix*; this became the guiding axiom of analysis for Theodor Adorno, Max Horkheimer, Herbert Marcuse, and a host of followers. Only a "negative dialectic," a logic of analysis that rigorously refused the comfort of all the conceptual identities that one might possibly produce given the regnant conditions of a bad totality, held out any hope that "representation" could be deterred from becoming "domination."[6] It was as if Marx's own healthy suspicion of Hegel's confidence in the dialectic's drive toward representability ("they cannot represent themselves, they must be represented," Marx famously observed of the French peasants) had been generalized, with no revolutionary impulse left uncorrupted, and no utopian fix in sight.[7] No one could self-represent, since this was itself a category of being that had been cannibalized by the culture industry of the West and put to use in fashioning individuals who would henceforth only imagine that they were self-fashioning, and therefore everyone would come to be represented by the categories of a social administration that possessed a purposive rationale of its own: the functional maintenance of the system. The Frankfurt School's major contribution was not exactly another "age of the world picture." Heidegger's bad totality and Adorno's remained different in certain fundamental ways, in that the Jewish Adorno had not one whit of Heidegger's faith that modernity's bad "world picture" could be destroyed by the rebirth of German consciousness. And yet, in both cases, representation/representability had clearly become the bogeyman of enlightenment, a viral threat to good mental (that is, both philosophical and political) health.

"Happy are those ages when the starry sky is the map of all possible paths—ages whose paths are illuminated by the light of the stars."[8] Georg Lukács, at the most Young Hegelian moment of his long and diverse career, put into basic existential terms what was later to be mourned by the Frankfurt School and disclosed as the fundamental illusion of Western (phonocentric) language by deconstruction: "'Philosophy is really homesickness,' says Novalis: 'it is the urge to be at home everywhere.' . . . That is why the happy ages have no philosophy, or why (it comes to the same thing) all men in such ages are philosophers, sharing the utopian aim of every philosophy. For what is the task of true philosophy if not to draw that archetypal map?"[9] In lieu of the word "philosophy," Lukács (and Novalis before him) could well have written "representation," since it is just the task of philosophy to be the mirror of nature, to "draw that archetypal map" of a heavenly order whose presence and palpability for human beings is immanent during those "happy ages" that have no need for representation, that is, when the sky is itself the map and hence immediately given, without recourse to the mediation, or representation, that philosophy (along with religion, literature, and purposive thinking about the relation of world and things) requires. If representation/representability itself harbors in its depths nothing but "homesickness"—nostalgia—then it is not difficult to see why Heidegger and Derrida hoped to "step back" from, or outside of, the era of nostalgic Western metaphysics and Western language, the closure of which had now become discernable; and why the Frankfurt School so fiercely lamented, in what Jürgen Habermas called the "performative contradiction" of their project, a spiritual homelessness that, they just as fiercely insisted, could not be overcome.[10] The Frankfurt School took up residence in what the later Lukács named "Grand Hotel Abyss," a "modern luxury hotel on the brink of the abyss" first described in Lukács's ponderous rejection of his former Romantic tendencies, *The Destruction of Reason*, as the piquant consequence of Arthur Schopenhauer's irrationalism and pessimism. Adorno and friends lived on their own Magic Mountain, shipwrecked along the hilly Pacific Palisades of the Los Angeles basin, even as the late Heidegger's work declared the age that produced such nostalgia, that is, the age of the world picture, of representation itself, more or less at an end.[11]

There is nothing surprising in the fact that the work of art became for both the Heideggerians and the neo-Hegelians, though for rather different reasons, the most effective antidote to, perhaps one should say purgative for, the disease of representation stalking modernity. In the case of the young Lukács, this antidote could not have assumed a more overtly theological form: "The novel is the epic of a world that has been abandoned by God."[12] Which is to say, as well, that the novelist's irony, "with intuitive double vision, can see where God is to be found in a world abandoned by God."[13] This claim would go through many permutations, but it lies at the root of Adorno's later and far more sophisticated argument that the seeming counterfactual illusion of artistic representation "is a refuge for mimetic behavior," that is, behavior sheltering within itself the only possibility of redemption in a world thoroughly colonized by its ability to be represented.[14] Unlike all other examples of representation, what the work of art preserved was nothing less than "immediate sensuous presence," so that the nonrational, nonpurposive magical illusion of mimesis—the production of similarity with nature, or the becoming similar to nature, without instrumental motive—ironically disenchanted the world falsely enchanted by all purposive representation, which was inextricably aimed at the domination (as in Heidegger's "world picture") of nature.[15] Adorno's impulses were not, perhaps, any less theological than those of the early Lukács: "[Aesthetic] form is the transfiguration of the existing, counter to which it represents freedom. Form secularizes the theological model of the world as an image made in God's likeness, though not as an act of creation but as the objectification of the human comportment that imitates creation; not *creatio ex nihilo*, but creation out of the created."[16] In a way that was fundamental not only to Adorno but also to Walter Benjamin before him, the "mimesis" of art was actually the dialectical negation (which at the same time means not simply the logical or disarticulated opposite) of "representation." Mimetic behavior was the remnant of an archaic ability to read in the starry sky, just as Lukács had intuited, "the map of all possible paths," as if each act of aesthetic imitation was not only the disenchantment of the endless representability of the modern age but was even more the recollection and reenactment of those "ages whose paths are illuminated by the light of the stars."

Benjamin would put the simultaneous distinction and (now lost to modernity) connection between mimesis and representation even more directly:

> Nature produces similarities; one need only think of mimicry. The highest capacity for producing similarities, however, is man's. His gift for seeing similarity is nothing but a rudiment of the once powerful compulsion to become similar and to behave mimetically.... We must assume that in the remote past the processes considered imitable included those in the sky. In dance, on other cultic occasions, such imitation could be produced, such similarity dealt with.... Allusion to the astrological sphere may supply a first reference point for an understanding of the concept of nonsensuous similarity. True, our existence no longer includes what once made it possible to speak of this kind of similarity: above all, the ability to produce it. Nevertheless we, too, possess a canon according to which the meaning of nonsensuous similarity can be at least partly clarified. And this canon is language.[17]

What Benjamin imagines is a quasi-evolutionary (or quasi-Hegelian) historical process by which the "occult practices" of reading "what was never written"—as embodied in the immediate presence of Lukács's starry "map of all possible paths," and hence in astrology, but also in haruspication and dance—give way to a "mediating link of a new kind of reading" based on runes and hieroglyphs. This is in turn overcome by modern phonetic writing, that is, the "semiotic aspect" of language by which signifiers (both written and spoken) are tied by (seemingly) arbitrary convention to their signifieds. In place of Benjamin's "semiotic aspect" we can substitute everything I have been calling "representation" or "the world picture": from Galileo's revolutionary mapping of the heavens, one devoted to a purely instrumental representation and account of them, to Newtonian mechanics, to the classificatory schemes of the Enlightenment, to the decoding of the atom and of DNA. For Benjamin, however, the "mimetic faculty" of archaic civilizations has not so much decayed, even though our ability to produce such similarity with nature seems much diminished, as it has been transformed. Vestiges of mimetic ritual and "nonsensuous similarity" remain embedded—sheltered, as it were—in modern, phonetic writing, which thereby appears as the last stage, or "highest level," of mimetic behavior, since phonocentric (semiotic) language thus seeded with the remnants (or rudiments) of archaic mimesis functions as "the most complete archive of nonsensuous similarity." This is also to say that semiotic language is a medium into which the earlier productive and interpretive powers of mimesis "have passed without residue," as if the entire process were a perfect enactment of what Hegel meant by *Aufhebung* or sublation. The forgotten elements of mimesis buried within the semiotic (or merely representational) use of language manifest themselves "like a flame": "the nexus of meaning of words or sentences is the bearer through which, like a flash, similarity appears... It flits past."[18] The difference, and it is a big one for Benjamin, is that in its latest incarnation as a lightning flash of similarity within the arbitrary conventions of reading and writing, mimesis is no longer tied to the ritual of archaic magic. Rather, mimesis-as-archaic-survival, once absorbed by the anti-magical prophylactic yet fallen medium of representational language, has "liquidated" the power of magic—one might say language has thus secularized magic—since such mimesis is no longer defined by the hieratic order and authority of occult practices. It is instead available to all who, with sufficient attention to those brief glimpses of mimesis in the fallen world of representation and to the uncanny echoes (as in onomatopoeia or graphology) of the thing in the word, of the spoken word in the written, or of the written in the thing itself, can indeed manage "to read what was never written," that is, to read once again Lukács's "archetypal map" of a heavenly order. To put all this in terms more Freudian than Hegelian, Benjamin's notion of "mimesis" is the repressed (or at least overlooked) primal unconscious of "representation," though it is a repressed that is happily destined to return, routinely, and with a quietly explosive force.

Benjamin's account of language is classic Hegelian Marxist thinking. It preserves within it the political allegory of an oppressed and seemingly powerless class, closer to archaic traditions, who nevertheless possess the ability to flare up, this time without the accoutrements of primitive magic, from inside the seemingly impervious order of modern representation (the order in which "those who cannot represent themselves must be represented"). Any full comparison of this account, or its allegory, with the Heideggerian-Derridean one outlined earlier is beyond the scope of this chapter. However, I still want to observe briefly here that what Heidegger called the "step back" from the Western "onto-theo-logical constitution of metaphysics," what he imagined as the *Ereignis* or epochal opportunity to rethink a catastrophic history linking Western philosophy and religion to the technology of nuclear warfare, and what Derrida imagined as the "closure" of that historical epoch with the deconstruction of logo-phono-centric language—I still want to observe that all this bears no little resemblance to Benjamin's desire to step back behind the apparent dominance of "the semiotic" realm, which is to say, of representation, in order to imagine pathways no longer allowed by the world picture of modernity. As Heidegger admitted, what may prevent the "step back" from metaphysics toward a proper thinking of its basic (or primal) elements—that is, "the active essence of metaphysics"—is, precisely, representation: "Everything that results by way of the step back [*Schrittes zurück*] may merely be exploited and absorbed in its own way, as the result of representational thinking. Thus the step back would itself remain unaccomplished, and the path which it opens and points out would remain untrod."[19] Heidegger's late *"Geviert"* (what I would call, perverting A. J. Greimas, the *mimetic*, rather than *semiotic*, "square," also translated as "fourfold," and italicized in the original) of earth, sky, divinities, and mortals— for example, "Mortals dwell in that they receive the sky as sky," and "Mortals dwell in that they await the divinities as divinities"—certainly recalls Lukács's own utopian sense that the happy ages are those "whose paths are illuminated by the light of the stars."[20] Lukácsian immanence is not that far from Heideggerian immanence. Benjamin's desire for a glimpse of a virus-like package of mimetic behavior that had been preserved despite, or because of, the protective carrier of representation enclosing it is not that far from Heidegger's sense that building and dwelling are in essence mimetic behaviors no matter how instrumental they may appear in our mere representations of them: "the bridge *gathers* [*versammelt*, italicized in the original] the earth as landscape around the stream," it holds the flow of the stream "up to the sky."[21] Heidegger's famously archetypal peasant "farmhouse in the Black Forest" is itself a mimetic object: the farmhouse admits and "*installs* the square" ["*richtet* das Geviert *ein,*" italicized in the original], both through its particular location on the mountain slope as well as in its structure.[22] "Here the urgency [*Inständigkeit*] of the power to admit earth and heaven, divinities and mortals *simply* (or *guilelessly*: "*einfältig,*" italicized in the original) into things, ordered the house," even to the presence of "the altar corner behind the communal table."[23] Central to Heidegger's later work is the need to allow human being, including dwelling and building, but also speaking and thinking, to participate in the mimetic square of the *Geviert* rather than in the representation (and hence domination) of nature elaborated in the world picture of enlightened thought.

In his brief commentary on a line from Hölderlin—"'. . . dichterisch wohnet der Mensch . . .'" (". . . poetically man dwells . . .")—Heidegger emphasizes the mimetic imagination, or what Benjamin had called the faculty for producing "nonsensuous similarity," in the act of making authentic poetry, which is to say in the act of authentically dwelling within the *Geviert* of earth, sky, divinities, and mortals: "The poetic is the basic capacity for human dwelling. But man is capable of poetry at any time only to the degree to which his being is appropriate to that which itself has a liking for man and therefore needs his presence. Poetry is authentic [*eigentlich*] or inauthentic according to the degree of this appropriation."[24] The authenticity of the appropriation referred to here bears a striking resemblance to the starry sky of Lukács, and the astrological "correspondences and analogies that were familiar to ancient peoples" in Benjamin's exegesis of the mimetic faculty.[25]

And the inauthentic is, precisely, mere representation, albeit representation that, in poetry, reveals the invisible, alien form of an unknown god lurking within, in exactly the same way that Benjamin's forgotten "mimetic behavior" can be glimpsed flitting past in the semiotic flow of a fallen, modern linguistic representation. In Heidegger's words:

> The poet makes poetry only when he takes the measure, by saying the sights [*Anblicke*] of heaven in such a way that he submits to its appearances as to the

alien element [*das Fremden*] to which the unknown god has "yielded" ["*schiket*," or "resigned himself to," in quotations in original]. Our current name for the sight and appearance of something is "image" ["*Bild*," or "picture," in quotations in the original]. The nature of the image is to let something be seen. By contrast, copies and imitations are already mere variations on the genuine image [*eigentlichen Bildes*] which, as a sight or spectacle, lets the invisible be seen and so imagines the invisible in something alien to it. Because poetry takes that mysterious measure, to wit, in the face of the sky, therefore it speaks in "images" ["*Bildern*," in quotations in the original]. This is why poetic images are imaginings [*Ein-Bildungen*, or "inner pictures"] in a distinctive sense: not mere fancies and illusions but imaginings that are visible [*erblickbare*, or glimpsed] inclusions of the alien in the sight of the familiar. The poetic saying of images gathers the brightness and sound of the heavenly appearances into one with the darkness and silence of what is alien. By such sights the god surprises [*befremdet*, or, etymologically, "alienates"] us. In this strangeness [*Befremdung*] he proclaims his unfaltering nearness.[26]

Heidegger's account of authentic *poiesis* takes its cue here from Hölderlin's proto-Lukáscian lines: ". . . Yet no purer / Is the shade of starry night, / If I might put it so, than / Man, who's called an image of the godhead" [". . . Doch reiner / Ist nicht der Schatten der Nacht mit den Sternen, / Wenn ich so sagen könnte, als / Der Mensch, der heißet ein Bild der Gottheit"].[27] Heidegger describes "genuine" images not as mere "copies and imitations," that is, as what I have been calling "representations," but rather as mimetic speech about the "sights of heaven" that allows the alien (but also archaic) appearance of the god to surprise us: such images are "visible inclusions of the alien in the sight of the familiar"; they are "the foreign element in which the invisible one preserves his presence [*Wesen*]."[28] But this way of putting things is remarkably near to Benjamin's account of the process by which archaic mimesis, now become alien amid the semiotic (phonological) representations of modern language, can be glimpsed as it "flashes" up off the page. Authentic poetry, like authentic dwelling and authentic being, is intimately related here to that nearly lost faculty for producing a mimetic (nonrepresentational) relationship with the world around us, one that, if only in brief moments of surprise, allows the now alien starry "map of all possible paths" to make itself visible to us. This is also what authentic "beauty" would have to be in Heideggerian terms, and it is finally what authentic "presence" must be if it is to escape, or step back away from, the history of metaphysics, which is neither more nor less than the history of representation that has inauthentically manufactured the illusion of presence for so long.

Representation versus mimesis; mimesis as the repressed Other of representation; mimesis flashing forth, like the primitive, pagan "fremde Gott" (strange God) of Thomas Mann's *Tod in Venedig,* out of the fallen and arbitrary signs of modernity, as the endless and increasingly swift parade of representations passes before us—all of this is fundamental to the story of European culture after Nietzsche, and especially to avant-garde literary culture and cultural criticism. It should come as no surprise if recent attempts to reinstall "beauty" and "presence" as categories worthy of critical reflection amid the ever more banal representations of "new" historicist contextualization would draw to a large extent on this story. Hence, even as "beauty" would seem to have been thoroughly undone by Pierre Bourdieu's sociology, and "presence" by Derrida's demonstration of the endless deferrals of signifier to signifier (and never quite to a genuine signified with no remainder), the deeper narrative of the struggle of mimesis with representation has withstood these onslaughts of critical reason. After all, one might say, Bourdieu's remarkable demystification of the "aesthetic" as nothing more than the efflux of class consciousness and the acquisition of "distinction," or cultural capital, depends on particularly modern notions of consumer culture and the largely eighteenth-century invention of "taste" as a properly philosophical concept. Construct your notion of beauty in a way that avoids these parameters, and the conversation about beauty will appear to reopen. Likewise, Derrida's demystification of "presence" depends on a specific "history of metaphysics" that culminates in Husserl and Heidegger, and on a logo-phono-centric model of language that imagines it can overcome the materiality of the signifier. Construct your notion of "presence" in a way that on the contrary emphasizes the materiality of things apart from any possible logo-phono-centric representation of them, that is, in terms of being as it unconceals itself apart from our effort to determine it, to situate it, to take account of it, or to put it to use, and the conversation about presence will appear to reopen as well.

In fact, two relatively recent books have taken just these paths, paths that are each in their own way examples of the bracketing of time and history that must occur to produce what Husserl described as the phenomenological attitude, though generally without the early Heidegger's attempt (however one judges its success) to recover a sense of being *in* time, that is, of the historicity of *Dasein,* or human being. It is my contention in the remainder of this chapter that both books wind up firmly reinscribing themselves in the modernist agon of mimesis versus representation, so that their rediscovery of the viability of the concepts "beauty" and "presence" is primarily a rediscovery of the lure of a redemptive mimesis in the face of the fallen world of representations. These books offer, that is, less a new approach to (happily or unhappily) devalued ideas than one more version of a story that has profoundly shaped critical thought since the late nineteenth century. They represent perhaps the surest sign that the post-postmodern cultural critic is having no little difficulty escaping the dominance of a modernist intellectual landscape, and remains (happily or unhappily) obsessed with the dichotomies that structured that landscape.

The opening lines of Elaine Scarry's *On Beauty and Being Just* are in fact a virtual hymn to mimesis, and decidedly not, as I will show, to representation, and they contain by implication all that I have tried to claim for the power of mimetic behavior untainted by the bad totality of a world of mere representations:

> What is the felt experience of cognition at the moment one stands in the presence of a beautiful boy or flower or bird? It seems to incite, even to require the act of replication. Wittgenstein says that when the eye sees something beautiful, the hand wants to draw it.
>
> Beauty brings copies of itself into being. It makes us draw it, take photographs of it, or describe it to other people. Sometimes it gives rise to exact replication and other times to resemblances and still other times to things whose connection to the original site of inspiration is unrecognizable....
>
> A visual event may reproduce itself in the realm of touch.... This crisscrossing of the senses may happen in any direction....
>
> This phenomenon of unceasing begetting sponsors in people like Plato, Aquinas, Dante the idea of eternity, the perpetual duplication of a moment that never stops. But it also sponsors the idea of terrestrial plenitude and distribution, the will to make "more and more" so that there will eventually be "enough."[29]

Beauty happens to Scarry with the same sudden decontextualizing "flash" of intensity that marked Lukács's prephilosophical starry sky, or the "flitting" of mimesis in Benjamin, so that "things whose connection to the original site of inspiration is unrecognizable" are reproduced in the same manner as Benjamin's "nonsensuous similarity": "the first flash of the bird incites the desire to duplicate"; "suddenly I am on a balcony and [a palm tree's] huge swaying leaves are before me at eye level, arcing, arching, waving, cresting and breaking in the soft air"; "you come around a bend in the road, and the world suddenly falls open"; "you may be sweeping the garden bricks at home . . . then suddenly a tiny mauve-orange-blue triangle, with a silver sheen, lifts off from the sand between the bricks where it has been sleepily camouflaged until the air currents disturbed it. It flutters in the air, then settles back down on the brick, demure, closed-winged, a triangle this big." And then Scarry draws, in all the innocence of a child's hand, a triangular representation of the moth, and we are suddenly reminded of the way Benjamin observed, in "On the Mimetic Faculty," that "children's play is everywhere permeated by mimetic modes of behavior. . . . The child plays at being not only a shopkeeper or teacher, but also a windmill and train."[30] The primitive drawings that accompany Scarry's words throughout her text all have this same function—to suggest that only a mode of "replication" beyond the semiotic properties of verbal representations, that is, iconic figures whose connection to the original is (almost) unrecognizable, could suggest what it means to want to duplicate the beauty that suddenly flashes forth once one assumes the naïve posture of the child wanting to become like the world. What at first appears to be only a rhetorical strategy designed to disarm or infantilize her readers is in fact a deeply rooted modern propensity to turn to mimetic behavior as the ground of a more authentic mode of existence. And the mark of this more authentic mode of existence is the endless perpetuation of mimesis, especially across the visual field (Scarry, remarkably, says little about beautiful odors or tastes, perhaps because, as in traditional Romantic accounts of the aesthetic, these would seem to be all too kinetic and crude). It is a visual field that also seems to be totally innocent of, completely untroubled by, what Heidegger called "the world picture," that is, the fallen world of representations that, for the average sentient adult, situates and defines the things of the world, often in an instrumental fashion, and hence circumscribes the apprehension of authentic beauty to sudden flashes on a garden path, over a balcony, around the bend of a road.

Moreover, Scarry's meditation in the second part of her book on the relation of beauty to justice depends on the same mimetic process that linked genuine, or poetic, dwelling in Heidegger to the *Geviert* of earth, sky, divinities, and mortals. Just as the peasant farmhouse replicates in its primal structure and location the larger cosmic relationship of earth to sky, and in its internal arrangements the intimacy of divinities and mortals, so Scarry finds an existential symmetry in the way political structures, when they are genuine—that is, "fair" (or just)—turn out to be a mimesis of beautiful form, which is to say, form that is equally "fair" (or pleasing) in its own way.

> But it may happen on occasion that the fair political arrangement itself (not just the laws prescribing it or guaranteeing it) *will* be condensed into a time and space where it becomes available to the senses, and then—like Augustine's water, sky, cakes, and roses—its beauty is visible. This may be true in a great assembly hall, where the representatives deliberate in a bowl of space available to perception. Now the claim has been made that the principle of rhythmic equality ... did in the ancient Greek world also take place in the sphere of social arrangements and—this is the next step—in social arrangements contracted down into a small enough physical space that it was available to sensory perception: namely, the trireme ships, the ships whose 170 oars and 170 oarsmen could, like a legislative assembly, be held within the small bowl of visual space of which a human perceiver is capable, and whose rhythmic striking of the water, in time with the pipeman's flute, could also be held within the finite auditory compass of a perceiver. But we have not yet arrived at the claim, and it is this: out of the spectacle of the trireme ship, Athenian democracy was born.[31]

Scarry goes on to cite a passage from the historian Bruce Russett to support her claim here about the mimetic nature of the trireme and the democratic assembly. But it is important to note that Russett's words are actually about Periclean reforms that shifted power to the poor (though free) Greeks who found employment in the increasingly large Greek navy, so that the ships were no longer manned by slaves, but by "full citizens." Hence, writes Russett, "With 170 rowers in each of at least 200 ships, no fewer than 30,000 supporters of democracy" were at work on the ships, and they were "generally from the lower classes."[32] That is, Russett's point is, precisely, not about mimesis—he says nothing here about what could or could not be "perceived" in the "bowl of visual space"—but rather about "representation": a substantial number of poor Greek citizens were now employed by the navy, and the new martial importance of this previously subordinate group gave the Periclean state a far more democratic character than it had had previously.

My point is that what Scarry sees in Russett has little to do with the question of political representation, or what one might call the purposive "world picture" of Periclean Greece, though that is primarily what concerns Russett, and everything to do with the sort of mimesis that Heidegger saw in the Black Forest farmhouse, where a cosmic, heavenly order of things was replicated in the existence of the genuine German peasant. Throughout her paronomastic treatment of "fairness" as a quality both of beauty and of distribution (of wealth or power or rights), what Scarry emphasizes is the "nonsensuous similarity" of beauty and justice, the mimesis in visual and auditory patterns across different realms of discourse of two conceptually quite different kinds of "fairness" (beauty and justice) that have throughout history so often *not* accompanied one another. It is a mimesis that would otherwise be obscured by the world of political and aesthetic *representations*, which is to say the realm in which being just and being beautiful generally do not conceptually represent one another. And it is a mimesis that emerges into legibility only when the microcosmic "spectacle of the trireme ship" suddenly appears to click into harmony, like some startling superposition in a 3-D stereoscope, with the macrocosm of Greek democracy (and by extension our own presumed ideals of social justice—though Scarry shows no concern for all those things, such as slavery, that undermine the naïve Western cliché of Athens as the cradle of contemporary, global justice).[33]

By comparison to Scarry, Hans Ulrich Gumbrecht has less to say about beauty per se, though the "aesthetic experience" is an important concern, than about the way beauty is itself a subspecies of "nonhermeneutic" "materiality" or "presence." The book is squarely aimed at what Gumbrecht takes to be the cardinal failing of the modern humanities and the modern academy housing them. His book is designed "to challenge a broadly institutionalized tradition according to which interpretation, that is, the identification and/or attribution of meaning, is the core practice, the exclusive core practice indeed, of the humanities."[34] But in his explicit reliance on Heidegger, and especially on Heidegger's denunciation of the "world picture" and its foundation in what I have called throughout this chapter "representation," Gumbrecht inhabits to a large extent the same intellectual space, with the same conceptual struggle of mimesis versus representation, that determines Scarry's argument about beauty. Gumbrecht is not so starry-eyed (in Lukács's sense) that he imagines he can do without meaning, or interpretation, or what Benjamin would have called the "semiotic" element of language and thought, altogether. After all, Gumbrecht is writing a book explaining his ideas to others who rely on the representational effects of his words, and he is throughout his text involved in a hermeneutic exercise: that is, he is interpreting what he takes to have gone wrong in modern humanistic education, and he is interpreting what might be done to set things right, even if such rectification means reining in a portion of our hermeneutic impulse. Rather, he hopes to create a larger space for "presence," for our nonhermeneutic apprehension of the world in all its sensuous materiality, for Being in its self-unconcealedness.

At times Gumbrecht seems to desire precisely what Immanuel Kant had said some time ago we had no ability to acquire, since human sensation had no direct access to phenomena unfiltered by the a priori categories of mind. In Gumbrecht's words, "Experiencing (in the sense of *Erleben* [experience as seeing or witnessing events as one lives through them], that is, more than *Wahrnehmen* [perception, observation or overseeing] and less than *Erfahren* [experience as coming to know, as learning from events]), experiencing the things of the world in their pre-conceptual thingness will reactivate a feeling for the bodily and for the spatial dimension of our existence."[35] And yet, as his parenthesis in the quoted sentence implies, Gumbrecht is not really after bare, unfiltered "perception." His object is something closer to what Heidegger meant by *Gelassenheit*: an extreme degree of serenity or composure. "*Gelassenheit* figures as both part of the disposition with which we should open ourselves to aesthetic experience and as the existential state to which aesthetic experience can take us.... I have come to describe, with a deliberately colloquial formula, that specific serenity as the feeling of *being in sync with the things of the world*.... This may be exactly what, from an existential point of view, the self-unconcealment of Being is all about."[36] In effect, though he denies any "cosmic" significance behind his use of *Gelassenheit*, Gumbrecht's longing for existential composure is a direct descendent of Lukács's desire for "immanence." (Gumbrecht describes his "desire to reconnect with the things of the world" as being as "strictly immanentist as one could possibly imagine."[37]) That is, Gumbrecht avowedly longs for being able to feel completely "at home" in the world beneath a starry sky that does not need to be read or interpreted or to have meaning, but presents its presence in our immediate (present) experience of it as always already a "map of all possible paths." Moreover, not unlike Scarry and the contrived innocence of her own openness to beauty and serene *Gelassenheit*, Gumbrecht limns Heidegger's "self-unconcealment of Being" in the language of new age wonderment, as a glassy-eyed naïf "in sync" with the world.

Most important for my present argument, Gumbrecht ends his meditation on the existential (and, he vaguely implies, the social and political) need for some redemptive moments of release from the "Cartesian worldview" that dominates modernity—which is to say, a worldview that is made up almost exclusively (in Heideggerian perspective) of representations (a "world picture") situated by or in front of a subject who interprets them—by turning, unsurprisingly, to the putatively repressed mimetic faculties of Western consciousness. His last pages are devoted to Kabuki and No theater, in which both the visual and the auditory fields (complete with "archaic drums") are defined not by interpretable representations, as on a Western stage, but rather by a setting that is frankly mimetic in the sense of Heidegger's essential bridge and Black Forest farmhouse, and by acting that is less an "interpretation" of fictional personae than a deliberately archaic spectacle of mimetic behavior. The kinship of Zen Buddhism and Heidegger's notion of the concealment and unconcealment of Being is explicit for Gumbrecht, who notes that "Zen understands 'nothingness' as a dimension where things are not shaped by forms and concepts, and therefore as a sphere that is withdrawn from the grasp of human experience (and this is the opinion of recognized experts)" ("experts" Gumbrecht never names), so that, just as in the Kantian formulation that denies us access to perception unfiltered by the categories of the understanding, "if the unshaped ever crossed this border, it would have to adopt forms."[38] Nevertheless, what Zen and (at least for Gumbrecht) No and Kabuki theater teach us is how to be open to the preconceptual, to the unshaped. It is no accident, I think, that this involves the apprehension of a mimetic tableau, in which the stage mimes an "immanent" order—complete with Heideggerian bridge and house—and the actors mime the unstable relation of mortals and divinities:

> In No and Kabuki, all the actors come to the stage and leave the stage across a bridge that leads to a "house" (a wooden container large enough for the bodies of several actors).... No drama and Kabuki drama look like the Zen motif of an impossible transition from nothingness into the world of forms and concepts.... But is this not, finally, a religious experience? ... It

is actually possible to find an answer to this question, an answer, however, that is as ambiguous as the demons are, those souls of the deceased who come back to the world and haunt the living. Demons seem to take even more time than the other characters to reach the stage in Kabuki and No. Once they arrive at the stage, they can adopt all kinds and forms of human bodies and human roles. But when they are supposed to be "just demons," the actors do whatever they can to blur any impression of formedness. Then their hair looks wild, the rhythms of their body movements seem to grow more irregular . . . and their tongues are sticking out. For the demons are of this world—and not of it. . . . The demons' tongues are flesh but, being part of these strange characters' ontic ambiguity, they are also words and language.

Gumbrecht's concluding image—of the Japanese actors' tongues that do not speak but rather mimic language in their fleshy materiality—marks a place, I think, about as far away from the Western world picture dominated by Cartesian representations, and hence from what Benjamin saw as the arbitrary signs of modern "semiotic" language, as Gumbrecht can find. It is a suitably Oriental space, one not so far from the static Orient of Hegel and François-René de Chateaubriand and Gustave Flaubert, in which mimesis reigns, and in which the "Western spectator" who finds the will to overcome his bewilderment and impatience at the difficulty of making sense of the proceedings begins "to feel the composure that allows you to let things come, and perhaps you cease to ask what these things mean—because they seem just present and meaningful."[39] E. M. Forster's Hindu Professor Godbole, in *A Passage to India*, could not have said it better. And it is in his embrace of the redemptive character of the mimetic arts—the mimetic arts of Forster's Orient, no less—that Gumbrecht offers his most striking image of the "presence" that the putatively "Western" compulsion for interpretation, and hence for representation, has occluded.

I want to conclude by suggesting that these most recent efforts of Scarry and Gumbrecht to move beyond the prison-house, the "world picture," of modernity wind up returning us to it with a sort of vengeance. But this only becomes apparent once it is understood that the leading edge of both literature and theory in the twentieth century depended on the idea that sudden, seemingly meaningless moments of archaic mimesis might provide either a form of resistance to or transcendence of the supposedly static, reified parade of representations offered up by modern rationalized society, one in which our need for "meaning" far outstripped our openness to Being.

Lukács's "starry sky," Benjamin's primeval astrology and dance, Heidegger's peasant farmhouse, Adorno's "objectification of the human comportment that imitates creation"—all reemerge in Scarry's "spectacle of the trireme ship" that replicates Athenian democracy and in Gumbrecht's Japanese theater, in which finally even the Western spectator exhibits mimetic behavior: "Perhaps you even observe how, while you ever so slowly begin to let things emerge, you become a part of them."[40] In their own ways, both Scarry and Gumbrecht hope to rescue the humanities from what Wallace Stevens once called a "Blessed rage for order, pale Ramon / The maker's rage to order words of the sea," the compulsion to make meaning out of perception, which is to say they want to rescue the humanities from their inability just to let things be and enjoy them: "A poem should not mean / But be," Archibald MacLeish famously admonished us, and Scarry and Gumbrecht concur wholeheartedly (if rather belatedly).[41] (In both poems, the goal is mimesis rather than representation; as MacLeish puts it: "A poem should be equal to: / Not true.")

One might then also recall the "epiphanies" that occasionally flash forth from the mundane repression of James Joyce's Dublin; Marcel Proust's tea-soaked crumb of madeleine that quite unexpectedly reawakens Marcel to "a precious essence" that "was me" quite apart from the unimportant vicissitudes of life; and the flickering "moments of being" that suddenly interrupt the eminently representational authority of "Proportion" and "Conversion" in Virginia Woolf.[42] But then one would also need to admit just how equivocal these irruptions of mimetic, or "nonsensuous," similarity generally wind up being: epiphanies that become instead for Joyce fusty products of a "Haunted Inkbottle"; Proust's unsettling recognition that "the memory of a certain image is but regret for a certain moment"; the tendency of a seemingly authentic "moment of being" in Woolf to trap the individual "into saying something that she did not mean."[43] In such cases, mimesis is never really as redemptive of "presence" or "beauty" or "justice" as we may like to imagine.

In the end, the underlying recourse in Scarry and Gumbrecht to archaic mimesis as an antidote to representation suggests, I think, something more than just nostalgic modernist pastiche. It implies the persistence within the modern humanities of a deeper discontent with the humanistic enterprise itself, which appears in their arguments as if it were something radically out of touch with the real, with the human body, with authentic sensation, with all that is beautiful and just, with feeling (once again? at long last?) "at home" in the world. For both, it is the apparent loss of the untutored (childlike) innocence of human perception that should matter most of all. Contemporary theory, it would seem, has once again discovered the Edenic fall of man into representational meaning that has so troubled European culture since the Romantics (and perhaps since the Gnostics). And, just as in Benjamin's Kaballistic insight that arbitrary linguistic signs harbored the remnants of mimetic magic and that even the merest commodity may contain redemptive "splinters of messianic time," it may be the sudden flitting of a moth on a garden path or the "aesthetic epiphany" aroused by "a beautiful play in American football and baseball, in soccer and hockey... the epiphany of a complex and embodied form" that provides the moment of escape from Cartesian space and from what Benjamin called "homogeneous, empty time."[44] Benjamin imagined that those messianic splinters prefigured a wholesale transformation of the social order, a complete reversal of a very bad historical totality indeed. Perhaps Heidegger too hoped, albeit from something like the other side of the political coin, that the end of onto-theo-logic would usher in a new existential reality. Such visions of total transformation would appear now to have been consigned in turn to the ash heap that propels Benjamin's Angel of Destruction backwards into the future. But the "starry night" that Heidegger inherits from Hölderlin and Lukács is still apparently as intimate and available to many of us as any of Benjamin's fallen but star-struck commodities, legible in the mimetic urges stirred by the palm tree outside a hotel balcony, or in the televised immediacy of a Sunday afternoon football game—a peasant hut in the Black Forest is helpful, but not required.

3

Meaning, Truth, and Phenomenology

Mark Bevir

Jacques Derrida rejects the Western philosophical tradition as logocentric. It is a discourse of reason centered on a misplaced faith in presence. Derrida argues in particular that neither meanings nor truths are simply present to consciousness. He suggests all concepts are metaphors haunted by absent others, and all consciousness deploys such metaphors, so we cannot have access to brute facts. Derrida's rejection of logocentrism precludes his offering a set of doctrines defended using the very discourse of reason he rejects. Often he conveys his views through deconstructive readings of other philosophers. He develops his view of meaning through a reading of Ferdinand de Saussure, and his attack on truth through one of Edmund Husserl. This chapter approaches Derrida's critique of logocentrism through these writings. I argue that aspects of his criticisms of Saussure and Husserl are valid, undermine appeals to presence, and so pose problems for some theories of meaning and truth. In addition, I argue that his criticisms of Saussure and Husserl cannot sustain a complete rejection of meaning and truth. Provided we conceptualize meaning and truth in the right way, we can avoid the problems Derrida raises. In other words, we can continue to appeal to meanings, truths, and even presence, as long as we recognize that we establish them within our web of concepts.

Saussure and Meaning

When Derrida famously proclaims "there is nothing outside of the text," he is arguing there is nothing outside the text for us; but then, of course, to say there is nothing outside the text for us is in effect to say there is nothing outside the text.[1] According to Derrida, we cannot have knowledge of anything beyond language because language cannot represent the world. Words do not have stable meanings; they do not refer to fixed concepts so they can not embody knowledge of the world. Derrida thus problematizes the question of meaning in a way that promotes an antirealist skepticism. He argues that signification always entails an element of *différance*; that is to say, whenever we tie a signifier to a signified, the nature of both signifier and signified depends on something absent and other than itself. Again, we cannot say what a signifier refers to without evoking an absent, and once we evoke an absent, we cannot say what it refers to without evoking another absent, and so on. As Derrida explains:

> It is because of *différance* that the movement of signification is possible only if each so-called "present" element, each element appearing on the scene of presence, is related to something other than itself, thereby keeping within itself the mark of the past element, and already letting itself be vitiated by the mark of its relation to the future element, this trace being related no less to what is called the future than to what is called the past, and constituting the present by means of this very relation to what it is not.[2]

Derrida rejects stable meanings on the grounds that signifiers and signifieds depend on what they are not. This differential nature of the sign destabilizes meaning in a way that precludes our breaking out of an endless play of signifiers.

Derrida adopts a differential view of the sign in his reading of Saussure. According to Saussure, language is an abstract system of signs, where a sign conjoins a signifier, or form, with a signified, or concept. The sign "pet," for instance, consists of the signifier made up of the letters *p*, *e*, and *t* together with the signified "a tamed animal kept as a favorite."

Saussure argues that signs are arbitrary and differential in two respects. First, signifiers are purely differential because their link to a particular signified is arbitrary. There is no reason why a given set of phonemes should convey a certain concept: for example, we could use the signifier "tet" just as easily as "pet" to denote "a tamed animal kept as a pet." This arbitrary feature of the sign implies that signifiers are indeed differential entities defined solely by their difference from one another. After all, although a signifier need not be linked to any particular signified, it must differ from other signifiers. Any set of phonemes we use to denote "a tamed animal kept as a favorite" must differ from those we use to convey other concepts.

Second, Saussure suggests that signifieds are as arbitrary and differential as signifiers. Saussure develops this suggestion using only phonetic examples because he thinks a semantic one would be too complex.[3] A common way of explicating his position is, however, to instance color concepts. Imagine we try to teach students the concept red by pointing to red things and saying "red." If we show them an orange and ask if it is red, they will not know. We cannot explicate a color concept merely by instancing examples of it. Why is this? According to Saussure, we experience reality as an undifferentiated continuum: our reality is a jumble of images all of which flow into one another. We experience color, for example, as a continuum moving from what we call red to what we call yellow and so on.

Next Saussure suggests that because our images of reality form an undifferentiated continuum, we have no reason to divide them up using one set of signifieds rather than another. We could conceptualise color, for example, using a set of signifieds such as X containing what we conceive of as red, orange, and about half of yellow, Y containing the other half of yellow and a tiny fraction of green, Z containing most of the rest of green, and so on. Our signifieds thus provide just one possible way of dividing up our flow of impressions: they are less a uniquely right or naturally determined set than an arbitrary way of dividing up the jumble of images constitutive of our experiences. Nonetheless, Saussure continues, we could teach our students the meaning of red by introducing them to our colour concepts as a set. If we did so, they would know whether an object was red, orange, yellow, green, blue, or whatever. It appears, therefore, that color concepts are differential since we make sense of red by knowing it is not-orange, not-yellow, not-green, not-blue, and so on. Certainly, Saussure concludes that because signifieds are arbitrary, they must be differential: "The conceptual side of value [a unit in language] is made up solely of relations and differences with respect to the other terms of language."[4]

When Derrida reads Saussure, he takes the arbitrary and differential nature of the sign for granted so as to question the idea of a stable link between signifier and signified, and thus Saussure's phonocentrism, his privileging of speech over writing.[5] For Derrida, speech represents stable meanings, while writing represents the undermining of stable meanings. A faith in speech stands for a belief in our ability to grasp meanings clearly: speakers know what they mean. A fear of writing stands for a neglect of all that unsettles the link between a statement and its meaning: we wonder what written texts mean. Saussure constantly treats writing as a lesser form of speech by, for example, using phonology as a model for linguistics, and describing phonetic scripts as superior to alternatives such as hieroglyphs. According to Derrida, Saussure's phonocentrism entails a neglect of the disruptive effects of writing.

Saussure presents the sign as a fluid construct except when he introduces a stable link between signifier and signified as exemplified in speech. Derrida argues that the existence of this stable link is brought into question by passages in Saussure's own text. These passages exhibit the logical course of Saussure's recognition of the differential nature of the sign. Saussure's differential view of the sign makes language (*langue*) essential for the appearance of speech (*parole*). Here *parole* occurs only in a system of differences devoid of positive terms, and such a system resembles the traditional view of writing as the sign of a sign. Indeed, Saussure explicitly evokes this resemblance when he uses writing as a metaphor to explicate the nature of *langue*. Thus, although he says he wants to exclude writing from his linguistics, his own text shows he has to use writing as a metaphor to sustain his argument; his own text shows the centrality of writing and thereby undermines his explicit belief in a stable relationship between signifier and signified. The ubiquity of writing implies all meaning is problematic. As Derrida explains, within every system there comes a point "where the signifier can no longer be replaced by its signified, so that in consequence no signifier can be replaced, purely and simply."[6] Because signifiers are not tied clearly to signifieds, every use of a signifier resembles writing; every use of a signifier raises as a genuine problem the question of what it refers to. The use of signifiers always corresponds to writing understood as an opacity that divorces expression from meaning. The use of signifiers can never correspond to the ideal of speech understood as a transparent medium for consciousness. Because we cannot reduce a signifier to a corresponding signified, any attempt to say what a signifier signifies must leave something or other out. There are no stable meanings.

Perhaps Derrida's argument works against Saussure. Perhaps the differential nature of the sign implies signifiers are not bound to fixed signifieds so there are no stable meanings just an endless play of signifiers. But, even if Derrida's argument works against Saussure, his general conclusion would remain parasitic on Saussure's differential view of the sign. Derrida takes as given a view of the sign that I think is mistaken. Saussure adopts a differential view of the signified as a consequence of his postulating *langue* as the proper object of a science of linguistics. Because he defines *langue* as a self-contained system, he cannot identify its individual parts by their relationship to things beyond that system. Thus, his account of the signified rests not on a philosophical argument about how things are, but on a methodological gesture designed to establish linguistics as a science.[7] The argument for a differential theory of meaning rests solely, therefore, on the evidence provided by examples such as color concepts. This evidence, however, shows only that some concepts form a continuum we could divide up in another way. It shows only that some concepts are differential: they refer to a continuum, so we know what part of the continuum one refers to if we know what part of the continuum the others do not refer to. It does not show that all concepts are purely differential: not all concepts need be part of a continuum, and, what is more, we might know what one that is on the continuum refers to even if we do not know what the relevant others refer to.

Derrida, albeit implicitly, makes an unwarranted leap. He moves from showing some signifieds are differential to the conclusion that all signifieds are purely differential. The illegitimate nature of this move appears in two failings in his purely differential theory of meaning. The first is that even concepts forming a continuum can be defined positively as well as differentially. That we can define color concepts negatively as not one another does not establish we cannot define them positively in terms of their referents. Consider again students we want to teach the meaning of red. Imagine we tell them an object is red if the light it reflects lies somewhere beyond a specified point on the spectrum. Imagine also we give them an instrument to measure the nature of the light given off by any given object. Under these circumstances, they could identify red objects without any problem; they could fix the meaning of red by knowing what objects red refers to, and they could do so even if they did not know the meaning of other color concepts. Clearly, therefore, we do not have to define red differentially. We can define it positively as the color seen at such and such a band of the spectrum. Red is a relational concept: we fix its meaning in relation to other signifieds that provide us with a theory of the nature of color. Nonetheless, red is not a purely differential concept: it is not composed solely of the contrast between it and other concepts. Of course, we still can say red is the part of the spectrum that is not-blue, not-green, and so on. We can do so, however, because our theory of color implies that color concepts form a continuous spectrum because anything giving off light gives off color and light forms a continuous spectrum. It is, therefore, a fact about our world (that light forms a continuous spectrum), and not a fact about meaning (that we define signifieds as different from one another), that enables us to equate red with not-blue, not-green, and so on.

The second failing of Derrida's purely differential theory of meaning is that most concepts do not form a continuum so we can define them only in positive terms. Consider the signified "malaria." No doubt we cannot teach someone what we mean by malaria solely by pointing to examples and saying "malaria." But this shows only that the meaning of malaria depends on a theoretical understanding of the world; malaria is a relational concept. It does not show that the meaning of malaria derives from its not being various other concepts: malaria is not a purely differential concept. Indeed, we can define malaria positively as, say, a fever caused by the presence in the body of the protozoan parasite of genus *Plasmodium*. To do so we need only to accept a theory about the cause of certain physical symptoms. Once again we can bind a signified to its referent in the context of theories composed of other signifieds. What is more, the relevant theories this time actually preclude a differential definition of malaria akin to that we can give of red. We could say only that malaria means something like "not the absence of a certain type of parasite." Malaria is not a differential signified, just a relational one.

Derrida's purely differential theory of meaning rests on a false dichotomy. He assumes that because individual signifieds do not have a context-independent link to their referents, we can identify them only negatively as different from each other. Actually, however, there is another alternative: we could identify them positively in terms of an external reality, where the way we understand this reality presupposes the applicability of various theories. When Derrida says "the absence of the transcendental signified extends the domain and the play of signification infinitely," he ignores the possibility of our theories providing a way of ending such play without appealing to a transcendental signified.[8] There is no reason why we should assume that the absence of a one-to-one correspondence between signifieds and their referents entails the absence of any correspondence whatsoever. That a signified cannot refer to reality in isolation does not imply it cannot refer to reality within a context composed of other relevant signifieds. On the contrary, the positive relations between signifieds enable them to refer to reality. Derrida errs when he says "language is entirely intertextual—words refer to one another in wholly contingent manners without touching any translinguistic reality."[9]

Derrida's critique of stable meanings might seem to rest not just on his analysis of the signified but also on his practice of deconstruction and his games with language. Really, however, the procedures Derrida uses to problematize meaning all fail along with his purely differential theory of meaning. Derrida deploys deconstruction, metaphors, and the like in order to show how arguments for stable meanings undermine themselves. Crucially, an argument might undermine itself in two different ways. First, there might be a logical contradiction in the intellectual content of an argument. Such contradictions trouble all philosophers. Second, there might be a contradiction between an argument's intellectual content and the way it is made. This is the sort of contradiction Derrida alights on when he deconstructs texts. Yet his justification for worrying about this second sort of contradiction depends entirely on his purely differential theory of meaning. Only if there are no stable signifieds will we treat signifieds as akin to signifiers: only if there are no stable meanings will we treat the intellectual content of an argument as akin to the way it is made. If there are stable meanings, we will consider the validity of the intellectual content of an argument independently of the manner of its performance. Thus, because signifieds are not differential, Derrida cannot problematize meaning simply by pointing to a contradiction between what a text says and how it says it. (He could problematize meaning only by pointing to logical contradictions in all arguments for stable meanings, and this he does not do.)

Consider Derrida's reading of Saussure. On the one hand, Derrida points to a contradiction between the content and performance of Saussure's *Course in General Linguistics*. Derrida argues that Saussure undermines his own argument for the priority of speech over writing because he explains the nature of speech by reference to writing. But there is no problem here. Saussure thinks speech is prior to writing, but because the latter is more familiar to us he finds it useful to explain the nature of the former by reference to the latter. We can use one thing to explain another without thereby being committed to regarding the latter as prior to the former. On the other hand, Derrida points to a contradiction in the content of Saussure's ideas. Derrida argues that Saussure's doctrine of the arbitrary nature of the sign undermines Saussure's belief in the stable link between signifiers and signifieds. If this is so, it is a logical contradiction, so Saussure's attempt to fix this link fails. Nonetheless, the failure of Saussure's attempt to bind signifiers to signifieds does not entail the failure of all such attempts. On the contrary, my relational theory of meaning allows us to bind signifiers to signifieds within a given theoretical context. There are stable meanings; it is just that they are in part products of our theories.

Husserl and Truth

Derrida proceeds from a rejection of stable meanings to a critique of the very idea of truth or objective knowledge. He argues that because we cannot have access to stable meanings, we cannot take anything as a given fact—a simple presence—so we have no foundations on which to ground truth-claims. "The dream at the heart of philosophy" is to bring the play of signifiers to an end by appealing to "the assured legibility of the proper."[10] Philosophy exalts a myth of presence: something is given as true to consciousness; it acts as a stable foundation for claims to knowledge. But, Derrida continues, the dream of philosophy can never be realized because there are no stable meanings; nothing is simply given to consciousness; nothing can secure truth-claims.

Derrida's critique of truth appears in his reading of Edmund Husserl. According to Husserl, phenomenology gives us a method for investigating the objects of consciousness.[11] Consciousness provides the starting point for philosophical inquiry because it is the one thing that is simply present to us and thus undeniable. When we focus on consciousness, we define its objects as correlative to thought, so we reject the distinction between things we perceive and our perception of them. Philosophers, therefore, investigate things in themselves by bracketing off all assumptions about a world beyond consciousness. Husserl denies, however, that this phenomenological concentration on the content of consciousness generates only subjective knowledge. He distinguishes between aspects of consciousness that characterize thought as such and ones that are contingent features of the thought of particular individuals. Phenomenology relies on a process of reduction to make this distinction and thereby focus on the objective features of consciousness as such. It gives us access to truths that are simply present to consciousness as such. In *The Origin of Geometry*, Husserl uses his phenomenological method to analyze geometry.[12] Although a truth of geometry is realized as true only when it becomes the object of a particular consciousness, it is true a priori in that it is a necessary feature of consciousness as such. A truth of geometry originates in the act of reason that discovers it to be true, and it is recognized as true in each subsequent act of reason that grasps it as such; but its status as an a priori truth present to consciousness as such remains unaffected by errors in the acts of reason that discover and recognize it to be true.

Against Husserl, Derrida argues that no stable objects are simply present to consciousness. Any appeal to truths present to consciousness entails an element of subjectivism—a concern with their genesis in the individual mind—from which errors can be excluded only by an appeal to writing. On the one hand, Husserl secures meaning and truth, "the ideal transparency and perfect univocity of language," by appealing to idealized objects that are indefinitely repeatable, that is, a view of the object as a given presence always and everywhere the same.[13] On the other hand, he secures the object as a given presence by appealing to writing, which, according to Derrida, undermines the stability of meaning that Husserl wants to establish. Husserl tries to avoid this difficulty by distinguishing expressive from indicative uses of language. When we use language expressively, we convey intentional meanings immediately present to consciousness. When we use language indicatively, we merely point indirectly to such meanings. According to Husserl, we can accept writing when it is a transparent medium that facilitates the pure expression and transmission of thought, but not when it acts as an opaque barrier to truths held in or recognised by the mind. Derrida, however, objects that writing always has an indicative character. Using Saussure's terminology, he says, "whenever the immediate and full presence of the signified is concealed, the signifier will be of an indicative nature," and, of course, Derrida's view of meaning suggests the signified is never fully present but rather always constituted in part by an absence.[14] We cannot grasp concepts except through the opacity of the words we use to convey them; writing is always indicative so it cannot secure claims to truth in the way Husserl proposes.

In Derrida's introduction to Husserl's *Origin of Geometry*, for example, he argues that Husserl can describe geometric truths as present to consciousness only by referring to the writing down of these truths.[15] If geometric truths were immediately present to consciousness, we would be unable to allow for the mistakes some individuals make in recognizing them. Thus, Husserl has to recognize that objectivity here depends on graphic representations securing the iterability of geometric truths. Husserl has to imply, contrary to his own argument, that only writing gives geometric truths the secure permanence of objective knowledge. Derrida's point here is that although Husserl argues geometric truths are self-evident to consciousness, he still has to invoke the writing down of these truths in order to secure them as objectively true—his text undermines his explicit argument.

Although Derrida attacks Husserl's idea of a pretheoretical consciousness by appealing to a differential theory of meaning, a relational theory of meaning, such as the one I have proposed, also implies that we should reject Husserl's metaphysics of presence. A metaphysics of presence postulates a one-to-one correspondence between concepts and their referents. It implies that signifieds do not need a theoretical context to bind them to their referents. Some signifieds are given to consciousness as brute facts independent of all else. A relational theory of meaning implies that this is not so. If all signifieds are relational, they all require a theoretical context to bind them to their referents. A relational view of meaning implies that the objects a concept picks out must depend on other concepts, so no concept can pick out objects in the absence of other concepts. The content of consciousness cannot be pretheoretical.

Consider the example of the concept "red." Husserl's metaphysics of presence would require some of our concepts to refer to objects in splendid isolation; perhaps we just see some objects are red, so we conceive of them as red. But I have argued that this is not so; to recognise something as red our student needs to master other concepts. Red is an abstract category that on its own cannot tell us which objects we should and should not place under it. More generally, all signifieds must be relational because when we identify an object as belonging under a given category we classify it in a way that presupposes theories about the world. Theories are implicit in all the objects that appear before consciousness. Nothing is given to us as a simple presence. Crucially, because all signifieds are relational, they can be tied to objects only in a theoretical context, so the truth-value of a statement must depend on our theoretical commitments. Nothing is given to consciousness outside of all theoretical contexts. Theoretical assumptions enter into our understanding of every aspect of the world, so we cannot possibly rest our knowledge on pure descriptions of pure experiences empty of all theoretical content. Phenomenologists cannot base objective knowledge on experiences that are simply given to consciousness since even experiences as they are given to consciousness must be experiences of theoretically constructed objects. Because our world is theoretically constructed, the dream of philosophy fails; we are left without the possibility of an absolutely certain set of beliefs. We are left, as Derrida puts it, with the fact that our "world is written only in the plural."[16]

Derrida is right, therefore, to reject Husserl's concept of objective knowledge as certainty. The relational nature of signifieds, the theory-laden nature of experience, means that no fact is given to us as an indubitable presence. Where Derrida goes astray is not in embracing an epistemological modesty that recognizes the uncertainty of knowledge, but in embracing an antirationalism that seems to deny knowledge any validity whatsoever. Here my relational theory of meaning implies that we can have access to stable objects, where the stability of these objects depends on our theorizing, and although the theory-laden nature of consciousness precludes our justifying knowledge in some ways, it does not preclude all such justification.

The theory-laden nature of consciousness implies there are no given facts so we cannot compare the content of consciousness with something else, neither the world as it is nor a quasi-Platonic world of ideal forms. Because there are no given facts against which to judge the theory-laden content of consciousness, knowledge cannot be absolutely certain. For a start, because no single piece of knowledge is given to us as true, the validity of knowledge cannot rest on its individual parts. Instead, we must justify knowledge as a whole; objectivity must be, at least in the first instance, a property of a body of knowledge. Individual bits of knowledge must be objective by virtue of belonging to an objective body of knowledge. Moreover, because we cannot compare the content of consciousness with something else, we cannot justify a body of knowledge by appealing to an external reality; we cannot say knowledge is valid because it corresponds to the world as it is. Instead, we must justify knowledge by comparing it with other bodies of theories we might adopt. Any ascription of objectivity must be a result of a comparison between rival bodies of theories. Finally, because knowledge cannot be absolutely certain, any ascription of objectivity must be provisional. When we say a body of knowledge is objective in comparison with its rivals, we do so at a moment in time. Later changes in the rival bodies of knowledge available to us could alter the result of our comparison and thus lead us to renounce the body of knowledge we now take to be true. Because no body of knowledge can stand as a complete account of the world, we must treat ascriptions of objectivity as provisional results of current practices.

My relational theory of meaning implies, therefore, that any acceptable theory of objectivity must proceed by showing how a body of knowledge can meet criteria of comparison in a way that should lead us to accept it provisionally as true. What we take to be objective knowledge must depend not on things present to consciousness, but rather on our activity as theorizers. For a start, our theories tell us what counts as an exemplary perception of an object. Although exemplary perceptions incorporate theoretical assumptions, they still provide us with shared facts, where these facts are propositions the members of our community accept as true, not truths simply given to consciousness. Our theories assure us of the validity of certain facts, so we can use these facts to justify the rest of our knowledge. Moreover, our theories provide us with criteria of comparison by which to decide between rival accounts of these facts. We can compare competing bodies of knowledge by examining things such as how well they fit the facts, the number and range of facts they fit, their internal coherence, how many hypotheses they generate, how well the hypotheses they generate fit the facts, and the boldness of the hypotheses they generate. Our theories define criteria that give us a normative standard by which to define a particular body of knowledge as objective. Finally, because the body of knowledge we take to be objective is thus the one that best meets our current criteria, later developments obviously could lead us to modify or renounce it.

Objective knowledge is, therefore, a product of a comparison between rival accounts of agreed facts.[17] No doubt a comparison between competing bodies of knowledge will not always find one to be notably superior to all others—the value of relativism is to remind us of just this fact. Although we have an objective standpoint from which to reject flat-earth theories—a comparison of various theories using established criteria is adequate for this task—there remain several other theories we treat as more or less equally valid; a comparison of them using established criteria does not yield a clearcut decision. Nonetheless, our inability to decide between various bodies of knowledge does not require us to adopt Derrida's antirationalism. Not only have we decided between some equally valid theories and other accounts of the world, we also have a rational conclusion to the debate between these equally valid theories. We should not say that the choice between them is an arbitrary one, but rather that an objective standpoint is one that recognizes their equal validity.

To avoid Derrida's antirationalism, however, we still need a reason to take objective knowledge, as I have defined it, to be true. Here, because objective knowledge arises within the context of a social practice, the question of whether or not we should accept it as true depends on the stance we take to this practice. Modern philosophy offers several plausible theories for accepting the results of our epistemic practice: pragmatists suggest we accept objective knowledge as true because it works; some falsificationists suggest we do so because the theory of evolution tells us to trust the mechanisms by which we acquire it; and Ludwig Wittgenstein would have us do so because of the central role it plays in our form of life.[18] I do not think that these theories are intended to secure individual facts as certain—they are intended rather to apply to the whole body of knowledge thrown up by our epistemic practice—but even if I am wrong about this, it is easy to see how they could be made to apply to a body of knowledge. Any one of them, therefore, could provide a suitable response to Derrida's skepticism and sntirationalism. Derrida does not try to counter them because he thinks his attack on all fixed signifieds undermines them just as it does Husserl's faith in a metaphysics of presence. Yet I have argued that signifieds can be fixed by an appropriate theoretical context, and this means that theoretical justifications of our epistemic practice do not fail along with the idea of truth as absolute certainty. The fact is that the unwarranted leap in Derrida's theory of meaning also undermines his skeptical antirationalism. The absence of signifieds fixed independently of their context really does imply there are no brute facts—nothing is present to consciousness as a thing in itself. Thus, Derrida is right to reject Husserl's account of phenomenology as a method of uncovering a priori truths by investigating objects that are present to consciousness as such. However, the existence of signifieds fixed by an appropriate theoretical context implies we can construct facts by our theoretical activity, and this opens up the possibility of a defence of objective knowledge conceived as the product of a social practice. Thus, Derrida is wrong to reject the very idea of objective knowledge in favor of a skeptical antirationalism.

Reconstituting Phenomenology

My arguments clearly suggest that we need to rethink the nature of phenomenology so as to free it from the myth of presence. I want to conclude by looking briefly at how we might do this. The key thing is to accept that the objects of consciousness are always in part theoretically constructed. Throughout I have argued for a relational theory of meaning, and this theory echoes much of Derrida's critique of Husserl's concept of presence. Nothing is simply given to consciousness; every object that appears before consciousness is in part a theoretically constructed one. Phenomenology, therefore, cannot give us knowledge of objects that are simply given to consciousness. Rather, it must explore objects that are constructed in part by our theoretical activity. To accept this is not necessarily, however, to conclude that a phenomenological concentration on the content of consciousness can provide us only with subjective insights into our individual minds. On the contrary, the conclusions that we derive from our phenomenological investigations will be valid for all those who construct objects with the aid of the same theories we use. We can still accept, therefore, much of Husserl's position: we can accept that phenomenology begins with a rigorous inspection of one's own consciousness and intellectual processes; we can accept that in performing this inspection philosophers exclude all assumptions about the external causes and consequences of these processes; and we can accept that this inspection leads not to subjective knowledge but to a grasp of ideas or meanings common to several minds. What we cannot accept is his claim that these ideas or meanings are common to every mind. We have to regard them instead as common to any mind that shares our theoretical assumptions. Phenomenology does not give us certain a priori knowledge. It provides us instead with knowledge that will be taken as true by all those who share our particular form of life.

I deliberately used the phrase "form of life" here because I want to highlight the extent to which adopting a relational theory of meaning—rejecting Husserl's myth of presence—might lead us to rethink phenomenology along lines made familiar by Wittgenstein.[19] Certainly there are significant parallels between my brief account of phenomenology as the study of a consciousness composed of objects that are fixed by our shared acceptance of certain theories, and Wittgenstein's account of philosophy as the study of the nature and use of our shared language. For a start, both accept, with Derrida, that there are no brute facts, so if stable meanings and truth exist, they must do so within the context of a body of theories or language. Moreover, both assert, against Derrida, that the relevant body of theories or language really does provide us with stable meanings, and thus a basis from which to defend an account of objective knowledge as a product of a comparison between rival bodies of theories. Finally, both a reconstituted phenomenology and Wittgenstein therefore face the question of what reason we can have for taking the knowledge generated by our epistemic practice to be true. Wittgenstein, of course, tries to find such a reason in the relationship that we have to our form of life, and I think this is indeed the best way to proceed. Nonetheless, phenomenologists might perhaps choose simply to bracket off the question of why we should accept the theories we do, in much the same way as Husserl brackets off the question of the relationship of the objects that appear before consciousness to an external reality.

Although there are similarities between my account of a reconstituted phenomenology and Wittgenstein's approach to philosophy, there are also important differences between them. In particular, my reconstituted phenomenology goes to work on concepts and theories, rather than language and its uses. Moreover, I think that this focus on concepts and theories enables us to avoid some problems associated with ordinary language philosophy. Various ambiguities in Wittgenstein's later work have encouraged some of his followers to adopt an extreme linguistic approach to philosophy. There are moments when he seems to argue that philosophy is a study of words, rather than concepts: philosophy, he implies, tells us about how we use words in our ordinary language, not about how we should theorize the world; and it aims to unravel the intellectual confusions created by the bewitching effects of language, not to extend our theoretical understanding of the world.[20] The reconstituted phenomenology I am advocating, in contrast, makes it quite clear that philosophy goes to work on our concepts so as to improve our theoretical understanding of the world. For a start, my reconstituted phenomenology would deal emphatically with the way things are, rather than the way we use language; it would explore our concepts in relation to our theories about the world, rather than in relation to the way we deploy them in our language. Whereas extreme linguistic philosophers can appear to be studying words as they are used in ordinary language, a reconstituted phenomenology would look at the theoretically constructed objects that appear before consciousness. No doubt phenomenologists might still examine ordinary language as a way of exploring these objects; after all, the theories we use to construct these objects will be ones embedded within a language. When they do so, however, they clearly will be discussing questions of linguistic usage only in order to discover things about the concepts, or objects, that appear before consciousness; their concern will remain the concepts and theories that constitute our understanding of the world. A reconstituted phenomenology, in other words, would focus less on using standard forms of speech to clarify actual norms of usage than on evoking unusual situations to clarify our grasp of the limiting cases to which we would apply various concepts and theories.

In addition, therefore, the principal aim of my reconstituted phenomenology would be to enhance our understanding of the world, rather than to exhibit to us the bewitching effects of language; it would try to derive further theories about the world from our existing ones, rather than to remind us of how we normally use words. Extreme linguistic philosophers sometimes imply that all philosophical problems arise when philosophers place words in contexts other than those they occupy in ordinary language: because the words do not belong in these contexts, they do not have any true meaning therein, and this absence of true meaning generates apparent paradoxes. Thus, they continue, linguistic philosophy dissolves philosophical problems simply by revealing them to be pseudoproblems that arise when we fail to grasp properly the way ordinary language operates. Philosophers, they conclude, should not develop theories, but rather remind us of how ordinary language operates so as to stop us worrying about meaningless paradoxes. In contrast, a reconstituted phenomenology would explore the theoretically constructed objects that appear before consciousness in order to reach a better understanding of their nature; it would explore our current understanding of the world so as to make our concepts clearer and then use them to develop further theories about the world. Because the theoretically constructed objects of consciousness constitute our understanding of the world, we can deepen and extend this understanding by exploring both their nature and their relationship to one another. This is what a reconstituted phenomenology would seek to do. In many ways, of course, it is also what Wittgenstein tries to do; certainly the philosophical problems he considers rarely resemble cases in which we use one word when we should have used another. They are more like cases in which we know what words to use but are confused about the concepts we thus apply; and the resolutions he provides to these problems rarely consist of clarifications of the way we use language—they are more like explorations of the limitations of theoretical models of the world suggested to us by our language. What I have tried to do, therefore, is to bring phenomenology and Wittgenstein's approach to philosophy closer to one another. I have tried to do so by freeing phenomenology from Husserl's myth of presence and by suggesting that we see Wittgenstein as interested in concepts and theories rather than words and their uses.

4

Of Photographs, Puns, and Presence

Susan A. Crane

> The present is the filling of a moment of time with reality: it is experience, in contrast to memory or ideas of the future occurring in wishes, expectations, hopes, fears and strivings.
>
> Wilhelm Dilthey

What does it mean to be in the presence of a photograph? Or, to restate it in a way that amplifies the complex potential of the question: What does it mean to recognize that one is fully present in the presence of a presented photograph? Some readers proofread compulsively; I do that, but I also hear heteroglossia impulsively, and I tend not to resist the intrusions because they prompt creative thinking.[1] In English, "present" is a heteronym: a multivalent term, which, although native speakers are unlikely to use it inappropriately, opens up wordplay which is also not irrelevant to a discussion of "presence." "The present" is a continuous moment in time which is also always in transition between past and future, and, as Michael Roth has astutely pointed out, it is precisely the photograph's inability to represent that duration that makes it a curious object for historical reflection.[2] So the presence of the photograph apparently stabilizes the flux of time—and in one of its heteronymic forms, makes a gift of its presence, as the gift that keeps on giving, insisting on the presentation of the present in that reiterated static form. Then too, to be present is to exist at a place and time; its antonym is absence. To be present in the present means to acknowledge distance from the past and to be in a physical location in a space/time continuum. What is not present may not exist; but what is not in the present still was or could be, either in the past or the future. The present is absolutely full of contingencies, making what ought to be most obvious, most illusory. For some critics, this awareness is as incapacitating as the postmodern proclivity for puns is annoying.

Unlike other documents and artifacts, historical photographs uniquely lend themselves to a historical gaze that renders them "present" in a universalizing, familiarizing, and ultimately objectifying manner. Viewers of historical photographs may feel that they recognize photographic subjects or landscapes, built environments, and assortments of objects even if they have never seen these before, in ways that suggest but do not require historical translation. Compellingly, photographs offer not only the "punctum" or frisson of realization that the reality of the past is tantalizingly available; indeed, "every photograph is a certificate of presence."[3] They also are apparent witnesses whose testimony renders visible lives and lifeways that are otherwise distanced by time. Borrowing a distinction from Georges Didi-Huberman, the "visible" ingredients of photographs, their formal elements, are inextricably entwined in their representational capacity, the "visual" impact.[4] In this way, photographs are uniquely both artifacts and bearers of representation. Historians are still learning how to account for photographs as more than mere illustrations of times past. Photographs challenge existing categories of evidence and testimony, and yet historians are still by and large not trained in visual analysis. Visual culture studies have emerged in the past thirty years as a corrective, and only since the turn of the century have historians acknowledged a "visual turn" necessitating new forms of analysis.

How the historian's gaze shapes the meanings associated with photographs needs to be interrogated specifically, in order to determine how the copresence of the real and the "reality effects" challenges the theoretical conceptualizations that Hans Ulrich Gumbrecht, Eelco Runia, Frank Ankersmit, and others have offered regarding the notion of "presence." Recently, in debates formed around a postmodern surge away from the assignment of meanings to texts, the notion of "presence" has reemerged as an antidote to the "there's no there there" aspect of discourse analysis. Gumbrecht's 2004 book on the "production of presence" describes a path taken by some literary critics in the 1970s through the 1990s to return to a humanist view of the material world; the book's revealing subtitle indicates an ambition to understand "what meaning cannot convey." As the cultural historian Lloyd Kramer put it, such theorists are "searching for something that is here and there and also gone," seeking the ineluctable.[5] Eelco Runia asserts that "what may be called 'presence' ('the unrepresented way the past is present in the present') is at least as important as meaning."[6] Frank Ankersmit's interventions into the debates about presence have highlighted the significance of the visual image, but it was remarkable that none of these literary critics or philosophers of history who were concerned with "presence" reflected on the extraordinary status of one specific kind of historical object: the photograph. The photograph's apparent ability to "be there" was accepted relatively unreflectively. How photographs, and particularly atrocity photographs, can be here and there and also should be gone, can now be addressed.

Parts and Holes

There's something charming about contemporary philosophers of history and literary critics desiring to reclaim "presence"—charming, in that historians might wonder what delights had been withheld by the presence of the past, which is always what attracted them to it in the first place. According to Runia, in his article "Presence," "we have long been led astray by the phenomenon of "meaning"—first by pursuing it, then by forswearing it" (Runia, 1). What mattered with meaning, what drove historians in their quest, were the ethical and national-political consequences of knowing about the past. The professional problem of how, then, to present those consequences led some historians and critics away from what had captured their interest to begin with—the "reality effects" Roland Barthes saw in photos, or Alain Badiou's "passion du réel" (cited by Runia, 5). Instead, modern professional historians inaugurated an era of historical narrative framed by the voice of the omniscient narrator who "would reveal all" in a carefully constructed story. Runia notes this trend, and Hayden White's epochal accounting of it, as well as a countertrend that originated sometime in the 1960s, away from hegemonic master narratives and toward poststructural "turns" away from meaning. He cites the debates around the "limits of representation" of the Holocaust in the early 1990s, polarized at a UCLA conference led by survivor-historian Saul Friedlander, as having had the unwitting effect of drawing "attention to the limits not of representation but of *representationalism*" (Runia, 3). Calling the historical narrative's ability to represent the past into question opened up new fields of historical inquiry.

Runia doesn't cite Gumbrecht, but they share a keen desire to feel the presence of the past as an epiphany—the sort of sublime historical experience that Ankersmit provided a theoretical framework for, and which I have attempted to describe as a motivational force behind historical preservation.[7] The early nineteenth century's historical collectors shared a Romantic sensibility that designated a sense of having been recently disconnected from the past and a longing for reconnection; not coincidentally, as Lloyd Kramer also notes, Gumbrecht shares this Romantic historical consciousness.[8] Epiphanies, by their very nature, elude containment in representation—they can be spoken of, but the experience is ephemeral and there is pain and loss associated with being sufficiently past that experience and ready then to share knowledge of it. Choosing to seek out opportunities for historically sublime experience might redeem the curious passivity that Ethan Kleinberg noticed in Ankersmit's and Gumbrecht's description of the historical sublimity: "there appears to be nothing to do but wait for sublime historical experience or presence to come to us."[9] Whether regrouping at conferences at the same site that initially was so inspiring, or publishing Romantic tracts on how to visit a museum gallery properly so that the sublime experience of historical consciousness would remanifest itself, intellectuals came back together in hopes of rekindling intellectual sparks—in hopes that repetition reproduces inspiration rather than redundancy. Kindred Romantic spirits, whether in Dresden in the 1790s or Dubrovnik in the 1970s, learned the same lessons: each experience of the sublime is unique, not replicable; and the presence experienced as "inspiration" is fundamentally unrepresentable because of its inherent connection to the inaccessible knowledge of divinity, what in theological terms is referred to as the "apophatic." Although Gumbrecht resolutely states that he in no way has become a "religious thinker," both kinds of critics are tempted by what eludes language, the revelation that speaks without words, which leaves an indelible impression that also itself begins to fade the moment it is recognized.[10] They call this "presence."

Particularly noteworthy is the way that Gumbrecht grounds his representation of "the production of presence" in his own life. For Gumbrecht,

Runia, and many others who may not choose to comment on it in print, academic conferences are more than line items on a curriculum vitae. A series of humanities conferences on topics such as "the functions of fiction" in Yugoslavia during the 1970s and 1980s fostered Gumbrecht's memorable encounters with both the physical beauty of the Adriatic beaches and the intellects of like-minded academic colleagues.[11] The reader senses that for Gumbrecht, place and intellectual stimulation were intertwined; "being there," on the Adriatic coast, allowed them, to paraphrase Greg Dening, to be at play on the "beaches of the mind" and amplified Gumbrecht's sense that he and his colleagues had made breakthroughs; they then longed to repeat that stimulating experience.[12] As often happens with the historical sublime, efforts to repeat, relive, or recirculate accounts of the epiphany experience did not live up to the initial inspiration, but Gumbrecht and his colleagues continued to meet and hope for further illumination. Those hoping to experience "presence" are as apt to be frustrated in their pursuit of the historical sublime as they are to be frustrated with the limits of meaning making.

Runia locates his desire for presence in personal experience less explicitly. He recognizes a characteristic desire for presence enacted within the historical discipline in the formation of collective memory studies, which he acknowledges but really has no interest in pursuing; this recent trend in historical studies, however, indicates for Runia one of the frustrations of pursuing the past as presence. His preference is that the past should now be "accessed" in other ways. "Innovative historical thinking," in Runia's terms, "does not start with focusing on history, but ends up with it." Runia makes his approach to presence in a thoroughly unappealing way via a bizarrely mixed metaphor:

> Innovative historical thinking . . . does not plunge into history right away, but starts with trying to ascertain in what respects the present cannot be understood *but by* turning to history. The past that is easily accessible, that spreads its legs and offers itself to fornication, that circulates—as a kind of "shareware"—through society, *that* past is, well, perhaps not exactly *dead*, but surely not much more than a reflection of what we already know. (Runia, 8)

The past is figured as some kind of Whore of History; and she isn't even worth the money, she's just what you "ended up with" when the present wasn't charming enough. She's only available as an Internet sensation, to boot (to kick around? to boot up?): freely accessible to all, and therefore useful but worth less; anyone can "have" her. Runia continues:

> The past, however, that is absent from our own mythology, the past that is withheld verbally, the past that is a subconscious *Aktuelle Macht* rather than freely circulating "shareware," *that* is the past that waits to be made sense of. (Runia, 8)

The present, in other words, is Princess History—that is, a sleeping beauty there before you who is worth rescuing—and suddenly the philosopher of history's interest in "presence" is something rather less endearing than Prince Charming's. Leopold von Ranke too referred to his sources as damsels in distress; some things never change.[13] But Runia's unfortunate choice of metaphors should give us pause, particularly since the bulk of the essay is about metonymy. Runia wants to emphasize, for instance, how historical monuments like the Berlin Holocaust memorial metonymically stand in for omnipresent memories that would otherwise remain unarticulated (Runia, 17). Metonymies, he argues, have their own histories and are repeatedly invoked even though, or perhaps because, their referential presence alludes to that which is otherwise always beyond our grasp, what might enable that elusive ephemeral experience of the sublime. Historical reality, he argues, "is incomparably more absent and incomparably more inaccessible than we like to think, though it is also—in metonymy—incomparably more present and accessible"; like a stowaway "the past 'survives' the text; as a stowaway the past may spring surprises on us" (Runia, 27). Metonymies tantalize with a promise of access that was far too easily obtained in the past we all thought we already knew; it is also the figure of speech, ironically, that draws most heavily on the intimacy of the relationship between signified and signifier. Runia finds the allure of presence among the stowaways much more sexy than the old whore of the past.

And Runia wasn't even looking at photographs. Historians have been chasing skirts and conducting love affairs with their archival sources at least since Ranke went to Italy, and desiring the experience of presence has clearly sensual aspects. Considering photographs as historical evidence or purveyors of potential presence merely turns up the heat. Julia Thomas knows that "photographs flirt":

> This is why historians love them, and why they drive us crazy. Unlike texts, which we usually approach with delicacy and suspicion, photographs often disarm us. They appear to offer immediate access to past realities and yet, when we try to embrace vanished worlds through them, we meet with resistance. We are left feeling baffled, even jilted, as photographs coyly withhold the full knowledge we desire.[14]

Thomas urges us to consider how "the evidence of sight" misleads historically conscious viewers into thinking they've achieved access to the past. Seeing is not only believing: seeing is experiencing, a quintessential moment of physical presence that, curiously, Gumbrecht and Runia don't consider. Relying on experience as a source of historical understanding, as Joan Scott worried, risks idiosyncrasy and presentism—in highlighting what *we* as historically conscious beings make of the presence of the past, we lose objectivity and historical context. But as Thomas points out, sight *is* personal, experienced by individuals in the process of using their brains (which is difficult to stop or prevent), and if we could not see it, the photograph would be absolutely useless as historical evidence.[15] The evidence of sight is not all we have; it is an essential starting point, but it must be combined with other historical knowledge. In effect, we have to acknowledge our blindness, as Thomas argues, in order to begin to appreciate what we have not been able to see with our eyes: the presence of the past.

Runia's lack of interest in collective memory studies, combined with his passion for the metonymic, raises a further issue. Collective memory studies have focused attention on the persistence of meanings formed as memories that often as not run against the archival and historical grain. The problem of representationalism actually arises outside the discipline rather than from within. The publics that are "consuming history" in the forms of movies, video games, Renaissance festivals, and living history museums are happier in pursuit of the present-day meanings of the past, than are historians who bemoan the limits of representation; they blithely ignore and transcend them, all the while studiously and carefully reenacting pastness.[16] Immersion in the virtual past, through video games such as Sid Meier's "Civilization," may characterize current experiences of presence in ways that appall historians unless, like Claudio Fogu, they respect the fact that historians are never the only ones making meanings out of the past.[17] This disjunction between historians' conceptions of the complex and diverse nature of the past, and public interests in buying, wearing, eating, or viewing reenactments is remarkably characteristic of our own present. History's presence is available to both, but only historians agonize over the meaning of this.

Shards and Wholes

What does it mean to be in the presence of a photograph? If, as Wilhelm Dilthey suggested, "the present" is not a moment of time filled with reality, but an experience of time and reality called "now," how can we understand the static presence of a moment in time, ripped from the continuum, of which we can now have an experience? How can we look at a photograph, which automatically represents something taken in the past and from the past, without a wrenching sense of disjuncture, or at least a hearty appreciation of an oxymoron? Like other historical documents and artifacts, photographs are three-dimensional objects whose reality and persistence over time categorically define "the presence of the past." And yet they are unique documents in that they sustain several kinds of historical moments: the recorded moment caught by the camera and its operator; the moments of its photographic development and reprints; and the multiple moments of being viewed. Texts too can relay multiple historical moments of recording and reception, but photographs simultaneously undermine their own historicity—they lend themselves to instantaneous recognitions that we make in the present, from their presence, leading viewers into a misguided perception of having direct access to another time instead of merely visual access to an object, a photograph, that is old. When we read a historical document, we may hold or see a thing that is old, the material that transmits the text from which we will make historical inferences; but when we hold or see a photograph, the fact that it is old and the immediacy of our seeing recognizable forms and contexts combine in an uncanny cognitive dissonance. Viewers of historical photographs often perceive that they can see into the past without barrier, as if historical distance were only imaginary. The photograph's uncanny ability to re-present the past in the present merits particular scrutiny by historians.

Conceptual difficulties abound in even the most innocent reference to "history," and one of the first stumbling blocks has to do with the distance between the past and the present. Where is it? Can you draw a line between the two, as in the sand? Things and lives transcend the past into the present, through lived experience and temporal duration, through generations of memories and collective experiences. I propose that we need to define "the past" as "present"—to the extent that it persists in the mind of the historically conscious individual. This conception of "the present" is intangible, and if it can be said to "exist" it does so mentally. So one of the first confusions that need to be overcome is how to represent the intangible—and that is why scholars have felt compelled to talk about meanings rather than presence. The mind of the historically conscious individual is a thing, which processes information neurologically, and as such can be observed and can make observations. But despite significant advances in neurology, we still can't "see" a thought or how biochemical processes produce an impression consanguine to the world outside ourselves. So we have to rely on humanistic conceptions of representation that are always inadequate to reality, and this is how we get historical objects: they do not merely exist, but have been identified as such by historically conscious observers. Dilthey's nineteenth-century conception of history as a "mind-constructed world" remains apt for historians who want to make the visual world a touchstone of historical analysis. It is perhaps not insignificant that Gumbrecht blames Dilthey specifically for a hermeneutics that "mortgaged the future of the humanities with the sole purpose of keeping certain problems at bay."[18] Insofar as hermeneutics was a method of reading that facilitated contemporary access to texts written for audiences in the past, it was an optimistic process; but Gumbrecht and his contemporaries became concerned that this access was itself prohibitive to alternative strategies of reading. Granted, Gumbrecht acknowledges that his generation of post-'68ers may have overstated the extent to which Dilthey, particularly as a scholar of Friedrich Schleiermacher, constrained opportunities for meaning to be produced within the hermeneutic horizon. It may well be, however, that we can profitably return to Dilthey for a philosophy of history that supports appreciation of the mind-constructed world of presence. Dilthey was extraordinarily sensitive to "being there" in the time-space continuum of life. As Dilthey wrote, "The ship of our life is, as it were, carried forward on a constantly moving stream, and the present is always wherever we are on these waves—suffering, remembering or hoping, in short, living in the fullness of our reality."[19] For Dilthey, history is "not something separated from life or remote in time from the present."[20] The past is what happened; history is what we make of it—our interpretations, understandings, and meanings—as well as the experience that allows us this knowledge, because "the past is a permanently enduring presence."[21]

When photographs were first created in the nineteenth century, stunned observers intuitively, almost instantly, realized that a technology now existed for capturing both "presence" and the present. The line in the sand, usually blurry, suddenly seemed to have been demarcated. The desire to know the past through historical objects could now be fulfilled in an entirely new way. Observers were confounded by the discovery of a method by which to permanently capture the most fleeting element of historical consciousness: time. But what was seen as a breakthrough that would aid and replace memory instead wound up creating new obstacles to historical knowledge. As Robin Kelsey has provocatively shown, photographs have an uncanny ability to capture random moments, ripping them from time and disconnecting time from the way we actually experience it, as a continuum. Both emblematic and blurry images equally share in the phenomenon of what was in fact not only evidence of an event, but evidence of the photographer's fortuitous "chance."[22] Photographic representation alienated observers because it presented the past once removed—(and this is a double pun)—once removed: the past once it no longer existed; and the past at a distance (and the past in a form that no one in the moment might have seen). The photographer's "chance" creates a "presence" only tangentially related to the event experienced by participants. How can such an object—neither in its three-dimensional form nor in its two-dimensional aspect for its typical recirculation in print or online—how can such a "thing" reveal what is by nature an experience of temporal duration? Chance moments caught in photographs are frozen time; historical events transpire.

Frank Ankersmit has called for a new philosophy of history that reflects and incorporates the nature of visual sources and our perceptions of them, a suggestion I would like to second.[23] Historians have turned back to influential nineteenth-century philosophers of history such as Ranke, rediscovering in these pioneers of modern historical thought a recognition of the visual impact of historical sources that has been papered over (pardon the pun) by later writers. Ranke, for instance, had from an early date believed that the significance of historical study lay in its ability not only to "represent the past as it really was" but also to "bring past life before one's eyes"– and this well before the invention of photography.[24] The question of why the visual image was devalued in favor of the text (which is, after all, itself a visual object) remains to be properly excavated and discussed, and it is becoming more relevant. Ankersmit suggested that "the study of history is more a 'depiction' than a 'verbalization' of the past," foregrounding the historical nature of the visual.[25] Philosophers of history are of course quick to point out that any reflection on history is a verbalization of historicity, or a bringing to speech of historical consciousness. Visual sources confound historical consciousness because they blur the distinction between past and present, but in their alterity (that is, they come from the past that no longer is; they are in the present but retain a trace of the past) photographs in particular are uniquely situated to confront historians with the most fundamental problem regarding historical sources.

To put this another way, I would like to invoke Paul De Man's reading of Walter Benjamin's 1927 essay "The Task of the Translator."[26] Some critics may see Benjamin's writings on photography as themselves modern historical relics, or relics of modernist sensibilities we have moved past, but I continue to find inspiration in his work and so did De Man.[27] More clearly than one would expect from an obscurantist of deconstruction, De Man used Benjamin's insights to create an evocative image of historical consciousness. He reads particularly closely Benjamin's description of a broken vase (or amphora). Benjamin's essay revolves around the relationship between the original text and its translation, emphasizing the creativity generated in the second language by its ability to translate the foreign into the familiar. German translators, for instance, succeed when they turn German into Hindi, Greek and English, not vice versa, so that the German language is enriched by the addition of the richness of the original language's "presence" in translation. De Man takes this insistence on generativity and puts it under the microscope of close reading: he takes the fragments of the broken amphora and examines them under the lens of historical consciousness. The amphora lies shattered, and Benjamin (who has in mind the translation of languages) compares the cleanup and restoration of the object to the creation of a translated text. De Man faults Harry Zohn's translation of Benjamin, the standard for many years, for creating this rendition of the process:

> Fragments of a vessel which are to be glued together must match one another in the smallest details, although they need not be like one another. In the same way, a translation, instead of resembling the meaning of the origi-

nal, must lovingly and in detail incorporate the original's mode of signification, thus making the original and the translation recognizable as fragments of a greater language, just as fragments are part of a vessel. (Benjamin, 78)

De Man prefers Carol Jacobs's translation:

Fragments of a vessel, in order to be articulated together . . . must follow one another in the smallest detail. So instead of making itself similar to the meaning, to the *Sinn* of the original, the translation must rather, lovingly and in detail, in its own language, form itself according to the manner of meaning of the original, to make both recognizable as the broken parts of a greater language, just as fragments are the broken parts of a vessel.[28]

I use plates more often than vases, and while I don't want to lose the antique resonances of the amphora, I would paraphrase De Man this way: when you break a plate, and try to put it back together, you never get another whole plate—you get a broken plate. Even if you swept up every speck, every bit of dust from the mess, you still have a bunch of nonidentical fragments that cannot be restored to the complete plate in its original, intact state. The beauty of De Man's reading is that he lets Benjamin—who was famously rather attached to an image of an angel being blown backwards into the future with a pile of trash, all those fragments of historical progress and the past itself, heaping up before him—dwell on the mess, the fragments, and what the craftsmanship of the translator is capable of restoring: not an imperfect version of a previously perfect whole, but a new version of the former object. This new object, an object of vision as much as of meaning, is full of cracks, and the only thing holding it together is the fullness of the translator's vision.

Not surprisingly, Benjamin saw exact parallels between the task of the translator and the task of the historian. The translator uses whole language, the human capacity for language, to rearticulate the amphora. The historian provides the meanings that lie at the interstices, in the cracks, adhering to their edges and not quite holding the whole thing together. De Man thinks "glue" is too literal a translation for Benjamin's notion of rearticulation, but I think he may have missed a resin-ance. Benjamin died before hot glue was invented, but its bonding agency is more what I have in mind: although hot glue acts as the ultimate bonding agent, it melts under extreme heat and everything it held together will disarticulate once again. (I speak of hot glue with the painfully acquired personal experience of a desert dweller; bear with me, this metaphor will only stretch so far.) Historical criticism, which scrutinizes artifacts for information about the past, and uses those artifacts to create historical meanings, holds both as strongly and as tenuously: strongly, as long as the meanings are viable, significant to the present, and abiding under the rules of ethical engagement with memory and evidence; tenuously, in that historical meanings melt under revision—and this is no accidental etymological coincidence. No interpretation has sacred tenure. Historical interpretations proliferate because the past in all its fragmentariness can never be fully rearticulated, and because the past is constantly being renewed by the onward force of the present: "the past" is constantly being created; "history" is the coming to terms with what we think of what is left. History is a broken plate that historians have pieced together so we can look at it and see something meaningfully whole, since the intact original is not available. De Man says Benjamin made the original a dead thing, that he killed it in order to reveal that we received it as dead. Plates aren't living things. But what if the original plate was a photograph that represented genocide victims or bodies placed deliberately in pain?

If I'm belaboring the fragmentariness of the past and the broken plate philosophy of history, it's because photographs and especially atrocity photographs have the evidentiary capacity to undermine our received notions of the nature of historical evidence. The broken shards that make up our pasts in the forms of documents and relics have all been made legible through the historian's ability to translate past meanings into present ones. If that evidence became opaque, or if we lost the ability to make the translation, history as such would be fundamentally altered. Photographs, in which the facticity of the photographic object in the present coheres with the factual nature of its content, remain visible whether or not the meanings and contexts associated with their content are transmitted or transmissible. A photograph can be touched, in the original as well as in the reprint; the contents can be described. Its physical properties do not change over time, unless it decays, and so long as you can tell what the image was depicting, you can engage in preliminary formal analysis of it. But once you move on to the level of critical analysis of the contents, you can no longer rely on the photograph alone to understand the contexts of its production and postproduction; of what it might represent; and of what other photographs went along with this particular broken plate (I am trying to resist puns here about the role of plates in early photographic reproduction). Just as no historian of any repute would rely on a single document to ascribe truth to anything about the past, so too no one should look at a photograph and assume it speaks anything of its visual content self-sufficiently.

According to the theorist Georges Didi-Huberman, the visual "loosens our grip on the 'normal' (let's say rather: habitually adopted) conditions of visible knowledge."[29] Drawing on early Renaissance paintings and Christian iconography, Didi-Huberman argues that "the visual" opens up transcendent, potentially revelatory insights: "Either you are merely the visible, in which case I will abhor you as an idol, or you open onto the radiance of the visual, in which case I will acknowledge in you the power to have touched me deeply, to have made a moment of divine truth surge forth, like a miracle."[30] Partly because visual content is historically contingent, and partly because it is indicative of an elusive, most likely unknowable wisdom, "the visual" in the photograph indicates an uncontrollable effect on possible knowledge. Roland Barthes famously viewed photographs as reminders of death; I am trying to highlight, as did Julia Thomas, the photograph's ironic capacity to hold knowledge beyond our grasp, mainly in order to remove photographs from the category of self-evident historical objects and into a more abstract, and metaphysically risky, realm of historical knowledge.

A photograph of an atrocity depicts something awful to behold, because it participates in the atrocity. This is especially true when the photographer takes the photo to document pride or achievement, delectation or gratification, or to facilitate someone else doing so, but not only in those cases. Following philosopher Cathy Card, I define atrocities as paradigms if/when they are uncontroversially evil, cause intolerable harm regardless of motive, and consist of culpable wrongdoing on a scale of magnitude that perpetrators are far less likely to perceive as evil than are their victims.[31] Atrocity photographs, by my definition, cause intolerable harm when they are made *and* when they are viewed and recirculated to compound culpable wrongdoing, *regardless of motive*. This seriously complicates any consideration of being in the presence of this genre of photograph. Thus it may matter less whether viewers of Holocaust photographs, for example, are replicating a Nazi gaze—an argument I considered seriously in a previous article—because *regardless of motive* they are indulging the creation of pain in the depicted victims and the photographer's intention to replicate that pain interminably by recording it.[32] If this seems overstated – surely most documentary photographers do not intend to perpetuate the pain of the victims, but rather to record it so that awareness will lead to justice—consider what was the point of taking a picture of pain, when it serves neither diagnosis, nor treatment of that pain, nor justice for the dead?[33] I would like to suggest here four related propositions that I feel sum up the status of atrocity photographs as historical evidence:

1. The body in pain is inarticulate. Elaine Scarry's profound insights from over twenty years ago remain resonant for historians viewing atrocity photographs.[34] Historical subjects in photographs are mute, but even if we could hear the victims' voices, the vocal register of human pain would not be universally understood; it would require translation.
2. Photographs render their subjects mute. They remove agency from their subjects, and cause them to be depicted in a format that literally takes away their voices, inarticulate or otherwise.
3. Photographs silence pain. Historians or critics who hope to honor the dead, bear witness to the victims' suffering, and testify to the horrors of evil need to be reminded that the *photograph references the silencing of that pain, never the recovery of the victims' voices.* As the German Jewish poet Gertrud Kolmar, who was killed in Auschwitz, wrote in the final line of "Die Dichterin": "You hear me speak. But do you hear me feel?"
4. Photographs do not restore life. Omer Bartov's book *Erased* (2007) vividly illustrates how inadequate photographs are to the resurrection of the past, in this case of extinguished communities of Polish Jews.[35] The photographs he uses show the husks of buildings and empty spaces to illustrate atrocities at those locations. As such, they are not "atrocity photographs." Bartov's model is perhaps the best for those who wish to honor the victims, but even this cannot revivify the past.

These four propositions are my tentative way of proceeding with an earlier effort to make it ethically viable *not* to look at atrocity photographs. There is also precedent for this in art. For instance, the photographer

Alfredo Jaar took thousands of pictures of the Rwandan genocide, which he then hesitated to publish. Instead, in his *Real Pictures* series from 1995, commissioned by the Museum of Contemporary Photography in Chicago, he placed more than half of his photos in one hundred black archival boxes with white text on their lids describing the depicted events, which were themselves being withheld from view. The boxes were then stacked up and installed in the museum, which the critic Paul Williams described as a monument to the genocide.[36] And while it is clearly intended as a monument, Jaar also revealed a profound sense of the historicity of his exhibit. In an interview, Jaar described his work this way: "The camera never manages to record what your eyes see, or what you feel at the moment. The camera always creates new reality. If the media and their images fill us with an illusion of presence, which later leaves us with a sense of absence, why not try the opposite? That is, offer an absence that could perhaps provoke a presence."[37] Absent atrocity images are not to be ignored or neglected as historical evidence, but neither are they to be recirculated. Their presence stymies historical understanding because the evidentiary capacity of the image is neither transparent nor universally accessible, and is easily decontextualized; their absence would remind us of the ineffability of presence—and isn't that what Gumbrecht and Runia hope to experience? Don't the absent images ironically serve as better evidence of sight than the metonymic traces we already have?

Puns play on words by calling up several meanings at once while simultaneously requiring that we look askance at the literal meanings—so puns actually require us to look away from the evidence of meaning in favor of the evidence of heteronymy.[38] Multiple meanings produce multiple objects, and we need to collect them all together to rearticulate presence. When Didi-Huberman argued for the imperative importance of viewing four specific atrocity photographs—those taken by the Auschwitz Sonderkommando of victims who were forced to strip outdoors and then proceed to the gas chambers—he noted that it was crucial not only to view them but to view them together.[39] The photographs' significance was embedded in the way that they were taken clandestinely, with smuggled cameras and from hiding within doorframes, which rendered two of them blurry and indistinct. Of these images, one has become iconic because it was able to depict naked women whose identities could almost be ascertained, but also because it is less blurry. When this image is reproduced singly, Didi-Huberman argues, it lends itself to a representation of innocent victimization more generally; however, the solo reproduction, especially if it is cropped and edited to highlight distinct women, actually reduces the possibility of seeing the heroic agency of the photographer. By wiping out the evidence of how difficult it was to make that image, reproductions of the one photograph twist its metonymic significance: instead of offering a metonym of Holocaust victimhood, it reproduces a part of the Nazi destructive process. Each part, removed from the whole, destroys the historical context; as Kelsey argued, the photograph itself is a record only of fortuitousness, not of the past in the making. Didi-Huberman suggests instead that the four images must be seen together, to restore historical agency and resist replication of the Nazi gaze. Drawing on French cinema, he argues that montage is a superior form of historical representation. In effect, he reintroduces the means of coming to terms: through the missing aspect of duration in the critical discussion of presence.

If we are going to look at atrocity photographs, then, we should do so only in sequence and in context—in the broken plate of history, as one shard among many—and not use them in isolation, or as if speaking for themselves or for the pain of depicted victims. Perhaps only in this way does the atrocity photograph as historical evidence allow itself to be translated into presence. Perhaps only in this way, but perhaps in others, can we be in the presence of the photograph.

My thanks to Julia Adeney Thomas and Ethan Kleinberg for their valuable comments on drafts of this chapter. Portions of this work were presented at conferences sponsored by the Monash University Centre in Prato, Italy (June, 2010) and the University of Freiburg in Freiburg, Germany (July 2010).

5

THE PUBLIC RENDITION OF *IMAGES MÉDUSÉES*

Exhibiting Souvenir Photographs Taken at Lynchings in America

Roger I. Simon

I.

In a speech at Fisk University, James Allen offered the following reflections on his decision to make available for public exhibition the collection of lynching photographs and picture postcards he and John Littlefield had accumulated over a twenty-year period: "For every victim that lies pasted in some racist family's photo album ... or stored in a trunk with grandma and grandpa's Klan robe, or still pinned to the wall of a service station in some holdout sorry-ass little town—if we can acquire and place their photos in an accurate, respectful context, identify and record them for the first time, I feel some slight awareness of what is meant by resurrection."[1] With these extraordinary remarks, Allen puts forth the idea of a public exhibition as a very specific form of remedy and restitution, a practice of rendition that

---

Roger I. Simon passed away soon after the completion of his final draft of this chapter. The chapter thus stands as it was completed at that time.

brings the dead into presence.[2] Much like Walter Benjamin's notion of a *weak* messianic power to which the past has a claim,[3] Allen offers his exhibition practice as a way of returning haunting specters that have been entombed, formerly secreted and sealed away from any transformative place in contemporary consciousness and conscience. These specters are *weak* in that they cannot force the future either with social movement or revolution, but, in the struggle to redeem the past, the curatorial claim is that they do possess a force that might unstick the present from its seemingly necessary future.[4] The fundamental premise of this idea is that properly recontextualized, the recovery and subsequent formal display of past images of the perpetration of racist brutality and murder have something progressive to offer to contemporary America and its future possibilities.

Since the year 2000, there have been seven different exhibitions in the United States that have presented images from the Allen and Littlefield collection of 140 photographs taken at lynchings in the United States between 1870 and 1960, an overwhelming number of which targeted African Americans.[5] Not just clandestine acts witnessed in secret by a few, many lynchings were public events attended by scores of men, women, and children. Often at these events, commercial photographers would appear and take photographs not only of the person(s) subjected to torture and death but also the crowd who witnessed the spectacle. The photographs would then be sold as souvenirs, often in the form of picture postcards. Rather than creating a traveling exhibition more or less uniformly presented at different venues, various museums in the United States have differently drawn from the Allen and Littlefield collection, staging and supplementing the presentation of selected photographs in, at times, quite dissimilar ways. This quite unusual situation, wherein multiple exhibitions have drawn differently from the same archival source, provides the opportunity to explore how different museums have pursued the practice of re-framing the presentation of the photographs. Clearly the initial circulation of the photographs in this collection among those who bought them as souvenirs was not intended to provoke guilt, pity, or ameliorative action but rather to instantiate racial solidarity, terrorize African Americans, and produce income for the photographers who took the photographs.[6] With this history of the production and circulation of the photographs in mind, the contemporary exhibition of these images has attempted (though in different ways) to render what were once viewed as tokens of racial dominance and superiority into socially instructive scenes documenting instances of historical injustice and shameful barbarity. All the exhibitions of these lynching photographs have assumed that, properly sited and presented, the rendition of these deeply troubling, difficult images enacts a valuable form of public pedagogy.

Still this pedagogy is not without its questions. The first in this regard stems from an acute ambivalence associated with the practice of publically displaying photographs of death and suffering, even when it is done as a demand for justice or a warning as to the horrendous consequences of human aggression, or both. On the one hand, such "socially concerned" photographic exhibitions are still commonly accepted as indexical depictions of reality. Such depictions are not only offered as information but often are intended as an indictment, a moral charge directed at the people, ideologies, and structural conditions responsible for the actions and circumstances depicted. Through a pedagogy of display, it is assumed that photographic images can inform public opinion and mobilize action to promote justice via either prosecution, restitution, or reparations, as well as instantiating a normative order that would constrain such violence in the future. This privileging of photography is grounded by an epistemological trust as to the representational truth of an image as well as the hope that it will awaken compassion and the desire for understanding. On the other hand, there remains a deep anxiety in regard to the propriety of this assignation of technology with the rendering of suffering and dying. This specifically takes the form of an unease regarding photography's complicity in sensationalism and exploitation. While defending the necessity of their public exhibition, Dora Apel has exemplified this concern in relation to the contemporary display of lynching photographs. She argues that "although the photos display the vulnerable black body and risk reproducing the prurient interest and humiliating effect of racist violence, we, as a nation, cannot afford to be innocent of these photos. The loss to historical understanding incurred by refusing to see them would only serve to whitewash the crimes of white supremacy."[7] In these comments, Apel recognizes the difficulty in reading these photographs "against the grain," against the photographer's gaze refracted within the composition of the image. Certainly it is important to register that the onlooker may be affected not only by what they see but how they are made to see it. Despite this acknowledgment, within her nationally framed historical consciousness Apel empathically defends the decision to exhibit the photographs. As she states, "through the act of 'bearing witness' to these photographs today, the traumatic history they represent is re-framed through the shifted context of contemporary exhibitions, providing new insights into this deeply troubling part of American history and countering a demonstrated will to historical amnesia."[8]

Yet such arguments as Apel's do not dispel a serious skepticism regarding the consequences of viewing images of suffering. This disquiet is rooted in a suspicion that the act of viewing photographic images of suffering and death will be taken in itself as a sufficient act of ethical witness, sufficient as an act of reparation and repair and thus not requiring further thought and action. The worry here is that the opportunity to view images of suffering will initiate a self-satisfied complacence that is complicit with the very conditions that have produced suffering in the first place. Thus the concern that, after attending an exhibition of photographs from the Allen and Littlefield collection, viewers may come to feel that they need to look no further to understand the events rendered by these photographs, that structural violence requires only a personal emotional response, and that the represented calamity has already been resolved and can therefore be dismissed.[9]

Such concerns provoke difficult questions for any institution intending to publicly display images of suffering and death. In such a context, much is at stake as to the exhibition practices within which photographs are rendered, constituting as they do the visual event that stages the encounter between images and viewer.[10] This is nowhere as evident as it was in the *Without Sanctuary* exhibitions mentioned above. Certainly, these exhibitions were intended to be more than social rituals wherein those possessing a consciousness of the history of racial injustice in America would gain some satisfaction by experiencing the grief and indignation provoked by viewing irrefutable documentary evidence of the horror of lynching. On quite different terms, the *Without Sanctuary* exhibitions were presented as visual events that offered the possibility of provoking a witness that might substantially alter the continued existence of what s/he witnesses.[11] Mark Simpson puts the matter succinctly: "Riven with fissures and contradictions, lynching's historical crisis exceeds any response that aims to mourn or condemn past crimes without confronting their uncanny powers of return—that settles for static remembrance and not dialectical reckoning."[12] These are pregnant comments whose implications are worth unpacking. In a more general vein, Simpson's comments suggest the need to think through how the historical repair initiated by the rendition and re-framing of images of the past will guard the specificity and singularity of past and present, facilitating a dialectical connection among temporal events that avoid the collapse of diverse forms of victimization into each other. These comments suggest that such a re-framing must avoid any epistemological complicity with the presupposition that the wrongs of the past have been eclipsed. This is to say that we must be wary of viewing difficult images of the past from the emotionally reassuring vantage point that assumes such actions are not possible today. But as important as these considerations are for thinking through what is at stake in contemporary exhibitions that have set out to re-frame lynching photography, Simpson's comments offer a more specific and direct thought proposal. Drawing on Walter Benjamin's notion of dialectics at a standstill, Simpson argues that an exhibition intended to serve justice must "arrest the memory of lynching in order to face and know its present spectres."[13]

But how might an exhibition of photographs provoke such an "arrest" of memory, one that provokes a dialectical "relation of the what-has-been to the now"? Needed here is something beyond the historical meaning of the photograph, the denotation as to the "who, what, where, and when" indexed by an image. Certainly, the contemporary displays of the Allen and Littlefield lynching photographs were intended not only to inform museum visitors about particular violent events in U.S. history and to memorialize those victimized but to publically indict particular acts of murder and the systemic racism that legitimated them. However, the significance of these photographs does not just rest on what history they signify but also on what their contemporary presentation does physically to those who view them. This is not just a matter of collateral emotional damage. That the photographs were often colloquially described as "shocking" is an inadequate but still telling indication that the public presentation of these difficult images rendered a presence that cast forward a force whose very tactility embodied an indeterminate provocation of affect. This affect is not just that which might be attributed to a viewer's moral consciousness, a consciousness that was apparently nonexistent in the photographer. As I will argue below, it is also the result of something more intuitively felt when confronted with images of a body in pain. Understood on such terms, the rendition of these photographs constituted a visual event within which museum visitors were confronted by what Gilles Deleuze termed "encountered signs," signs that were felt, not just recognized and understood.[14] Critical here is that such a force not be understood as solely leading to the experience of sensation as such, but that the "affective force" of an image holds the possibility of compelling thought. As Deleuze wrote: "More important than thought there is 'what leads to thought' . . . impressions which force us to look, encounters which force us to interpret, expressions which force us to think."[15]

It is the possibility of affect that "leads to thought" that sets the stage for the explorations in this chapter. Thus my concern with the following two interrelated questions: (1) how might the presence encountered within the rendition of a series of lynching photographs be understood as a force to thought, and given this, (2) how might we understand the various exhibition logics organizing the public presentation of these photographs as containing, channeling, and disciplining the movement and substance of the relation between affect and thought.[16] These questions point to the importance of studying the various ways exhibitions have presented the photographs from the Allen and Littlefield collection and how it is that this exploration goes to the heart of contemporary considerations regarding public history and museology. Fundamental in this exploration are the problematic relations between affect and thought, image and word; relations that are central to comprehending any given instance of the public pedagogy of exhibitions. Such concerns are common to many other exhibitions that have attempted to publically render photographs taken by perpetrators of humiliation, suffering, and death. Most pertinent for my purposes here are the recent variations in public pedagogy organized by the Institute for Social Research in Hamburg. I am referring to the 1995 exhibition *Vernichtungskrieg: Verbrechen der Wehrmacht 1941–1944 (War of Extermination: Crimes of the German Armed Forces 1941–1944)* and its subsequent "correction" in 2001, in the guise of a new exhibition entitled *Verbrechen der Wehrmacht: Dimensionen des Vernichtungskrieges 1941–1944* (Crimes of the German Wehrmacht: Dimensions of a War of Annihilation, 1941–1944). These exhibitions offered documentary evidence and historiographic argument about the Wehrmacht's participation in war crimes on the Eastern Front during World War II. My concern will be how a consideration of the different employment of photographs in these two German exhibits might inform what is at stake in regard to the relation of affect and thought evident in exhibitions of lynching photographs presented at Pittsburgh's Andy Warhol Museum and at the Chicago Historical Society. To develop this analysis,

I first consider some of the major fault lines between these two different renditions of images from the Allen and Littlefield collection, and then consider it in light of the exhibitions on the crimes of the Wehrmacht.

II.

The Andy Warhol Museum (AWM) opened its *Without Sanctuary* exhibition on September 21, 2001. At the exhibit's entrance, visitors were greeted with two introductory panels placed on a dark maroon-red wall. The first of the texts provided an explanation of the contents of the exhibition, a statement of its provenance as part of the collection of Allen and Littlefield, and the museum's justification for publicly presenting the material. The exhibit was characterized as a moment of disclosure offering images that "have rarely been shown publicly" and thus revealing not only "a previously untold history, once hidden among ephemera," but as well "the power of photographs, whether documentation or art." In an effort to historically situate the photographs, the second panel provided visitors with a definition of lynching, the time and place coordinates for the majority of lynching activity, an explanation of why African Americans were the primary victims, and which Americans have been at the forefront of antilynching struggles.

Beyond the introductory text panels was a gallery in which were displayed ninety-two postcards containing images of lynchings, all of which were drawn from the Allen and Littlefield collection. The postcards/photos were placed in black frames with a large black mat and hung at eye level on muted cream walls with subdued lighting. The collection was presented chronologically and hence sequenced by the date of the lynching pictured in each photograph. However, where one started one's viewing of the images was indeterminate and, therefore, there was no specific path that structured a visitor's movement through the exhibition. This gallery also included several flat table cases for pamphlets and other ephemera as well as additional wall mounted material relevant to the history of lynching being presented through the photographs. The labels for each photograph were in black lettering on white background placed below the frames. Label texts provided a title, a date, and a location indicating where and when the photograph was taken, and technical information regarding the printing of the image. In addition to the gallery display of the lynching photographs, the sizable interpretive segment of the exhibition was made up of four distinct spaces. These spaces functioned to supplement the presentation of the photographs not only in the sense of ameliorating something sensed as a lack but in providing further experiences intended to extend and enrich (and hence transform) visitor's viewing of the photographs. This supplement to the photographs should not be understood as simply an "add on" that was secondary in importance to the primary material displayed. Rather, supplementation in this exhibition design was intended as a practice that put into place a structure through which the affect and meaning of any one segment of an exhibition might be either contained or transformed through its relation with others.

The first interpretive space beyond the photograph gallery was a forty foot long time-line entitled "African-American Experience, Struggle and Achievement: 1885–1995." Next was a gallery containing three displays including an exhibit focused on Billie Holiday and her signature antilynching song, "Strange Fruit," a display providing information on antilynching advocacy during the 1930s on the part of a local newspaper, and the presentation of an artwork specifically commissioned for the exhibition. This gallery also included ample space devoted to collecting an extensive range of visitor responses, including portfolios for written comments and a recording booth for video comments. A third supplementary space extended off this gallery and was a small cloistered area intended for reflection. It was quiet, dim, and provided benches and tissues. Outside this gallery and off the main hall was a fourth space whose purpose was to encourage visitor dialogue and social action. Part of this gallery was designated for daily facilitated public dialogues addressed not only to the exhibition but also to current concerns regarding race in America. This area contained concentric rings of chairs intended to create a degree of conversational intimacy. Even during hours when dialogues were not taking place, the presence of these chairs signaled the Museum's emphasis on public conversation concerning the significance of the exhibition. Next to this "forum" was a large table with blank postcards and writing implements. Here visitors could write a postcard addressed to themselves reflecting on their experience in the exhibition and offering any commitments they were prepared to make regarding future action for either personal or social change. Throughout the exhibition a changing selection of these written cards were on view tacked to a bulletin board mounted in the gallery. After the exhibition closed, the postcards were then mailed to their authors, effectively reminding visitors of their museum experience and the feelings, thoughts, and commitments it might have provoked. As well, this gallery contained one other seating area with a large table displaying reference material intended to support local and national social justice activism.

When the Chicago Historical Society (CHS) opened their version of the *Without Sanctuary* exhibition in June 2005, the gallery space allotted for the photographs was over double that at the Warhol Museum. Nevertheless, in displaying only fifty-five lynching postcards and photographs compared to the ninety-two displayed in Pittsburgh, the CHS presented just over half the number of images that had been presented at the Warhol. However it was not just the difference in the number of images shown that marked the divergence in display between the two exhibitions. As the following description of the CHS exhibition indicates, the two exhibitions markedly differed in the logics through which each created quite distinct visual events. Rather than the dramatic, emblematic red-and-black entrance space designed for the Warhol exhibit, the text that marked the entrance to the CHS exhibition was graphically rendered in various fading gray tones. Close by the entrance sign a large picture showed thirteen-year-old Emmett Till seated next to his mother, accompanied by a text noting the murder of Till as a significant event within the history of the American civil rights movement, and a statement explaining that the museum was supplementing the *Without Sanctuary* photographs with material related to Till in commemoration of the fiftieth anniversary of his death. Linking Till's murder to the Allen and Littlefield collection no doubt helped justify the presentation of disturbing images of racial violence, images so graphic that the CHS posted an explicit warning that the exhibition might not "be appropriate for young children." Further introductory texts included a statement from CHS president Lonnie Bunch providing his justification for the museum's presentation of the photographs, as well as a text explaining the historical significance of lynching as a post–Civil War violent tactic that whites used to terrorize and intimidate blacks in order to suppress their progress.

Straight on and quite prominent when entering the exhibit space a blue wall displayed the first of the photographs on display, a series of images devoted to the lynching of William James in Cairo, Illinois, in 1909. As one stood facing the wall containing the photographs of the James lynching, to one's right, in immediate spatial proximity, supplementary materials provided an indication of the strong historical contextualization given the photographic display. This set of materials included a map indicating the distribution of lynching of African Americans in various states and counties in the United States as well as various artifacts and documents referencing the post–Civil War Reconstruction era. Beyond this initial display area a series of open spaces contained the remaining fifty lynching postcards and photographs. In contrast with the chronologically ordered, minimally interpreted presentation of images at the AWM, the rest of the lynching photographs displayed at the CHS were ordered by a narrative arrangement in which specific sets of photographs were organized into thematic groupings and placed in six distinct sections of the exhibition. These six sections included: (1) an explanation of the existence of lynching photography; (2) the way lynching operated as a form of terror; (3) definitions of what constitutes a lynching; (4) information on who the people were in the mobs that perpetrated lynching; (5) specific information on the existence of lynching photographs and how they were used; concluding with (6) a segment showing and hence acknowledging that, besides African Americans, others who were considered "racial outsiders" in the United States were also lynched (although these were clearly a small minority of the total victims of lynching). The thematic substance of each of these sections was rendered through particular juxtapositions of wall text, images, and image labels. Also dispersed throughout the exhibit were additional texts printed on the walls providing various poignant statements reinforcing exhibition themes.

In addition to the presentation of lynching photographs, the CHS provided a memorial space offering a respite from the intensity of viewing the photographs. This space contained a blue-teal semicircular wall on which were written the names of five hundred lynching victims. Turning away from the memorial space and extending further into the exhibit was a display of artifacts and memorabilia about antilynching activism, focusing on the work of Ida B. Wells and the NAACP in the early decades of the twentieth century. The final segment of the exhibition comprised photographs, drawings, and text that marked the anniversary of Emmett Till's lynching. This space included several enlarged photographs (the only images in the exhibition so altered in scale) including a portrait of fourteen-year-old Till before his death as well as of his brutally beaten and disfigured face photographed in his open casket during his funeral. Accompanying the images were text panels giving a brief account of the circumstance of Till's murder, the subsequent public funeral, and the 1955 trial and acquittal of two men charged with his murder. Courtroom sketches and ink-and-wash drawings made during this trial were also on display. Just before the exhibition exit a small area contained two visitor comment books and take-away memorial cards inscribed with the names of each of the victims referenced in the exhibition. Visitors frequently took these cards and the museum had to reprint them several times during the duration of the exhibit. The wall near the exit displayed a quote by Martin Luther King Jr., "The arc of the moral universe is long, but it bends towards justice."

III.

It is evident that the *Without Sanctuary* exhibitions presented by these institutions gave a very different weight and sensibility to the photographs in the Allen and Littlefield collection. There were major differences between the exhibitions in the number of lynching photographs displayed (AWM, ninety-two; CHS, fifty-five), the logic employed to sequence them (AWM, chronologically; CHS, thematically), and the degree to which they were situated within a narrative context (AWM, entrance signage and minimal object labels; CHS, extensive labels providing general and particular narrative contexts for specific images as well as expository and hortatory wall text). To illustrate this last point, consider the contrasting labels placed under one specific photograph that each institution entitled *The Lynching of Rubin Stacy, July 19, 1935, Fort Lauderdale, Florida*. At the Warhol Museum the text placed subsequent to this title was the following: "Onlookers, including four young girls. Gelatin silver print, 8 × 10 in. (20.3 × 25.4 cm.), In the Allen Littlefield Collection at Special Collections at Woodruff Library, Emory University." Quite differently, at the CHS, the following text appeared:

> After he allegedly assaulted a white woman, the police arrested Ruben Stacy and slated him for transfer to the Dade County Jail in Miami. According to Deputy Virgil Wright, more than 100 masked men overpowered his deputies during the transfer. The mob seized Stacy, shot him and hung him from a roadside tree, and continued to riddle his body with bullets. According to the *New York Times*, subsequent investigation revealed that Stacy, a homeless tenant farmer, had gone to a house to ask for food. The woman became

frightened and screamed when she saw Stacy's face. The number of young witness participants at Stacy's lynching is almost as troubling as this unjust murder. Capturing the disconcerting tone of this photograph, James Weldon Johnson describes the epidemic of the lynching of African Americans as a "problem of saving Black America's body and white America's soul." The NAACP later used this photo in their anti-lynching propaganda.

Although not all the photograph labels at the CHS provided as extensive a narrative as that above, it does indicate the decision of the museum to provide as much textual narrative as feasible regarding each event portrayed in a photograph. The exhibition at the CHS clearly attempted to individuate those people whom the photographs indicated were victims of lynching terror. This effort is further brought into focus when one considers the differences in the selection of photographs for display. At the Warhol Museum twenty-one out of ninety-two photographs were accompanied by texts in which victims were unidentified (close to one in five) while at the CHS only four of fifty-five (less than one in ten) were not identified. This obviously facilitated the museum's desire to provide visitors with texts that offered brief individual "stories" of the circumstances surrounding specific lynchings. The AWM displayed only photographs from the Allen and Littlefield collection, but in Chicago curator Joy Bivins, to further the narrative character of the CHS exhibition, added images available from other archival sources in order to provide an image set deemed most appropriate to the exhibition logic organizing the display. In one instance, Bivins chose *not* to show an image that was presented at the Warhol Museum. The Allen and Littlefield collection contains eight different picture postcard images of the William James lynching mentioned above; the AWM displayed all of these while the CHS showed only six. One of the postcards purposely excluded was printed with the label "Half Burned Head of James on Pole" in Candee Park, in Cairo, Illinois. In an interview with Bivins, she indicated that this image wasn't needed to tell James's story and hence she decided that presenting the gruesome photograph would be exploitative of both James's murder and the emotional sensitivities of visitors.[17] Further justifying the excision of this photograph from exhibition, Bivins also made it clear that she thought it appropriate to temper the emotional assault inherent in viewing these photographs by excluding this particular instance of bodily mutilation. Thus, while the exhibition at the CHS did not defer the presentation of quite disturbing images, each of those presented were justified by their illustrative function and the way they fostered the narrative coherence of accounts of individual lynching, or the overall thematic historical narrative that organized the entire presentation of the fifty-five photographs.

In a different vein, the staff at the Warhol Museum minimized the presentation of context in order to maximize the act of closely looking at the photographs. They acted on the assumption that reducing labeling and other explanatory text would intensify the visual and emotional experience of confronting the actuality of the images. As Warhol Museum director Tom Sokolowski put it, "In terms of the imagery, other than basically labels that were really taxonomic, we didn't have a lot of text because we wanted you to look at the images. And we tried to make our labels clear, in a style that was appropriate for the audience."[18] This emphasis on reinforcing an intended intensely visual experience available in the photographs is also conveyed in the director's comments describing the exhibition layout and overall design: "We wanted to take out this cold, harsh analytical thing because while these were documents, we wanted to raise the heat a little bit. Also, we wanted people to get close to the images, and this was necessary because the images were so small. You had to step into the row and you really had to be close up. We felt that was very important."

IV.

As I have argued above, at stake in these instances of the contemporary exhibition of lynching photographs is the very basic question of how those responsible for presenting such exhibitions might re-frame a selected set of images so that they function to contest the very purposes for which they were taken in the first place, purposes perhaps still resonant with certain aspects of contemporary life.[19] In both instances, each institution recognized that the contemporary exhibition of lynching photographs was not just a matter of the public presentation of historical documents but also a practice of rendition that returned a presence felt as a potentially overpowering heteronomic force. In his justification for presenting the exhibition at the Chicago Historical Society, Society president Lonnie Bunch explained that his intent was not to "embarrass, cause pain, or be unpatriotic" but rather to recognize that these "shocking, unimaginable images reveal much about the terror and lawlessness that shaped race relations in America in the 19th and 20th centuries"... thus "*forcing us* [my emphasis] to confront a shameful part of our history, a part many of us would rather forget."

The question remains, how then might we conceive of this force and its consequences? If the photographs were felt as a "shock to thought,"[20] on what terms might such a shock be conceived as a force that compels thought rather than a traumatic disruption that leads to the extended abandonment of thought? Furthermore, on what terms might the coupling of affect and thought be disciplined to prevent the reproduction of intensified frameworks of racial superiority or, in a different vein, feelings of shame that, while instancing moral norms, would abort the thought necessary to a "witnessing that might alter the continued existence of what it witnesses?"[21] Such questions are posed within the recognition, for those of us privileged enough to not witness violent death on a regular basis, that photographic images of disfigurement and death are commonly felt as *images médusée*. My preference for the French idiom here lies in the way it succinctly encapsulates the intertextual reference to the myth of Medusa, a reference that, in my view, helps articulate something of the affective force of lynching photographs. Within Greek mythology, Medusa was the monstrous Gorgon whose visage, if looked at directly, was capable of turning one to stone. When Athena instigated Perseus to kill Medusa, she warned him to never look at the face directly but only at its reflection in a polished shield. Following this advice, Perseus was able to cut off Medusa's head. Although an *image méduse* cannot bring forth the immediacy of a horror that would turn one to stone, it still emits a force that can startle and stupefy, leaving one feeling appalled, confused, and speechless. Despite this, as Georges Didi-Hubermann has suggested, the horror reflected by Perseus's shield remains a wellspring of knowledge on the condition that it is engaged as a device (*dispositif*) of image production.[22] This means that, rather than seeing a photograph as a pacification of the horror of reality, its force to thought lies in how an image both reveals and occludes the horror not only of the atrocities it records but also the gaze within which it is recorded.

More than one visitor to the *Without Sanctuary* exhibitions reported leaving the exhibit in a highly agitated state feeling that they should think more deeply or do something productive as a result of viewing the photographs, not knowing, however, what could possibly be adequate to such felt responsibilities. The last thing organizers of the *Without Sanctuary* exhibitions intended was for visitors to leave with the sense that seeing these photographs served little purpose as they were images of past events that one could do nothing to change, images of suffering that one can barely imagine and of which one is in no position to relieve. In parallel with James Allen's comments cited at the beginning of this chapter, but in a somewhat different idiom, Joseph Jordan, curator of the exhibition of Allen and Littlefield photographs held in Atlanta in 2002, noted that "if we put these photographs back into the trunks, or slide them back into the crumbling envelopes and conceal them in a corner of the drawer, we deny to the victims, once again, the witness they deserve. We deny them the opportunity to demand recognition of their humanity, and for us to bear witness to that humanity."[23] In Jordan's view, the public exhibition of recontextualized recovered images is a way of allowing the dead "to speak," to "demand recognition" and in doing so make claims on those living in the present. In presenting the grotesque public spectacle of racial murder, Jordan's curatorial intent was not simply the rendering of a living memory of those subjected to historically documented racist violence but also included the rendition of socially organized events of singular suffering and dying.

All versions of the *Without Sanctuary* exhibitions attempted to render these moments of suffering and dying as a felt presence that claimed one's attentiveness, demanded one's acknowledgment, and held out the possibility of provoking thought. The public display of lynching photographs brought forth the presence that was exposed and embodied through the rendition of a disfigured human singularity subjected to the violent hands of those pictured as celebrants at the scene of death. Rendered here, in J. L. Nancy's words, "is not, presence pure and simple; *not* the immediacy of the being-posed-there, but rather, that which draws presence out of this immediacy insofar as it puts a value on presence *as* some presence or another."[24] The value exposed through the presence rendered by these images is not just that grasped in the moment of recognition of an objective depiction of suffering, but includes the tactile impact or force felt as the sensation that accompanies the exposure to the rendition of people undergoing extreme degradation and pain. In this sense, the photograph exhibitions under discussion here are as much transactive as they are communicative. As Jill Bennett helpfully observes, "images have the capacity to address a viewer's own bodily memory; to touch the viewer who feels rather than simply sees the event" depicted.[25] The photographic image of a lynching has the potential to register more than it is meant to denote. This "more" is not just a felt loss (of the adequacy of a known history, of a trust in the uprightness of the nation) but a felt responsibility that one cannot remain indifferent when faced with the pain of another.[26] In this sense, such a photograph is not just to be understood as representation of the world but a visual perlocution that registers and produces sensation. This is affect, not as opposed to thought, but as a possible means through which a claim is made on a viewer to both acknowledge the pain of another *and* begin the thought required to come to terms with the felt presence of that pain in the present. The affective force brought forth in the violent images of lynching do not simply interpellate the already morally predisposed viewer as a particular kind of subject (expressing horror at the act of racial violence, sympathy for the victims, and outrage at its perpetrators), but rather it instantiates a tactile connection that, *despite who we are*, has a bodily impact on us. Thus the response to images of suffering addressed here are not limited to the dynamics of identification with people now dead, but exist at that moment when the rendition of the disfigurement of another is felt bodily as a deep disturbing anxiety often reflexively signaled as a uncontrollable wince, cringe, or squirm.[27] To respond to this presence is both to acknowledge past injustice *and* the continuing affective heritage of the lynching photographs. On such terms the consequences of seeing the lynching photographs cannot be determined in advance; the substance of the thought that will be provoked is uncertain. Nevertheless, central here is the realization that violent images of lynching are not just "shocking" but also compelling; they require an acknowledgment of another's pain that might lead to some yet to be decided thought and action commanded by the felt experience of viewing the photographs. Provoked by the rendition of historical documentation, this thought and action can be performatively understood as a continuous negotiation with and in the present in its indeterminable links to the past.

The possibility of thought in the engagement with the *images médusée* of lynching is not just a matter of the impossibility of a photograph as an adequate representation of pain but is also influenced by the way an exhibition takes such limits into account. The presence rendered in the images in the Allen and Littlefield collection exposes a revelation that, in revealing, withdraws what it reveals.[28] Within the photographic image, suffering is transactively revealed and withdrawn at the same time. Thus there is a "hollowness" at the heart of a presence such as that rendered through the lynching photographs,[29] an occlusion of what happened that is both an unimaginable horror *and* an opening to thought. If viewers think that the answer to the question of what the photographs show is entirely known in advance, their viewing will remain a relatively sterile ritual in which one looks at a photograph without seeing its image. The challenge in viewing an exhibition of images from the Allen and Littlefield collection is to not simply discover what it is one already knows, but rather that which one has yet to know, and must yet know. Arguably, the curatorial frame for such an exhibition must attempt to facilitate meeting this challenge in order to avoid rendering lynching photographs as a spectacle of violence or simply a grotesque synecdoche that reminds viewers of where notions of racial superiority can lead. To further grasp what conditions might be necessary for this affective force to compel the dialectics that are a necessary component of a critical public history, consider for a moment what was perhaps one of the very first public renditions of lynching photography. This visual event took place on the streets of Seattle one Sunday afternoon in 1893. Jacqueline Goldsby provides the following account in her extraordinary book, *A Spectacular Secret: Lynching in American Life and Literature* (2006).[30]

Samuel Burdett, a forty-four-year-old black veterinarian active in local politics and African American organizations, was whiling away an hour seeing the sights in the city he called home. Burdett came upon a crowd, that, in Burdett's words, "was attending to some sort of entertainment." "Curious," he approached the group, threading his way to the front "where a man was mounted on a stand or platform of some sort." At the center of the circle, Burdett saw that the attraction was a carefully planned display of the newest technology America had to offer, an exhibit "for civilized citizens to enjoy according to their individual relish for the awful—for the horrible." Burdett recalled in anguish that the presentation "consisted of photographic views, coupled with phonographic records of the utterances of a negro who had been burned to death in Paris, Texas, a few months earlier." Mounted on easels and placed in chronological order, the photographs tracked the Paris lynching of Henry Smith, from the discovery of the corpse of the young child he was accused of raping and murdering to the capture, torture, and cremation of his body. Adjacent to these images was a gramophone with several listening devices—what we would today recognize as headsets. As its disc plate spun, listeners could hear a recording of the confrontation between the dead child's father and the child's alleged assailant, including Smith's response to the torture imposed upon him and the responses of the large crowd who had chosen to witness all of this first hand. Intrigued by this remarkable, totally new combination of sight and sound, Burdett, "like others who were there on that street corner in Seattle," "took up the tubes of the phonographic instrument and placed them to [his] ears." Horrified by both what he saw and heard and the very public street scene of such a display, years later in the context of his antilynching writing Burdett struggled with the words to express an experience that was profoundly unnerving.

At the very least, the contrast between the scene described by Burdett and the curatorial project offered by Lonnie Bunch graphically underscores that the frame of analysis for the discussion of the practice of exhibiting souvenir photographs of racist violence cannot be the unconfined photograph alone but rather must center on the "visual event" of the photographic exhibition. As Mieke Bal has astutely stressed, photographs are not autonomous objects that travel through space and time in self-same identity.[31] Clearly, the particular contexts for viewing any given set of photographs may offer very different purposes for their contemporary presentation hence altering the significance of the photographs as a social sign. But clearly it is not just the denotative and connotative aspects of the photograph that are altered by its rendition within a given visual event; altered as well is its affective force. The Seattle exhibition rendering the lynching of Henry Smith throws into relief the absence of presence in the photographs that were on display, supplementing them with recorded sounds in an attempt to fill in what remained hollowed out in the image. The sounds integral to this event attempted to draw the viewer nearer to what the lynching photographs in the Allen and Littlefield collection cannot show. This approaches Jean-Luc Nancy's notion of "super-representation," a regime of rendition in which what is aspired toward is the exposure of a world without fissure, without withdrawn invisibility, that can be placed right before one's eyes. In super-representation, its object is "completed within what is manifestly present."[32] In such a regime, the image actually gives out an affective force that exhausts itself in the trauma of its blow with the consequence that there is little provocation to thought.[33] There is no impetus to meaning other than the conformity of the world to its awful representation.

In contrast to this, the exhibitions at the AWM and CHS were visual events that contained their own "forbidding," events that were subjects of their own retreat. Rather than exhibitions intended to provide access to the past, each exhibition in its own way attempted to couple affect and thought while endeavoring to restrict the indeterminancy of this relationship within the terms offered through specific exhibition logics. At the CHS the force of the image was restrained (but not finally contained) by the extensive text offering both a historiography of lynching in America and a series of *"petite histoires"* that rendered intelligible individual narratives of racial violence. The extensive text employed by the CHS made it possible to read one's way through the exhibition, enabling visitors to both look and look away at the same time. The risk taken by the CHS was manifest in the creation of a visual event in which the photographic images could fade into historical knowledge, channeling the affective force of the images on to an undialectical memorialization of those subjected to a tragic injustice. Possible jeopardy arose from disregard for how the visual composition of the images themselves might give pause to consider the contemporary significance of the circumstances of the production and circulation of the photographs as photographs. Arguably, at the AWM the affective force of the images of lynching was heightened by the minimal historical context provided.[34] Standing in the photograph gallery at the Warhol, it was much more difficult to both look and look away. Yet it was quite clear that much work was done at the museum to restrain the indeterminacy of the affect provoked by these images and to channel these sensations into affirmations of the struggle against racial discrimination. The restraint of this indeterminacy also produced the risk, inadvertently perhaps, that enjoining individuals to virtuous behavior would be accompanied by an undialectical looking away from the singular photographs of lynching that focuses instead on the personal actions one might take to fight racism. The possible unanticipated consequence of this would then be a short-circuiting of the thought provoked by an attentiveness to "the way of seeing" offered in the photographs. The photographs of lynching from the Allen and Littlefield collection are not only documents of events that have happened in a certain place and time but also bear witness to modes of encountering the world that are deeply problematic. Although these archival photographs may seem to offer a practice of looking that appears foreign or even unimaginable, what is worth considering is whether they can be considered as more closely related to "ordinary," contemporary positions of engagement than their contents seem to suggest. Mobilized differently, the affect-thought coupling consequent with viewing the lynching photographs might otherwise consider how such "inconceivable" ways of seeing resonate with modes of perception that are complicit with the foundational relations responsible for much of the present-day problems of racial inequality.

V.

What is at issue in the two risks articulated above can be further discussed in relation to two recent exhibitions presented by the Hamburg Institute for Social Research (ISR). The first of these, *Vernichtungskrig: Verbrechen der Wehrmacht 1941 bis 1944*, opened in Hamburg in 1995 and subsequently appeared in thirty-three cities in Germany and Austria until, in response to public controversy, it was suspended in 1999. Based on archival photographs not previously shown in public, the exhibition presented evidence of extensive war crimes committed by ordinary German soldiers serving on the Eastern Front during World War II. The intention of the ISR was to confront the treasured image of the German army as fighting a difficult war, but one guided by military—and not racist and inhumane—principles. For this reason, the exhibition offered many images that documented an army that was complicit with, and often an active agent in, a program of extermination. Although the exhibition gave rise to an extremely intense national controversy, my concern here is not the controversy itself and the larger question of postwar German memory, but the exhibition's particular use of photography. This first exhibition employed over fourteen hundred photographs, many taken as personal mementoes. In a substantial number of these photographs, soldiers and their comrades were present in the images—laughing, triumphant, or businesslike and cold while carrying out acts of humiliation, incarceration, and murder. The most controversial curatorial decision was to place a large number of these photographs in thematic groupings without labels for individual images. These groupings were labeled by the activities depicted in the photographs making up each group, for example, tormenting Jews, the operation of gallows, shooting operations, deportations, and so forth. These groups of photographs were placed on curved display walls whose negative space defined a large Iron Cross (the medal for bravery and honor awarded to German soldiers since 1813). Curator Hannes Heer stated that the exhibition was intended to "'block the work of forgetting' and 'immortalize' [the] death[s] caused by the Wehrmacht's extensive involvement in the Nazi war of annihilation."[35]

Bernd Hüppauf has argued that the visual power of the images in this ISR exhibition contributed greatly to a process that was changing the German collective memory of World War II, "freeing its history from the isolation and disciplinary constraints of conventional historiography given a new concern with images, especially the photographic image."[36] But it was just on these terms that the exhibition was accused of irresponsibly creating the general impression that all German soldiers had been criminals. Charges that the exhibit misrepresented (or some suspected, even fabricated) the photographs on view ultimately led the ISR to suspend the exhibition. This charge crystallized in regard to a small number of photographs wherein the deaths of those murdered were incorrectly attributed to Germany army personnel given other evidence that these murders had been done by the Soviet secret police. Although these accusations were directed at a very small number of the images, the public controversy placed the credibility of the entire exhibit (and its sponsoring institution) in question. Under these circumstances, ISR director Jan Phillip Reemtsma suspended the exhibition and appointed an independent commission to assess what errors (if any) had been committed in its production. Although the commission absolved the exhibit organizers of forgery, they did criticize the exhibition for its intellectual sloppiness and lack of historical rigor. Faced with this report, Reemtsma ordered the exhibition redone. A new curatorial team was appointed and subsequently in 2001 a completely new exhibition opened, *Verbrechen der Wehrmacht. Dimensionen des Vernichtungskrieges 1941–1944.*

Taking up twice the space of the previous one, the new exhibition contained considerably more text but only 450 photographs. Gone was the use of the Iron Cross as a display space; instead, a large number of individualized glass booths presented documents and text. Within the revised exhibition logic, the photographs functioned primarily as denotative illustrations of the principal message supplied by the text. Only 10 percent of the photographs that appeared in the first exhibition were present in the second and all photographs were individually labeled and accompanied by a large amount of contextual information—mostly in the form of written documents. The smaller role ascribed to photography was the result of a more rigorous historiography that required extensive cross checking to identify the content of any given image, reflecting the desire of the new curators to provide contextual information for all the photographs shown. A further shift in emphasis occurred so that the new set of documents and text narrowed the focus of criminality primarily to German officers, rather than to all soldiers.

Both ISR exhibitions argued that the Wehrmacht was involved as an organization in crimes perpetrated in the course of the war on the Eastern Front and that the war itself, taken as a whole, was criminal. However, they did this in very different ways. Reemtsma has argued that the photographs in the first exhibition accomplished a great deal. Shortly after the first exhibition opened he acknowledged "that the exhibition makes an appeal to emotions and was organized with the intention both to document atrocities committed by the German army and to create feelings of consternation and bewilderment."[37] Much later, after the second exhibition had concluded, reflecting on the entire experience of presenting the two exhibitions, Reemtsma wrote that although the first exhibition showed much of the reality of the war of annihilation, forcing people to think and ask questions (about perpetrators and witnesses, about those who photographed what they saw), ultimately this exhibition could not answer the questions that were being asked. While implicitly acknowledging the affective force to thought of the first exhibition, Reemtsma concludes that this force was problematic given that the exhibition could not properly channel the thinking it helped initiate. In his reflections on exhibition design written in 2004 he noted that visitors were left alone with their queries, "since the first exhibition did not anticipate the extent to which photographs would be taken as a representation of complex realities, rather than as isolated segments of reality in need of interpretation."[38] In other words, in his view the affective force of images of atrocities had yet to be contained by the demands of proper historiography. It is not surprising, therefore, that Reetmsa concluded that the second exhibition "took up the problem the first exhibit initiated and rectified it as far as possible." Responding to the criticism that the second exhibition was tantamount to a "walk-in book," he wrote: "is that really an objection? The only question is whether the book has, in fact, been walked into and read."

What Reemtsma's remarks convey is that the redeployment of photographs within the exhibition logic of the second exhibit involved more than ensuring that the images shown could be reliably offered as documentary evidence in support of a particular historical narrative. As well, in the service of producing an exhibit as a historiographic argument, one that was as clear and well documented as possible, the redeployment of photographs was seen as a necessary attempt to contain the indeterminate affective heritage of the souvenir atrocity photographs taken by German soldiers. Given the intent of the second ISR exhibit, this need not necessarily be construed as a problem. However, as with the CHS and AWM exhibitions of the *Without Sanctuary* photographs, the ISR strategy was not without its risks. As Hüppauf and others have helped us understand, one of the risks of the second ISR exhibition was the fading of photographs into historiography. In such an exhibitionary circumstance, images are to be read exclusively as documentary evidence of actions taken by the German army and forgotten as traces of the conditions facilitating the operation of what Didi-Huberman calls the photographic *dispositif*. There is little question that the second ISR exhibition did its best to minimize not just the horror of the atrocities depicted but as well the horror of the gaze through which they were recorded.

Whether in the context of the public rendition of photographs of atrocities committed by the German army on the Eastern Front or the public rendition of photographs of atrocities committed by white racist mobs in the United States, when public history is practiced through such forms of visual pedagogy, it is crucial to consider not only what a photograph means but also what the public presentation of a photograph may do. This requires not only a rigorous historiographic method for the treatment of photographs as documents but a way of thinking that grasps how the visual perlocution performed by a display of photographs is structured by practices of exhibition through which their images come into view.

The consequences of the physical sensations that accompany the acknowledgment of the presence of bodies in pain rendered by photographic images of suffering and death are indeterminate. There is an affective force felt when viewing *images medusée*, though how this force is embodied and with what consequences cannot be specified in advance. Given this, the question remains: What would justify a visual practice of public history on such terms? To speak here of the courage to (and responsibility of) witness is not nearly enough. To claim that we owe the dead our witness simply avoids the question as to what would constitute an adequate practice of witnessing. Contemporary ethics would have us attempt to guard against reducing another's suffering to imaginative or quite real versions of our own by critically attending to the inescapable failure of comprehension that is always a component of ethical witness. Yet Theodor Adorno reminds us that "even the most radical reflection of the mind on its own failure is limited by the fact that it remains only reflection, without altering the existence to which its failure bears witness."[39] To witness in a manner that opens the possibility of altering the existence of that to which it bears witness requires a dialectical coupling of affect and thought. Exhibitions are visual events that stage such a possibility. Yet because the consequences of the affective force of an image are indeterminate, there are pedagogical (and political) risks associated with the practice of exhibition. It is important that the design logics through which exhibitions are structured be critiqued and considered for the specific ways they attempt to contain and channel affect, given any particular exhibition's pedagogical intents. What is needed is a greater understanding of what is gained and what is lost in such pedagogies of provocation and containment, for it is such understanding that will determine much of what might be made of the affective heritage ingrained in the visual histories of our contemporary world.

6

The Presence of Immigrants, or Why Mexicans and Arabs Look Alike

John Michael

Nothing seemed more in the news in 2011 than walls. Walls go up in Arizona, they come down—for a moment at least—in Gaza. They divide Israel from the West Bank (while redefining significant areas of Palestinian territory) and they seem destined to play a part in the future of Iraq where partition seems one possible solution to ongoing and shifting divisions among ethnic and religious groups. Though Hans Ulrich Gumbrecht argues in *The Production of Presence* that those who study culture and literature have been too concerned with meaning and not enough with presence, the implications of his argument also makes the meaning of these seemingly omnipresent walls more vividly apparent. For the presence of these walls all over the globe means something and that meaning makes a certain kind of presence more difficult to sense and more important to consider.

To build a wall along a border is a forceful materialization of an imaginary creation, a special kind of literalization of a fictional trope. A familiar cliché holds that from an airplane no borders are visible. To trace a border with a wall makes an imaginative division into a brutal fact. So the question of what these walls might "mean" comes up quite naturally. One might say that these walls around the world pose the question of their own meaning, or, in Gumbrecht's terms, that they are one crucial example of "the things of the world . . . [that] oscillate between presence effects and meaning effects."[1] They lend a certain unexpected pointedness to Gumbrecht's attractive polemic "in favor of a not exclusively meaning-based relationship to the world" and to his appeal for more attention to moments of intensity or "the intense quietness of presence."[2] Who has not experienced what Gumbrecht poignantly evokes as a longing for "those short moments of concentration on 'the things of the world' and the intense quietness that comes with it"?[3] But these walls, these particular things of the world, remind a sympathetic observer of the "tension between presence and meaning" that—more than a simple celebration of presence over meaning—Gumbrecht claims as the "leitmotif" of his book.[4]

The strain of Heideggerian nostalgia that inflects Gumbrecht's appeal for a return to a less mediated appreciation of aesthetic experience in the world finds that the division of the world into spirit and matter and of the subject into mind and body stands as the root cause of human alienation. Gumbrecht writes that Heidegger "articulated a widespread discontent with the intellectual loss of the world outside human consciousness":

> From Heidegger's perspective, at least, Husserl's phenomenology was merely the endpoint of a millenary philosophical trajectory in which the subject/object paradigm—that is, the conceptual configuration of the ongoing divergence between human existence and the world, based on the contrast between human existence as purely spiritual and the world as a purely material sphere—had led Western culture to an extreme state of alienation from the world.[5]

The production of meaning, the vocation of the humanist, seems the symptom of this alienation, for the work of interpretation holds the objects scrutinized at a distance however closely read they may be. What humanist has not sensed this barrier dividing the interpreting self from itself and from others? Who has not felt, as Jean Luc-Nancy put it in *The Birth to Presence* and as Gumbrecht cites him, that "there is nothing we find more tiresome today than the production of yet another nuance of meaning, of just a 'little more sense'" and also, as a corollary, "how hopeless it was for the humanities to try and justify their existence by pointing to some 'social function' or 'political yield'" to be gained from their hermeneutic endeavors or exegetical elaborations.[6] And yet, against the grain of Gumbrecht's attempt to turn attention from meaning to presence, the very presence of the world as it arrives through fallible senses and unreliable communication networks raises difficult ethical and political questions that have an aesthetic dimension and produce moments of intensity of their own. These worldly moments may call into question or reinforce the neat dichotomies of subjects and objects reinforcing or relieving alienation from the world. But they make present intensities that remark the tensions between presence and meaning and pose political and ethical questions, whatever relevance or force may be possessed by the answers to those questions that humanists may propose.

Gumbrecht himself seems alive to this problem when he acknowledges the ambivalent implications of those aestheticized images of the world the media daily present:

> But if watching a war that is an ocean and a continent away from us can definitely repress even the thought of what a war means to those who are physically close to it, if the floating images on the screens that are our world may become a barrier that separates us forever from the things of the world, those same screens may also reawaken a fear of and a desire for the substantial reality we have lost. Clearly our reactions can go either way.[7]

The presence of the world as a mediated object can become one of the barriers separating us from the world and it can become the beginning of a crucial imagining of some other thing, some less alienated relationship—reactions can and do go either way. So the question of barriers, of imagination, and of walls reappears here transposed from the world into the metaphorical substance of theoretical speculation. With all the real walls in the world, it seems difficult to say whether this transposition of material reality and figurative language is a symptom of too much or too little meaning, too much or too little presence. Or does it remark the inevitable and necessary tension between meaning and presence that Gumbrecht notes? Might attending to that tension help recover a less alienating relationship to the world and to those who suffer in it?

106   Chapter 6

I Less in Gaza

Consider a concrete case of how difficult the tension between meaning and presence in the contemporary world can be to negotiate. Presence and meaning, the meaning of war and the presence of walls, seem especially vexed in the contemporary Middle East, a part of the world that seems especially full of intensities but devoid of quietness. Consider this document from the media, a newspaper photo of a wall on the Egyptian border with Gaza at the end of January 2008.

I call this a photograph of a wall, despite the figures in the foreground, because the wall in this image dominates the composition. The wall is the story. In this remarkably unremarkable photo, the people standing in front of the overarching ruin of the Israeli-built barrier separating Gaza from Egypt—they might be a mother, daughter, and three younger children though this information is absent from the news—seem, with their plastic sacks of provisions, actually to be dematerializing into the landscape. This is an effect of photographic overexposure, poor resolution, and dust, an accident

Figure 6.1 Rafah women, *New York Times*, January 27, 2008.
Photograph by Shawn Baldwin.

as it were, of various contingencies, but an aesthetic effect nonetheless. Similarly, the hard dark outline of the twisted iron corrugations of the wall, including the large square area that once no doubt housed the locked gate and now seems a frame around a mirror—so similar is the ground on one side of the wall and the other (though the piles of windowless concrete dwellings glimpsed through the hole belong unmistakably to Gaza)—dominates the photo and seems physically to press upon the figures in the foreground. In one sense, looking at this quintessentially ephemeral photo while drinking morning coffee, I could not be more distant from the sort of aesthetically charged moments, the moments of intensity, to which Gumbrecht asks his readers to attend. And yet this photo, and especially the nearly invisible eyes of its figures, especially the almost absent eyes of the children, arrested my gaze and forced on my sleepy senses a riveting intensity of its own. These are figures without eyes, whose subjectivity does not register in this medium, and who seem about to dematerialize into the landscape that overdetermines their meaning while it threatens to erase their presence. I thought something like this while I looked at this photo and thus the thought of what war means for those who suffer it began to take shape within my consciousness, spurred by an image that seemed to erase those whose presence I found myself wanting to know.

The "news," of course, is not about aesthetics but the world. But its messages continuously call that distinction into question. In practice we are hard pressed to distinguish these things. This is a photo that produced in me, at least, an aesthetic effect and that effect, visceral as it is, relates to a set of meanings that require articulation and a set of meanings that require disarticulation, meanings full of potential insights and actual distortions—glimpses through the barriers of difference and distance—pertaining to one fraught story in the news of the world today. One thing that struck me, between the eyes so to speak, was the way in which in this composition the wall seems present, the people seem or seem about to become, absent, dissolving into the landscape before my eyes. The disappearing bodies give the eyes of the children, especially the eyes of the boy who gazes at us and the girl who clutches some treat or package (a toy? lentils? apricot paste?) their nearly unbearable poignancy. Here there seems to be a geopolitical truth too often made absent from our "debates" about the world these people and we ourselves inhabit today; a truth ironically made present, made visceral for me for a moment, in this photo—borders matter, people are immaterial.

From our point of view in the distant West these Eastern conflicts often seem devoid of people but full of geopolitical meaning. That's one thing, one might say, this picture in the newspaper seems to "mean." Which raises a question that Gumbrecht might recognize as worthy: when faced with this picture, how do we restore the presence of eyes like our own, of subjectivities we can recognize, to the figures in it? How do we make the distant other present to ourselves with any immediacy? Can the mediated suffering of others ever be a moment of intensity for us? Can it ever have real meaning for those of us who are asked to witness it from a distance and through the media?

Among the many forms of exhaustion—economic, political, spiritual—circulating in the world today, perhaps the exhaustion with meaning should for a moment take center stage. In both Gumbrecht's *The Production of Presence* and Jean-Luc Nancy's *The Birth to Presence*, from which Gumbrecht takes his point of departure, the challenge to meaning, the attention to "what meaning cannot convey" to cite Gumbrecht's subtitle, comes not from an exuberant embrace of the body but from a sense of having reached a point of exhaustion in or with the hermeneutic project. But what does Gumbrecht's salutary turn away from meaning and toward "moments of intensity" (a nod to Heidegger, certainly, but to Walter Pater as well) suggest we do about those moments of intensity with which the world news visits us daily. This is no criticism of aesthetics for turning its back on the world—or rising above it as Gumbrecht might say. Those moments of sublimity that art and nature afford seem far too precious not to cherish. But I wish to consider the ways in which meaning and aesthetics, ethics and intensity, our viscera and the world, remain difficult to disentangle in ways that elucidate the promise and the challenge of Gumbrecht's attempt to distance us aesthetes from a world based on meaning.

What might it take to make the woman in this photograph with her children on Palestine's southern border present to a reader on a given Sunday morning in midwinter in western New York State? For this is less a picture of human beings than it is a snapshot of a geopolitical situation and one that in the United States, at least, nearly everyone has very strong feelings about. So the presence of this photo, as arresting as it may be, does not stand independent of meaning. The meanings with which the image and the figures in it are surcharged interrupt or mediate the viewer's relationship to the people the photo represents. Few of us perhaps can actually see these people as presences in the sense that Gumbrecht asks us to experience presence at all. Simply put, that in itself poses a certain political and ethical problem. The difficulty of actually experiencing the other has, of course, been familiar for a very long time, and has left its trace not only on philosophy but on literature generally and on American literature in particular. I find myself increasingly convinced that this is fundamentally an aesthetic question. And, if in the history of modern Western thought and the history of modern Western art, one considers how presence manifests itself, the imbrications of presence and meaning, politics and feeling, become interestingly apparent.

Presence as the Immigration of the Other

One of the meanings carried by the image of the Palestinian woman and her family that makes them difficult to see attaches to the meaning of words like refugee and immigrant. The wall behind her, all will recognize, signifies the Gaza strip and the Gaza strip means people displaced by the foundation of Israel as a Jewish state, people who have lived in Gaza for a long time and who find themselves now strangers in what they consider to be their own land. One of the endless struggles over possession and dispossession that has enervated the region's tragic politics (and these tragic politics furnish another meaning for this photo of people and a wall) has to do with who gets to call themselves at home and who gets to be labeled an immigrant. Anyone who has followed any of the conflicts in the region over the last many years will recognize that the answer to this question does not simply reside in facts about who actually was in residence where or in legal possession of what in 1946 or 1967. It has everything to do with imaginative meanings assigned to certain pieces of real estate by the hopes and aspirations and interpretations of Zionist settlers on the one hand and indigenous peoples who have only recently come to think of themselves as a nation on the other. For some Zionists in recent decades it has to do with meanings assigned to the Torah and for some Palestinians even more recently it has to do with meanings assigned to the Koran. It is far too easy to make too much of the part religious differences play in this conflict. Similarly, it is easy to make too much of the cultural differences separating U. S. citizens and the "unassimilable" immigrants who seem always to be threatening the nation's security from within its borders. It can be difficult to assess, in either case, what difference these religious or cultural differences make to the material dimensions of the problem.

In the Middle East there is also no easy equivalence between the claims of Zionists on the one hand and Palestinians on the other, each side with its history of atrocities suffered and committed. Any examination of actual death tolls over the years, any comparison of the difference in living conditions obtaining in Israel and in Palestine, should convince any impartial observer that the Palestinian people, whatever else one might say, suffer disproportionately in this conflict. But unscrambling the historical claims of each and the present injustices each side perpetrates and suffers goes considerably beyond the discussion here. Focus for a moment on the manner in which the presence of an other, an immigrant, an alien entity within identity's enclosure, is far from being a special case in the confrontation of selves with others in the world and might in fact be the most perfectly evident case of what the presence of the other might mean in ethical and aesthetic terms.

Consider for a moment a certain genealogy that associates ethics and aesthetics. The presence of others, the question of ethics, has entailed, at least since David Hume and Adam Smith, aesthetics in a way closely akin to what Gumbrecht means by presence. For these thinkers and many others in the canons of Western metaphysics attempt to place the presence of others, that crucial aspect of the world, beyond questions of meaning by making the sense of the other an aesthetic or bodily experience. It is a question, of course, of that central discursive formation of eighteenth-century moral philosophy, sympathy.

Modern speculation on psychology begins with what is recognizably a question of aesthetics and of presence: namely David Hume's discovery, in his analysis of sympathy in his *Treatise of Human Understanding*, that others or their feelings are present within what John Locke had imagined to be the empty closure of the self:

> 'Tis indeed evident [Hume writes], that when we sympathize with the passions and sentiments of others, these movements appear at first in *our* minds as mere ideas, and are conceiv'd to belong to another person, as we conceive any other matter of fact. 'Tis also evident, that the ideas of the affections of others are converted into the very impressions they represent, and that the passions arise in conformity to the images we form of them. All this is an

object of the plainest experience, and depends not on any hypothesis of philosophy.[8]

Hume notes that in our plainest experiences we experience the feelings of others—their passions and sentiments—as a sort of rematerialization of the other within the sensory precincts of our own being. The feelings of the other migrate innocuously, first as mere ideas or—let's say—images and then take up residence with the possibly insidious immediacy of actual impressions, giving rise to the very passions and sentiments of the other within the borders of our selves.

For Adam Smith, famously, the question of sympathy grounds moral thought and, as in Hume, trespasses on the boundaries that we usually assume divide us from other people and the world. At the beginning of *The Theory of Moral Sentiments* Smith writes that when we witness "our brother . . . upon the rack . . .

> by the imagination we place ourselves in his situation, we conceive ourselves enduring all the same torments, we enter as it were into his body, and become in some measure the same person with him, and thence form some idea of his sensations, and even feel something which, though weaker in degree, is not altogether unlike them. His agonies, when they are thus brought home to ourselves, when we have thus adopted and made them our own, begin at last to affect us, and we then tremble and shudder at the thought of what he feels.[9]

For Smith, even more clearly than Hume, sympathy—our involuntary and unavoidable association of ourselves with those around us which, Smith begins by saying, even the greatest ruffians and the most selfish in some degree share—brings the other home to ourselves, breaches the wall that separates self and other and makes the other's pain to some extent involuntarily our own, so that "we . . . tremble and shudder at the thought of what he feels."

Here, I think, lies one important explanation for the odd proliferation of barriers and walls so prevalent today. Whatever geopolitical policies and material ambitions legitimate them, these walls create a protective distance that human sympathies always in some measure threaten to breach. Whereas they seem intended to keep foreigners out, they more importantly expel or abject the strangers who, we struggle not to think, are already at home in our hearts and minds. In the picture above, the woman's presence and her suffering are distanced by the meanings ascribed to the wall behind her. Even her clothes come laden with significances that conceal not only her body but also her being. The scarf on her head might signify Muslim piety and allegiance to Hamas, or it might afford the sort of protection against wind and weather that women of my mother's generation seldom left home without. In the context of contemporary American and Western understandings of Arab women, a headscarf cannot but resonate with religious and political meanings. Like the meaning of the wall—protective barrier or punitive enclosure—Arab women's heads in the East and in the West remain very much an issue of contention, and very few Arab women actually get to be present in the dispute.[10]

In the realm of politics, whose borders Gumbrecht's impatience with meaning would like to leave at least momentarily behind, sympathy and presence have long played a complicated part especially when artists have dreamed that an aesthetics (for what is the question of fellow feeling and compassion but an aesthetic question?) of sympathy might settle moral and political issues on a more solid basis than the seemingly endless and endlessly wearing contentions of news media and political debate seem to allow. In this connection, any student of sympathy within the borders of the United States thinks immediately of Harriet Beecher Stowe's *Uncle Tom's Cabin*, whose appeal to "right" feeling originates in the author's own fatigue with the meanings of the world, a fatigue similar to the weariness Gumbrecht and Nancy register as they turn away from meaning and toward presence. "See, then, to your sympathies in this matter!" she enjoins her readers speaking of slavery at her novel's end, "for your sympathies, if they be in harmony with Christ's, will preserve your sensibility and judgment from the perversions of "worldy policy" and its "sophistries."[11] Earlier in the novel, readers will remember, Stowe offers an object lesson in how such sympathies communicate (perhaps propagate would be a better word) through presence. In an oft-cited chapter, Stowe takes the reader into a U.S. senator's home. There she stages a debate between the senator and his wife on the vexatious issue of slavery. Mrs. Bird urges slavery's end and condemns the dehumanizing cruelty of the fugitive laws, but Senator Bird sticks to the worldly wisdom of sectional compromise, property rights, and patriotic duty to demonstrate the necessity of passing ever more stringent laws to punish fugitive slaves and protect the nation. "I hate reasoning, John," Mrs. Bird declares, and swears that at the first chance she gets to break the laws her husband has taken an oath to uphold she will do so. This argument ends only when the senator finds Eliza, the novel's fugitive slave mother and her child, materialized in his kitchen and discovers himself to be "quite amazed at the sight that presented itself."[12] The painful sight of the suffering and shivering woman actually present, really presented, and making herself a presence in his home proves too much for Senator Bird's defensive structure, his personal wall of worldly meanings: "The magic of the real presence of distress,–the imploring human eye, the frail, trembling human hand, the despairing appeal of helpless agony,–these he had never tried. He had never thought that a fugitive might be a hapless mother, a defenseless child."[13] He feels her pain and acts accordingly. Stowe tries to make that presence work on and for her readers as well, by representing the figure of the stranger, the fugitive, the other as a human presence, within the homely walls and hearts of her characters.[14] Through the wall-breaching power of sympathy, presence makes itself felt for the sophistical senator and the susceptible reader; the appeal of suffering cannot be denied and it silences worldly sophistries whose noisy disputations too easily alienate human sensibilities from the world. Senator Bird experiences here something like a moment of intensity, but it carries a meaning with it that gives the lie to the meanings of the world and, Stowe hopes, puts an end to further disputation. Here presence and art seem entwined with politics and meaning in ways that require further thought about the meaning or the appeal of the *New York Times* newspaper photograph, the production of presence, and the dialectical tension between presence and meaning that Gumbrecht's work indicates.

The Presence of Immigrants after September 11

The events of September 11th that those in the news love to say changed everything did not, in fact, change much (except for the lives tragically touched by Al Qaeda's murderous attacks) if what one means by change entails a fundamental redefinition of the world and America's place in it. There was an imperial American presence in the world before the towers fell; there is an imperial American presence in the world today. But the catastrophe did affect many things, from the weakening of civil liberties and the legitimation of torture in the United States to the destruction of lives and livelihoods in Iraq and Afghanistan. It has altered the relationship of the United States to other nations and has worsened the lot of immigrant workers within its borders. Of course, none of this, neither bad diplomacy nor mistreated foreigners, is new. Those of us who work in or on the United States know that a strain of nativist paranoia is precisely native to many strains of political discourses in the United States. and has been for a long time. What Paul Smith calls American Primitivism seems primitive not only because of its regressive appeal to brute, resonant simplifications but because a certain antipathy to outsiders—to specific outsiders—has marked the nation's national discourse since its founding. In the eighteenth century, before the nation was founded, Benjamin Franklin inveigled against Germans and other tawny races that might blight the purity of the pale-skinned America he imagined. Thomas Jefferson warned of Africans and other heterogeneous peoples who would distemper the temperate republic of which he dreamed and make it a "distracted mass."[15] Commentators as various as Harvard professor Samuel Huntington and populist firebrand Michael Savage continue this distinguished line of attack today. So much remains the same. But after 9/11 much seems different as well. And one of the effects of 9/11 is to mask that similarity and the difference too.

One important difference occurs at the level of American public discourse. After 9/11, the extremely Teutonic-sounding phrase "homeland security" became an American idiom. Under its cover popular pundits and administration officials explicitly linked problems of immigration—heretofore an economic and especially a labor problem—to problems of national security. Anxiety about terrorism colored worries about undocumented labor and did much to confuse both issues.[16] But immigration, like terrorism, seldom gets discussed in reasonable terms. Like terrorism, immigration has become part of a primitive sort of discursive panic. The response to this panic has been to look to the nation's walls, less with any real hope to seal the border (which would be disastrous were it possible) than with the phanstasmatic desire to stabilize a fraught situation by making, once and for all, the difference between "us" and "them" and thereby "our" own identity apart from theirs as palpable as possible. Of course, this process demands simultaneously a denial of the presence of those others already within the nation's borders and a fixing of them with the meaning of their otherness. In the terror over immigration, as in the terror over terror, the others to whose presence the discursive panic affixes meanings—Arabs and Mexicans in this instance—fail to materialize as human presences at all. This has the reassuring consequence of denying that "we" have any relationship to "them," their predicaments, or their grievances at all. There is certainly an ethics and a politics to these visceral reactions.

The codifications of national security have forged an odd identity between these two radically disparate peoples: Mexicans, who not only in the Southwest but everywhere in America are identified as a threat to American labor and livelihoods, and Arabs, who whether they remain in the Middle East or immigrate to Paris, London, or Detroit represent a threat to American values and lives. In the American psyche especially, the anxieties associated with these groups involve the problem of presence and its dialectical tension with meanings that distance presence from us. In both cases, representational effects short-circuit sympathetic connection. First, the individuals constituting either group disappear within a stereotype that makes the mere presence of a Mexican or an Arab perceivable as a threat. Here presence and meaning seem insidiously associated so that the signifier "Mexican" encompasses and confuses distinctions among documented and undocumented workers, solid citizens and jackals or pushers, and U. S. citizens and illegal immigrants.

For Arabs the categorical force of the signifier makes the differences of actual Arabs present in the world more difficult to discern. Consider the crimes committed in Darfur as an example of how the signifier "Arab" tends to operate today. Little explanation of the horrific events there seems necessary for the U.S. media other than to label the murderous Janjaweed as Arabs. The word Arab functions here less to offer a useful description of those who commit atrocities in water-starved Sudan than to link them with Arabs in the Levant, especially Palestinians, whose struggles against long decades of Western meddling and Israeli oppression have sometimes deployed terrorism as a weapon. It links them as well with those Arab Americans living in Lackawanna, Pennsylvania, or Detroit or in "any town" U.S.A. who form, in the collective American imagination and often on the nightly news, a nightmarish network of sleeper cells capable at any moment of wreaking terror in the heartland. The murderous raids of the camel herders on the farming villages of Sudan become another example of the murderous behavior of Arabs against their neighbors and an object lesson in why "we" must win the global war on terror. The civil war in Iraq, the bloody aftermath of Saddam's dictatorship and the U. S. invasion, offers more evidence. Arabs cannot even refrain from killing each other. Worries in the United States over the meaning of the Muslim Brotherhood's presence in the recent Egyptian revolution furnishes yet another example of how representations of Arabs as Muslim fundamentalists and murderous fanatics makes sympathy with their oppression and struggles difficult for many Americans.

Recent hearings on the radicalization of U.S. Muslims in the House of Representatives enjoyed wide popular support and indicate the pervasiveness of American's disidentification with Muslims generally and Arabs in particular. That these Arabs, representatives of a culture that seems resolutely foreign to the West, the last holdouts against the beneficent values of democratic modernism, Islamofascists, tribal killers of daughters and wives, religious zealots, should somehow become linked with those who come from a neighboring country to pick fruit, work in factories and restaurants, clean houses, and assume myriad necessary burdens that make modernity—as the United States knows it—possible, might, at first, seem surprising. But the media fascination with the recent violent lawlessness associated with Mexico's drug industry reminds us that the "Mexican" in the United States is often represented as a drain on public resources or worse, a threat to law and order, a gangster, a pusher, a pimp, and a thief. In fact, despite these representations, both Arabs and Mexican immigrants to the United States could in fact be seen as brilliant examples of assimilation. Each group has produced a fair number of quite reputable public figures ranging from former New Mexico governor Bill Richardson to Senator John Sununu. But Arabs and Mexicans have come to share an identity in the American imaginary as unassimilable others whose presence within the nation's borders threatens not only the nation's security but its very identity. It should not seem paradoxical to say that in this presentation of Arabs and Mexicans, Arabs and Mexicans remain largely absent, dematerialized by the geopolitical significance ascribed to them, like the woman and children in the news photo above.

In all this anxious discourse about these groups, specific representations of Arabs and Mexicans make themselves felt. Arabs have religious and familial beliefs and structures that, defenders of the West such as Bernard Lewis say, are fundamentally at odds with Western values. Mexicans, champions of American identity like Samuel Huntington claim, lack the Protestant work ethic and the ability to acculturate and therefore pose a serious threat to America's very character. Inexorably in these discourses about the nation's security, Arabs and Mexicans begin to look alike as representatives of pure otherness. Whatever the homeland means, its security requires that these others need to be kept out or cast out. Their presence threatens the nation's existence and values. Remember how quickly explanation for the attacks in New York and Washington, D.C., boiled down to the simple assertion that "they" hate "our" "values." Arabs and Mexicans, however hard many of them may work and however much many of them may succeed, hate our values too. But pure otherness is actually no presence at all. It is in the very nature of this very one-sided debate about national security, despite all the thrills and intensities it may possess for "white" Americans, that Arabs and Mexicans may not feel present in it at all. Can these significantly absent immigrants be made present in a way that might positively transform the nation's sense of its domestic state and its own presence in the world? In considering this question the presence of immigrants, the problem of security, and the value and limits of feeling begin to come into view.

Presence Limited

There is, in the remarkable confusion between Mexicans and Arabs, a lot a cultural critic could work with. The technique of demystification bequeathed to criticism by the Frankfurt School and designed to strip the masks of deception from the face of human suffering, to make that suffering present to the imagination, still has purchase in a world where the systematic distortion of significance still holds sway. U.S. popular culture at this moment sometimes seems, in ways Adorno could never have appreciated, prescient in this regard.

Consider an American film starring the comic character Larry the Cable Guy, which appeared during one of the frequent fever spikes in U.S. anxieties about immigration. While pundits and politicians debated the wisdom and practicality of constructing a wall between Texas and Mexico, *Delta Farce* (2007) played briefly in suburban multiplexes and found its place in the rental market. A synopsis of this very funny, thoroughly modest film suggests its relevance for the question of presence and sympathy, meaning and immigration. A group of alienated National Guardsmen in the Deep South looking forward to a weekend of what passes with these slackers as training—watching porn and eating chicken wings—suddenly find themselves called up to be shipped out to Iraq. On the way, however, the armored personnel carrier in which they are all sleeping falls out of the airplane and lands in the desert outside of a small Mexican town that is beset by bandits. Larry and his two companions wake up and, believing they actually are in Iraq (to an American, Mexicans and Arabs do look alike), successfully "liberate" the village. They discover their error about halfway through the film, but by that time they have learned to love the people among whom they find themselves and, overcoming their own alienation, manage to humanize both themselves and the militarized American culture they represent. In this fantasy film, the troops come home to resume their "normal" lives having exhibited honor, compassion, and courage, and having created, on however small a scale, a real cross-border transnational community.

A cultural critic might do a lot with this film, analyzing, for example, what it reveals and what it hides about representations of Mexico, about American imperialism, about attitudes toward Arabs, about images of working-class Americans, the military, official policy, popular culture, and alienation. I would note that I was surprised at how subversively sly and sympathetically progressive on issues of sexuality and race the film seemed. The Mexicans in the film, and oddly enough even the Arabs in Iraq who never actually appear in the frame, seem more present to the viewer and more sympathetically accessible than news stories and border walls seem to allow. If one of the dreams of sympathetic art—like *Uncle Tom's Cabin*—imagines spreading the ethos of compassion by making more people feel the presence of others and wish to feel right about their relation to them, then this film succeeds quite well.[17]

But now I must confess a weariness of my own, not with meaning but with the longing in contemporary culture and criticism for this ethos of niceness and right feeling. Right feeling, moments of sympathetic identification or imaginary fellowship, however necessary they are to the continuation of human communities, have terrible limitations in their purchase on the world. It required a horrifying civil war and over a century of frequently violent struggle and enforced legislation and litigation for the United States to begin to redress the evils of the racial caste system that Stowe attempted to make her readers feel. Mexican immigrants continue to suffer exploitation in the workplace; Arabs and Arab Americans remain prominent victims of civil and human rights abuses. These failures of just principle and sympathetic understanding occur despite President Barack Obama's advocacy for cross-cultural understanding and mutual respect. More than sentiment and sympathy, more even than intense moments of felt presence, seem to be required.

To return to the beginning point of this chapter: one legacy of 9/11 has been the radical reification of an identity logic in U.S. foreign and domestic policy, an intensified rigidity in American attitudes toward immigrants and the world, that have always been one component of American ideological life. This, interestingly, takes two opposed forms based on appeals to either brusque exclusivity (equating immigrants and terrorists as threats to national security) or hospitable openness (attempts to bridge borders and understand others).[18] In its nativist or conservative form, this cultural and state politics demands exclusion and control and the priority of "our" rights to privilege or defense. In its progressive or cosmopolitan form this cultural and state politics would (it doesn't presently exist, I think, except as sentiment) work toward inclusion and identification and the painful calculations of justice for those whose presence among us demands that we rethink material questions of equity, the nature of identity, and the need for security in a complicated and threatening world. I am deeply committed to the latter, but I wonder—as all before the awful bar of justice must—where a commitment to right will take us and to what extent the attractive appeals of sympathy will prove inadequate to the material requirements of the still incompletely realized other's presence among us.

Of one thing I am sure, any attempt to really do justice to the other will take us beyond both the discourses of meaning and presence that, Gumbrecht correctly notes, tend to occupy professional humanists. Giorgio Agamben reminds us that instituting justice and respecting rights entail the same mechanisms of state sovereignty and legislative policy that can and do create injustices and violate rights. This has led some critics to imagine that state power and juridical discourses can play only an oppressive part in global politics.[19] Yet, sentimentalizing the other, even feeling for the other, may fail to redress the miseries of dislocation and oppression, unless the other can be made present in a realm somewhat distant from the humanist's more familiar aesthetic concerns.

To truly alter the immigrant's place in the world may require admitting the other as a presence not so much in our hearts and homes as before the lawful procedures and protections of empowered institutions devoted to human rights in principle and in practice. Those rights include freedom from search, seizure, and torture, and the freedom to organize, to earn a decent wage, and to bargain with management.

One of the reasons that Arabs and Mexicans look alike is that American policies at home and abroad reduce both to that state of exception Agamben defines as being beyond law and community. Immigrants are threatened with the status of peoples whose sufferings and deaths can be given neither moral nor legal meaning, existing within society but separated from society's laws or feelings, incapable, because of this separation, of being murdered or sacrificed but dying none the less. This is an odd and tragic dynamic that permits presence but paradoxically only under the sign—or within the barrier of—exclusion. Agamben familiarizes us with the complex implications of sovereignty, law, and modernity in an increasingly normalized state of exception, and reminds us of one real reason that Arabs and Mexicans might make us feel afraid. They provoke terror not for the damage they may do to us but for the fact that in a world where states of exception become the norm, we, like they, might find ourselves naked before state power and common indifference, confined by the barriers of civil exclusions and erased as human subjects, but present as suffering bodies clutching a few objects we can never really call possessions.

A possible remedy for this terror entails more than a demand for more present feeling regarding one's ethical burden with regard to the other. It requires more importantly that we make these others more present as participants in the meaningful discourses and deliberations of the state. One of the ways in which we might recognize and attend to Arabs and Mexicans and so many others at home and in the world would be not to fixate on the fascinations of their identities (which are for those of us interested in art, culture, food, and other forms of present difference fascinating indeed) but to render each of them present to the law—if any true lawfulness remains—and empowered by the law in their negotiations with capital and the state—if the capacity of any true governance has not been fatally compromised. Although this doesn't sound like an especially liberatory project, and while it poses complexities of boundaries and justice, belonging and identity of its own, it might be an economic and political strategy that could begin to construct our economic and ethical debts in ways that might get paid. Those lawyers and activists who are exploring ideas of transnational citizenship for workers moving between the Middle East and Europe and between Mexico and the United States work beyond sympathy and aesthetics, beyond what professional humanists—whether they fixate on meaning or presence—usually do, to address and empower the other's existence as a legal subject in a lawful world.[20]

As agents within and not beyond the law, Mexicans and Arabs—however different their cases may be—might both still look alike, but they would look more like those of us still able to assume (though we may be wrong) that we are protected by a form of belonging that allows us to be present before the law and that protects us (we hope) from the most brutal forms of oppression and expropriation. Whether that assumption is tenable or that hope forlorn requires further discussion among an "us" that includes the presence of all interested parties. The outcome of that discussion, should it occur, will depend in large part on the specific states of exception—exceptions to full lawful presence or justice—that we allow ourselves to be terrified into accepting.

7

Transcultural Presence

Bill Ashcroft

The theory of presence may be one of the most exciting interventions in the humanities in a long time since it forces us to inspect something we normally accept without question: the centrality of interpretation. Interpretation has become *the* dominant feature of all the humanities, even history, and it has moved, since the appearance of quantum mechanics, into a central place in science as well. The discussion of "presence" has been firmly focused on the aesthetic encounter—an encounter producing a "meaning" beyond interpretation. But it may be a feature of other encounters in which "understanding" is reached outside of hermeneutics. I want to discuss a production of presence that is not so much a moment of aesthetic intensity as it is a moment of cultural transformation. Such presence may be seen to occur in transcultural encounters, particularly the reading of cross-cultural literature: a moment of sudden awareness in which the reader engages an excess, the "beyond" of interpretation in what may be understood as a sense of cultural "otherness." When this works most successfully, the otherness is one's own. This moment may overlap and merge with the aesthetic and indeed cannot be fully separated from it, but it encompasses a radical unfamiliarity that is perhaps better understood as an encounter with the uncanny, the *unheimlich*. The strangest feature of this encounter in the transcultural text is that this uncanny space becomes, potentially, a space of negotiation.

The word "transcultural" will require some explanation because I am going to talk about the experience of a nonhermeneutic moment of intensity that may occur in reading postcolonial poetry in English. Poetry is useful for this purpose because of all literary forms (with the possible exception of drama when performed) it best demonstrates the oscillation between what Hans Ulrich Gumbrecht calls "presence effects" and "meaning effects."[1] In this case the "materialities of communication" are focused in the sound and texture—the music of the lines—and it is precisely the materiality of the poetry that produces presence, or, more precisely, *presence effects* that elude interpretation. I will focus on the transformative use of English by writers who speak a different mother tongue and often come from what Gumbrecht would call a "presence culture." But the concept of presence may help us to solve, or at least circumvent, some tenacious theoretical arguments that attend the reading and interpretation of postcolonial literatures.

One of the conditions of the dominance of hermeneutics in the humanities seems to have been the pervasive dominance of boundaries in Western culture; boundaries between subject and object, signifier and signified, writer and reader, speaking and writing. These boundaries may be useful tools at times but just as often they confine and inhibit, yet their restrictions are pale reflections of the far more violent inhibitions effected by the borders of nation and state. In his novel *Shadow Lines* Amitav Ghosh offers a metaphor that might help us begin to think past these boundaries. In despair at the violence generated by the "shadow lines" of national borders, he uses the metaphor of the mirror to try to resolve the tragedy of national hostilities and perhaps even of nationality itself. The book seems to ask: "How is it possible to live in a way that might escape the borders of nation, maps, and memory?"—and for an answer it arrives at the subtlest of boundaries: that of the mirror. Mirrors appear both as objects and metaphors because mirrors disrupt the clear border of identity and difference. The clearest statement of this comes late in the novel after the narrator has pondered the absurd power of lines on the map. Speaking about the people who made the map that divided India and Pakistan, the narrator wonders:

> What had they felt, I wondered, when they discovered that there had never been a moment in the four-thousand-year-old-history of the map when the places we know as Dhaka and Calcutta were more closely bound to each other than after they had drawn their lines—so closely that I, in Calcutta, had only to look into the mirror to be in Dhaka; a moment when each city was the inverted image of the other, locked into an irreversible symmetry by the line that was to set us free—our looking-glass border.[2]

The mirror dissolves the persistence of all borders of identity. As a phantom border the mirror creates a spectral contact zone, indiscriminate but ultimately revealing because it reflects the continual possibilities of negotiation, transformation, and change. The mirror metaphor does not construct the other as the same, but rather subordinates identity to difference, reversing the othering process.

Michel Foucault uses the image of the mirror in an equally illuminating, though quite different way. The mirror is the perfect metaphor for the dissolving border between utopia and heterotopia:

> The mirror is, after all, a utopia, since it is a placeless place. In the mirror, I see myself there where I am not, in an unreal, virtual space that opens up behind the surface. . . . But it is also a heterotopia in so far as the mirror does exist in reality, where it exerts a sort of counteraction on the position that I occupy.[3]

This seems to capture perfectly the metonymic relation Foucault is striving for in the apparent contrast between the sacred space, the "placeless place" of the utopian, and the real, yet only partially desacralized, reflection of that utopia in the heterotopia. But we can see how valuable the mirror may be in understanding the dual nature of the literary text because the relationship between utopia and heterotopia mirrors the relationship between the imagined space of the literary content and the real site of its physical production. The mirror metaphor suggests that the border between these is illusory—imagined space and real site interpenetrate one another in the same way that the virtual and real dimensions of the mirror coexist. The literary text is a heterotopia, a real and tangible site of the imagination. But the mirror metaphor, particularly as Ghosh conceives it, also leads us toward transculturality because it reformulates the idea of the contact zone, the zone in which subjects in contact are both changed. The mirror proposes a recognition that is not sameness, but a dialogue beyond speech, a space in which both self and other are mutually constructed.

Ethnographers have used the term "transcultural" to describe how subordinated or marginal groups select and invent from materials transmitted to them by a dominant or metropolitan culture (e.g., Michael Taussig 1993). The word was coined in the 1940s by Cuban sociologist Fernando Ortiz (1978) in relation to Afro-Cuban culture, and incorporated into literary studies by Uruguayan critic Angel Rama in the 1970s. Ortiz proposed the term to replace the paired concepts of acculturation and deculturation that described the transference of culture in reductive fashion, one imagined from within the interests of the metropolis.[4] The concept of the contact zone in postcolonial studies has often been framed as a contestatory space because it is marked by "highly asymmetrical relations of dominance and subordination." However, the concept of transculturality I want to develop through the analysis of reading proposes a more constructive dialogue, a zone of contact that produces a new, "third" cultural space. This is why the metaphor of the mirror can be so useful in this enterprise.

The transcultural text is a space of negotiation, a heterotopic space in which the boundary between self and other blurs. The "real" text is also the space of utopian possibility—the possibility of meaning beyond interpretation. The "cross-cultural" text—a term that is comparatively static and linear—may be seen to be a "transcultural" text once we understand it to be a space in which meaning is negotiated, where, in a sense, both writer and reader are changed in constitutive collusion. Although we are interested in the production of presence in such a text, we need to get to it through an understanding of the meaning of the text as a negotiation between different voices, between what I call the writer and reader functions. Mikhail Bakhtin is interesting here because he contends that *all* novels involve a cross-cultural engagement between readers and writers. He is interested in the novel because for him the novel form provides a particularly rich medium for the many-voiced appearance of different languages. For the novelist the object is always "entangled in someone else's discourse about it, it is already present with qualifications" and is inseparable from the "heteroglot social apperception of it."[5]

Significantly, Bakhtin is talking about a putatively monoglossic text, unhampered by issues of cultural communication. For him, such a text is already heteroglossic, already engaged in dialogue *within* the text, a dialogue, which to all intents and purposes, is a *cross-cultural* dialogue between "belief systems." All forms involving a narrator

> signify to one degree or another by their presence the author's freedom from a unitary and singular language, a freedom connected with the relativity of literary and language systems; such forms open up the possibility of never having to define oneself in language, the possibility of translating one's own intentions from one linguistic system to another, of fusing "the language of truth" with "the language of everyday," of saying "I am me" in someone else's language, and in my own language "I am other."[6]

The dual dynamic of saying "I am me" in another's language and "I am other" in my own language captures precisely the dual achievement of the second-language writer. It is also captured beautifully in Amitav Ghosh's metaphor of the mirror. For such a writer, while emphasizing the way in which the space between author and reader is closed within the demands of meanability (the expectation that language will convey meaning), also demonstrates in heightened form, the writer's negotiation of the forces brought to bear on language:

> Every concrete utterance of a speaking subject serves as a point where centrifugal as well as centripetal forces are brought to bear. The processes of centralization and decentralization, of unification and disunification, intersect in the utterance; the utterance not only answers the requirements of its own language . . . but it answers the requirements of heteroglossia as well; it is in fact an active participant in such speech diversity.[7]

For the postcolonial writer these forces are those of a culturally ossified way of seeing and the heteroglossia of a world readership. One of the preeminent advantages of cross-cultural writing in English is the capacity to translate ways of seeing into the "bilingual" text without making any concessions to the "way of seeing" of the reader. This is because the text is already a heteroglot profusion of ways of seeing. But it is also because the postcolonial text manages to extend Bakhtin's view of dialogue with the discovery that *true dialogue can only occur when the difference of the other is recognized.*

Constitutive Reading

The beauty of the mirror metaphor is that it shows how the cross-cultural text becomes a transcultural space of negotiation. Although I don't have room to fully outline it here, since we are not focusing on meaning and interpretation, I want to suggest a model of reading that demonstrates the way in which transculturality operates in the text.[8] To do this I want to propose that the dialogism of the text shapes it as a *social situation.* We tend to see the text as a *thing,* forgetting that the writing is an intense and socially mediated *act.* If we accept the reality of writing as a practice we can then understand that the text as a *social situation* in which the "objective" meanings of writing come about through a process of "social" accomplishment between the writing and reading participants. If we understand the "meaning event" as a negotiation of social actors who present themselves to one another as functions in the text, we can then posit the negotiation of *cultural* meaning in the cross-cultural text as a "transcultural" event. People living in different cultures may live in totally different, and even incommensurable, worlds: different worlds of experience, expectation, habit, understanding, and tradition. Nevertheless, meaning is *accomplished* between writing and reading participants in ways that may confound theories of cultural incommensurability.

Meaning, then, is a social accomplishment involving the participation of the writer and reader that "functions" within the "event" of the particular discourse. Both are subject to the requirements of meanability, but in various ways both writer and reader are subject to and incorporate *both* writer and reader functions. Hence we may refer to the achievement of meaning as a "situated accomplishment." It is much easier, of course, to see a conversation as a "situated accomplishment." But a conversation has a life of its own beyond the intentions of the participants. The apparently simple example of a casual conversation clearly demonstrates the complex array of structuring participations in the social event. But it is the 'event', the *situation* of its structure and structuring participations, rather than the contingent intentions or psychological states of speakers which imparts a direction and a meaning to the conversation.

Understanding and Cultural Experience

This brief intimation of the constitutive theory of textual meaning opens the way toward an engagement with the "beyond" of meaning in the text. Is presence also negotiated in the text? If so, how? How is that sense of cultural otherness that lies beyond interpretation engaged as a function of the reading process? Before addressing these questions we need to deal with a persistent misconception that dogs the reading of the cross-cultural text—the assumption of the incommensurability of the cultural experiences of writer and reader—the idea that the non-African reader of African texts in English, for instance, can never fully understand the text because he or she has no experience of the African world.

Jejune as this seems it is a surprisingly tenacious prejudice. A quite common assumption about understanding is that it must be a discrete experience, that there must be characteristic experiences of understanding when we "understand" that have corresponding identifiable mental correlates. Consequently how could we "understand" a writer, even writing in a common language, who has a profoundly different experience of the world? But we can test this assumption that understanding is an identifiable experience with two examples.

First, take the example of a conversation between two people of the same culture—nothing could better define *presence* than the conversants' presence to each other. Yet if we think about it, even in the most empathetic exchange the speaker and hearer are never fully present to one another. The experience of one conversant can never *become* the experience of the other, and the experience aroused by a word (even a simple word like "dog"), the associations it evokes, may be very different in people *within* a culture, but this does not prevent meaning occurring. Meaning and understanding of meaning can occur because the language encodes the reciprocity of the experiences of each conversant. It is the situation, the "*event*" of this reciprocal happening that "tells," that "refers," that "informs." There are many dimensions of this "social event," but it is the "event," the *situation* of its structure and structuring participations, rather than the contingent intentions or psychological states of speakers, that imparts a direction and a meaning to the conversation.

Take another example of a bricklayer who uses the term "Brick!" to his helper as an elliptical form of the phrase "Pass me the brick." Neither he, nor the helper need to translate the word "Brick!" into the phrase every time it is used, in order to understand it. The same process applies when English variants, neologisms, and borrowings are situated in the written English text. As with most words there may be many possible uses but it is the use in this situation that locates the meaning. When I understand what another person says, I am not required to have their mental images nor when they communicate meaning are they obliged to transfer to the listener the "contents" of their mind, nor any of the mental images and associations that may be aroused by that language. Ludwig Wittgenstein uses the famous example of the mathematical series to get a grip on the concept of "understanding." We understand the series, he says, when we are able to *go on* to continue it. Understanding is not therefore a specific mental experience occurring at a particular moment but is realized in the reader's ability to "go on," so to speak. "Understanding" may indeed occur in "Eureka" moments, but those moments of apparent sudden realization may not correspond to understanding at all.

The transcultural moment, if we may call it that, is not a moment of experience but a space of negotiated meaning. The particular facility of writing that uses English as a second language, and invites the reader into the mental and emotional horizon of the "other" culture, is to bridge the gap between cultures, to reveal that understanding is a function of the linguistic situation. The dialectic of writer and reader that functions within this situation is particularly significant. Such writing reemphasises the constitutive nature of the meaning event and the varied nature of the usage in which meaning is accomplished.

Metonymic Gap as Production of Presence

We still need to deal with Bakhtin's valuable insight that *true dialogue can only occur when the difference of the other is recognized*. Understanding does not demand a shared experience of the world, but how is the "mirror" effect—that process by which both recognition and otherness occur—installed in the text? We have already provided part of the answer by seeing the literary text as itself a "mirror heterotopia," a confluence of the imagined and real. Yet despite the constitutive nature of transcultural meaning, there is an element in postcolonial literature that introduces what appears to be a gap in the text, and this is a "gap" that exists beyond interpretation, that, in fact, seems to *resist* interpretation. By stressing the distance between the participating writers and readers, the text prevents itself from being so transparent that it is absorbed into the dominant milieu of the reader of English. Such writing, while it provides a path for cultural understanding that overcomes the exclusionary effect of anthropological explanation, also questions easy assumptions about meaning and its transmissibility, and actively reinstalls the reality of its own cultural difference in quite explicit ways.

I call this reinstallation of difference the "metonymic gap." This is the cultural gap formed when writers transform English according to the needs of their source culture: by inserting unglossed words phrases or passages from a first language; by using concepts, allusions, or references that may be unknown to the reader; by code switching; or by transforming literary language with vernacular syntax or rhythms. Such variations become synecdochic of the writer's culture—the part that stands for the whole—rather than representations of the world, as the colonial language might. Thus the inserted language "stands for" the colonized culture in a metonymic way, and its very resistance to interpretation constructs a "gap" between the writer's culture and the colonial culture. The local writer is thus able to represent his or her world to the colonizer (and others) in the metropolitan language, and at the same time to signal and emphasise a difference from it. In effect, the writer is saying "I am using your language so that you will understand my world, but you will also know by the differences in the way I use it that you cannot share my experience." The reader exposed to such language is unequivocally in the presence of a culture that is "Other" to his or her own.

The metonymic gap is a central feature of the transformation of the literary language. The writer concedes the importance of *meanability*, the importance of a situation in which meaning can occur, and at the same time signifies areas of difference that may lie beyond meaning, so to speak, in a realm of cultural experience in which the reader must see him- or herself as other. The distinctive act of the cross-cultural text is to inscribe *difference* and *absence* as a corollary of cultural identity. Consequently, whenever a "strategy of transformation" of the dominant language is used, that is, a strategy that appropriates English and inflects it in a way that transforms it into a cultural vehicle for the writer, there is an installation of difference at the site of the meaning event. In this sense such strategies are directly metonymic of that cultural difference that is imputed by the linguistic variation. In fact, they are a specific form of metonymic figure—the synecdoche.

This strategy may appear, as I have suggested, to be a strategy of *resistance* to reading and, indeed, it is very easy to assume a level of incommunicability as a characteristic of such writing. But from another perspective postcolonial poetry *insists* on presence by demonstrating how inadequate the mechanics of interpretation *alone* can prove to be in the experience of the poem. This is not to concede the fallacy of incommensurable cultural experience. Rather, it reveals presence to be a *mutually negotiated* cultural/ aesthetic experience, emerging as an extension (more truly a ground) of the transcultural negotiation of meaning. As we have seen, neither cultural meaning nor culture itself, despite a widespread misconception, is embodied in the language. But it may be *disembodied* in the language in the sense that the presence appearing in the text may lead the reader to engage in a dimension of cultural revelation that occurs through its materiality, its music, and its transformative difference. Presence may therefore be seen to be "negotiated" because it too is a meeting place for the writer and reader functions, but it is a meeting in the space of *silence* within the language.

The "Beyond" of Interpretation

The importance of the materiality of the transcultural text compels us to face the possibility that presence is not something added on to the interpretation, but something on which interpretation is grounded. At one point in his reflection Gumbrecht makes one of his many concessions to the inevitability of interpretation, to the fact that presence must be something extra, something in addition to interpretation:

> I think that the "beyond" in metaphysics can only mean doing something in addition to "interpretation" without, of course, abandoning interpretation as

an elementary and probably inevitable intellectual practice. It would mean to try and develop concepts that could allow us, in the Humanities, to relate to the world in a way that is more complex than interpretation alone, that is more complex than only attributing meaning to the world (or, to use an older topology, that is more complex than extracting meaning from the world).[9]

If we think of presence as initiated by the materialities of the communication, in our case by the texture, music, and linguistic transformation of the lines, then we must see the "beyond" of metaphysics as in fact the ground or starting point of an interpretation. Although we might engage presence, *after* we have engaged the meaning (or, as I have in this chapter, after we have examined the process of the transcultural negotiation of meaning), we must begin with the *substance* of presence, so to speak. In one respect this is obvious—we must start with the physical (or aural or visual) text before we can even read, much less engage in an interpretation. But I want to suggest, by means of a diagram of the hermeneutic spiral, that what we term as the *beyond*, that is, the non-semantic, may be seen as the *before*, the prelinguistic.

This idea of the hermeneutic spiral proposes that the presence of the text, and I am thinking particularly of the transcultural text, might become the ground of interpretation rather than the excess or the additional engagement with the text's "meaning." We see in the diagram below, that the X axis is the axis of articulation, and the Y axis is the temporal or historical axis of interpretation, an axis that leads to progressive cycles of the hermeneutic circle changing through time and in different historical and cultural contexts. In this simple diagram of the hermeneutic process we may see that the axis of interpretation begins *below* the axis of articulation. This is the realm of presence.

The depiction of the relationship between the dimension of presence and that of interpretation suggests that our approach to the work begins below the axis of articulation and continually returns to it. Presence may not therefore be the added-on factor to the hermeneutic process but the ground in which that process occurs. This is particularly so in music and art, as well as in song and recited poetry, but in literature it is particularly so in the transcultural text. Why presence has been so obscured by interpretation is probably explained by the historical dominance of the hermeneutic attitude in the

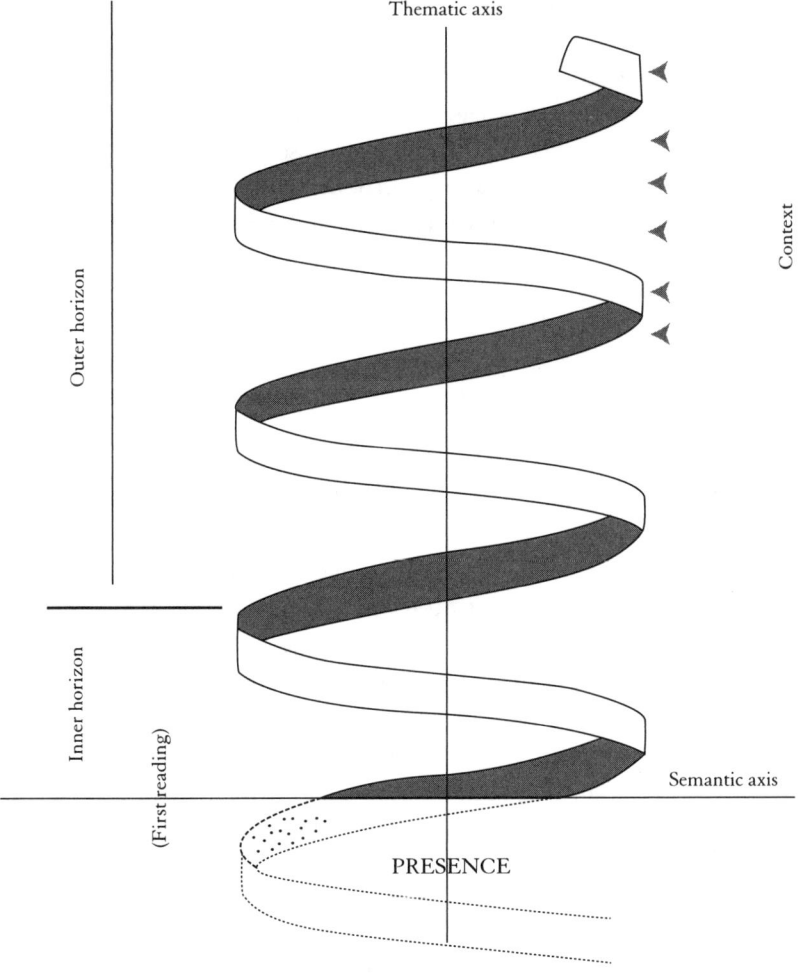

Figure 7.1 Hermeneutic spiral

humanities. The suggestion I want to make here is that the transcultural text, by insisting on presence, gives an easier access to this prelinguistic section of the hermeneutic spiral. We don't do away with representation, or with the requirements of meanability, but we find them considerably augmented by the production of presence in such a text.

The "Volume" of the Text

The space of negotiation, even though it is marked by the metonymic gap through strategies of transformation, even though it is silent, is still a transcultural space, a contact zone characterized by a considerable dynamic of change. Take the example of a verse from a poem by the Caribbean poet Linton Kwesi Johnson, who was born in Jamaica but lived in England most of his life:

> di lan is like a rack
> slowly shattahrin to san
> sinkin in a sea of calamity
> where fear breeds shadows daak
> where people fraid fi waak
> fraid fi tink fraid fi taak
> where di present is haunted by di paas[10]

While the poem transcribes the sound of the local dialect, Jamaican Patois, its orthography still "constructs" a reader for whom its variations pose no serious obstacle. Rather, the code variations become a part of the enjoyment of the poem. At first reading the poem might be formidable to a monolingual speaker, but the secret of the poem is its orality and its *performance* of a cultural reality that resists easy interpretation. There is much more *meaning* in the poem than an interpretative gloss would encompass and by balancing the requirements of meanability and difference the poem *insists* on presence. The "much more" that constitutes cultural presence is in fact beyond meaning for it exists in the *sound*, the music, of the lines, a dimension very aptly described by Hans-Georg Gadamer's term—"volume"—which Gumbrecht warmly cites in his own argument:

> But, can we really assume that the reading of such texts is a reading exclusively concentrated on meaning? Do we not sing these texts [*Ist es nicht ein Singen*]? Should the process in which a poem speaks only be carried by a meaning intention? Is there not, at the same time, a truth that lies in its performance [*eine Vollzugswahrheit*]? This, I think, is the task with which the poem confronts us.[11]

The "volume" of Johnson's poem is encompassed in the "performance" of the sound and shape of the lines, a materiality that opens up the nonhermeneutic dimension of reading. This is not an aesthetic volume alone: it is an extension, a "beyond" of cultural difference as well. Gumbrecht makes the point that this tension between the semantic and nonsemantic dimensions of the poem reflects the distinction between "earth" and "world" that Heidegger makes in his essay "The Origin of the Work of Art." "It is the component of 'earth' that enables the work of art, or the poem, to 'stand in itself'; it is 'earth' that gives the work of art existence in space."[12] We must imagine the cultural earth of the poem, then, to be that which is adumbrated by the physical texture of the lines. In the cross-cultural text the earth is that which is approached through the world, but because the "world" of the text is hybrid, the earth is engaged in a transcultural negotiation, a constitutive negotiation of writer and reader functions.

An example that demonstrates much more clearly how far short of the poem's "volume" a simple interpretation may fall occurs in James Berry's "Caribbean Proverb Poems":

CARIBBEAN PROVERB POEM I
Dog morning prayer is, Laard
wha teday, a bone or a blow
Tiger wahn fi nyam pickney, tiger sey
he could-a swear he woz puss
If yew cahn mek plenty yeyewater
fi funeral, start early morning[13]

A prosaic translation would be:

A dog's morning prayer is "Lord what will it be today, a bone or a blow?"
If a tiger wants to eat a child the tiger will swear he is a pussycat.
If you want to cry plenty of tears at a funeral, start early in the morning.

This translation might capture the proverbial sense of the lines but, obviously, not only is much lost in the sound, but an interpretation, or in this case a "translation," delivers virtually nothing. It is the sound and texture of the lines that give the *feel* of the creole culture, its sense of insouciance, its verbal and experiential plasticity (but even as I describe this cultural *feel* I know that my interpretation falls far short of the "volume" of the text, the cultural presence encountered by the reader). It is the capacity to expose the presence of Caribbean culture that gives the proverbs their particular character, and indeed, their aesthetic purpose. Thus we come to the conclusion that the very *poiesis* of the poem involves much that exists beyond simple interpretation and yet it is still a feature of the "meaning" of the poem.

Lines such as Berry's wrestle with the written text in a struggle that leaves the uncommitted reader stranded. This is what I mean by *insisting* on presence. But the sound of the language can still impress itself as needing to be heard without creating quite so much distance. For instance, Linton Kwesi Johnson's "Street 66" is a poem that impresses its orality, emerging as it does from the creole continuum:

> de room woz dark
> dusk howlin softly
> six-a-clack,
> charcoal lite defyin site woz
> movin black;
> de soun woz muzik mellow steady flow,
> an man-son mind jus mystic red,
> green, red, green . . . pure scene.
>
> no man would dance but leap an shake
> dat shock thru feelin ripe;
> shape dat soun tumblin doun
> makin movement ruff enough;
> cause when de muzik met I taps,
> I felt de sting, knew de shock,
> yea had to do an ride de rock.

The third stanza launches into the music of the vernacular voice:

> oughta dis rock
> shall come
> a greena riddim
> even more dread
> dan what
> de breeze of glory bread.

> vibratin violence
> is how we move
> rockin wid green riddim
> de drout
> an dry root out[14]

The language of the poem appropriates the writing for its own purposes, not just transforming the written form but adapting it to a voice whose very presence in writing creates the sense of cultural difference within the shared language. In this way the oral doesn't just enter the text but wrestles it to the ground. This act of violence is itself a feature of the cultural "resistance"— its "verbal insurgency" if you like—that gives the poem its character. This is a character we could certainly describe if pressed, but this would simply transfer presence into meaning (however inadequately) and thereby reduce the "volume" of the poem.

Sometimes the difference of the language and its avenue to presence is used as both the imagined or virtual dimension of the poem's meaning and the real substance of the lines. Valerie Bloom's poem "Language Barrier" a poem by Valerie Bloom, Jamaican born but a long time resident of England captures both dimensions of this heterotopic ambivalence:

> Jamaica language sweet yuh know bwoy,
> An yuh know mi nebba notice i',
> Till tarra day one foreign frien'
> Come spen some time wid mi.
>
> An den im call mi attention to
> Some tings im sey soun' queer,
> Like de way wi always sey 'koo yah'
> When we really mean 'look here.'[15]

But the musical quality is not limited to Caribbean poems. In Nissam Ezekiel's "Very Indian Poems in Indian English" a mild parody of Indian English actually comes in lines whose oral quality is compelling:

> Some people are not having manners
> this I am always observing,

> For example the other day I find
> I am needing soap
>
> For ordinary washing myself purposes
> So I'm going to one small shop
> Nearby in my lane and I'm asking
> For well known brand of soap.[16]

Clearly we are not talking about a moment of aesthetic intensity here, and the sense of cultural presence the sound of the lines delivers is relatively inconsequential. But nevertheless the poem demonstrates a widespread non-semantic and nonhermeneutic strategy: it exposes us to the culture in a way that operates quite beyond the level of interpretation.

Between Presence Culture and Meaning Culture

The "volume" of the text lies, then, in the materiality of the lines, which we might also relate to the performance, the music of the poem. Such music is very obvious in the hybrid creole poetry of the Caribbean but it also becomes a feature of the presence of cultural otherness in literature written from an oral culture. Such an oral culture conforms fairly precisely to Gumbrecht's idea of a "presence culture." In such cultures, words are granted a certain measure of control over the objects or situations to which they refer. Words are *sacred*. They have the *power* of the things they signify because they are imputed to *be* the things they signify. Language embodies the seamless connection between people and their environments. This type of language culture is distinguished by the general absence of metaphor, but the nature of representation itself is different. Words are concrete and the relation between the word and the thing is characterized by analogy and embodiment, or "presentation," rather than by representation. Thus the concepts of soul, mind, time, courage, emotion, or thought are intensely physical, as in the languages of Australian Aboriginals, South Pacific, and African peoples.

Gumbrecht provides a fascinating account of the distinction between a presence culture and a meaning culture in the Eucharist, the moment of transformation from the Middle Ages to modernity occurring when the

Host changes from an "embodiment" of Christ's body to a symbol, or representation, of the body of Christ. But another interesting survival of this unity of word and referent can be seen in Hebrew in the form of the Jewish phylactery, the piece of written Hebrew text from the Torah kept in a container and worn on the body, (preferably strapped to the head). The word of God is objectified as physical presence. The phylactery is not merely the representation of the wearer's closeness to the strictures of the Law, but the Law *itself* in its actual, unambiguous, and power-laden presence.

A consequence of the power of words to embody their referents is the importance of the link between the word and the physical breath. The "breath" remains the sign of the tangible reality, the bodily presence of words. Oral myths are the fundamental means of communicating history, traditions, morality, customs, and values. They are life giving and they can only be maintained by continual repetition. The anthropologist A. P. Elkin found that these oral myths in Aboriginal clans must be inculcated, indeed, breathed into all members of the tribe, and this is done in a very literal manner by constant repetition through infancy and childhood:

> Most striking of all, however, is the teaching of the sacred chants to the newly initiated . . . [I]n Arnhem Land, the elders grip the young fellow, and vigorously sing the chant into his very mouth, so that after several such "treatments," it becomes part of him.[17]

The breath is the metonym of language, the tangible link between words and world, the sign of their material embodiment of meaning.

Often, the coextensivity of the body with the world and the personal potency of the objects with which it is familiarly connected seem to play a greater part than language. Maurice Leenhardt, the missionary anthropologist in New Caledonia, expressed his profound surprise at the assurance of his old friend and informant Boesoou that it was not the notion of the spirit but of the body that the missionary had brought them.[18] Notions of spirit were completely compatible with the Melanesian view of the interpenetration of man and reality. The really new concept was of the body as "set apart" from a world external to it. In such a society the symbolic power of parts of the human body, such as excreta, hair, nail parings, skin, spittle, domestic utensils, and a whole host of objects and artefacts, play a central role in procedures to affect or influence the individuals to whom they are connected.

This is because, although they may seem symbolic, such objects are dramatically *metonymic* in the sense that they are possessed of the essence of the individual. They are not simply the parts that "stand for" or represent, the whole person, they *are* the whole. These nonverbal symbols appear to contradict the function of language in magical processes, but in fact they are given their potency precisely because they are employed with the accompaniment of spells and incantations, which are necessary to accord them the requisite power. Without the metaphoric power of language their potential symbolic functions remain unrealized. In being given verbal labels, the objects themselves become a form of language. The reason magicians spend so much time choosing objects and actions as surrogate words, when spoken words themselves have magical potential, is that objects become a more permanent and more manipulable *form of words*.

Although the sacred power of language assumes the status of a theme in much African, Pacific, and indigenous literature, the interesting question remains as to what extent this concrete property in the mother tongue intervenes in the use of English. What happens when the writer from an oral culture uses words in English? Even at the superficial level a different resonance in the language can be discerned in those literatures in English that draw their energies from such a source. To students of literature the effect is of a controlled economy of diction that often appears overly simple at first reading. Rather than a matter of overt technique, however, the English of the text appears to ascribe more metaphoric resonance to the words themselves, more "embodiment" of their subject than might immediately appear in the Western novel. We can assume that the greater importance of the tangible *form* of language in a presence culture leads to a greater prominence of presence in the cross-cultural text in English.

Another effect on English writing is the influence of orality on the rhythms of the written language, as may be seen in a passage from Chinua Achebe in which he describes the reactions of parents to a child who exhibits characteristics of a previous child who had died:

> Edogo's mind was in pain over the child. Some people were already saying that perhaps he was none other than the first one. But Edogo and Amoge never talked about it; the woman especially was afraid. Since utterance has the power to change fear into living truth they dared not speak before they had to.[19]

This passage is particularly interesting because not only does it use the rhythms of the Igbo language, it demonstrates the text in the process of negotiating the conceptual gulf between the Igbo sense of the power of language where "utterance has the power to change fear into living truth," and the English text in which this is conveyed, where words are representations. The language of the novel, with its adapted African rhythms, becomes metonymic of the culture it is describing. It stands for the difference of Igbo culture without actually circumscribing it, and becomes a sign standing for experiences that are ultimately incommunicable. Language operating in this way achieves something a simple translation could never achieve.

Consequently, we find a language that lays stress on metrical regularity and tonal cadence. The character's "mind was in pain," the metre smoothed out by the 'n' sound and carried into the next sentence. Instead of "perhaps he was the same," we find the more formal and attenuated "perhaps he was none other than the first one," in which the 'n' sound again carries the rhythms generated in the first sentence. The Igbo language has an eight-vowel system in which harmony is essential and this harmony is reflected in the harmony of the English consonants. This, allied to the African "mode," which uses both proverbs and what we might call a "proverbial diction," produces a text with a distinctive character.

Language operating in this way achieves something a simple translation could never achieve: it foregrounds the various forms of language use in the text and constructs difference in two ways. On the one hand, the linguistic features simultaneously install and bridge a cultural gap between African subject and English-speaking reader by replicating the rhythms of oral language in literary English. On the other, the reader, simply by opening the "African novel," makes an unspoken commitment to accept this formal, highly structured, metrically measured, and tonally smooth writing as African English. This dialectic is the essential feature of the literature of linguistic intersection and its particular facility in this context is its capacity to intimate a cultural reality though the music, the "bodily presence" of the words.

The engagement with the cross-cultural text occurs in a "transcultural space," a contact zone in which both reader and writer functions are changed. We can see how the writer of the second-language text sets up the conditions for this engagement through a use of language that pushes the attentive reader past the demands of interpretation. This is an elaboration of the power of all literature to present the luminous effects of its materiality. But what of the reading? Should readers approach the text in a different way to engage with presence? Whether obliged to or not there is a way of being open to the text without "representing," a way of (un)thinking that Heidegger calls *Gelassenheit*. As becomes very obvious when we examine this concept, Heidegger's admonition to engage in a form of meditation without willing, an attitude of "being open" (what he refers to as "releasement") is ideally designed to apprehend presence in the text. "Releasement towards things" and "openness to the mystery" are two aspects of the same disposition, a disposition that allows us to inhabit the world "in a totally different way."[20] *Gelassenheit* is enabled when we let go of willing, and, by letting go of it, we let ourselves in, in the sense that we are let-in into *Gelassenheit*. By letting-go of willing, we actually give ourselves the possibility of being open to *Gelassenheit* and, in *Gelassenheit*, remain open for be-ing itself.[21] What this may mean in a practical sense is being open to otherness in the transcultural text by being open to the materiality of its language, to remain in the "primordial, prehermeneutic context" of the hermeneutic spiral so to speak. This becomes part of a subtle ethical engagement where true dialogue is enabled when the difference of the other is recognized, as Bakhtin suggests, but where the reader goes further by refusing to capture that otherness in an act of interpretative willing.

How this form of reading might be achieved is much easier to ponder than how it might be conveyed to others in the classroom. One of the most appealing aspects of Gumbrecht's commitment to presence is his considerable concern with the capacity of university teaching to introduce the student to presence, in the process of "producing complexity." Good academic teaching

> should be deictic, rather than interpretative and solution-oriented. But how will such a deictic teaching style not end in silence and, worse perhaps, in a quasi-mystical contemplation and admiration of so much complexity? For an analogy that helps to clarify this point, we can turn to the "emphatic" new concept of "reading" that probably comes from the specific experience that readers have had with certain types of modern literature. Such "reading," both reading books and reading the world, is not simply meaning attribution. It is the never-ending movement, the both joyful and painful movement between losing and regaining intellectual control and orientation,

that can occur in the confrontation with (almost?) any cultural object as long as it occurs under conditions of low time pressure, that is, with no "solution" or "answer" immediately expected. This is exactly the movement that we are referring to when we say that a class or a seminar 'broadened' our minds.[22]

Alas, the fatal term here, from the point of view of the teacher, is the phrase "low time pressure." Where might this reading time exist in the contemporary academy with its bureaucratic obsession with strategic goals, outcomes, and throughput? But no matter how much time we might have on our hands presence proves to be notoriously resistant to teaching strategies, certainly to the "interpretative and solution-oriented." "There is no reliable, no guaranteed way of producing moments of intensity," says Gumbrecht, and "we have even less hope of holding on to them or extending their duration."[23] In teaching postcolonial poetry, for instance, we might invite the students to "get the feel" of Caribbean culture, we might discuss the oral nature of the creole continuum or the music of the lines, but this is a way of "talking around" the poem and there is hardly any way of defining or assessing such experience, nor any guarantee that it can be encountered. Nevertheless, it is important for the teacher of literature to recognize that a resonance between presence effects and meaning effects is going to be an almost inevitable consequence of the reading experience. And it focuses on an important feature of the transcultural negotiation: the opportunity to experience the self as other. Rather than a sense of alienation, the transformative strategies of the cross-cultural text, by enabling the student to see himself or herself as other, may offer an intense invitation to transcultural dialogue.

"It Disturbs Me with a Presence"

Hindu History and What Meaning Cannot Convey

Ranjan Ghosh

Presence is a state of prenarration; it is also implicated in postnarration. It is caught in the interstices of historical narration; it is an active resident in a prison house of historical representation. It challenges and questions the limits of representation in a variety of discourses.

All forms of representation bear the promise of a presence mothered by an absence. This absence can be conscious when the subject chooses to put something at the other end of the line or, without an alarm to the subject, the absence can simmer unwarily in the backyard and then ambush with a meaning under circumstances where factors required to judge its legitimacy are too feeble to question it.

Presence can be positive when, for instance, parliamentarians in arguing on the floor of the House keep the "absent" electorate in mind. It can be perilous when narratives of ethnic or communal glorification are mismapped and malappropriated to aggrandize the particular needs of a community at the exclusion of the "other." Ideas from the past that can never be pinned down to strict objectivity and, incidents from the past that are more a part of popular consciousness and products of our cultural inheritance than possessions attested to by archaeologists, become naturalized residents of our daily existence. The past becomes immovable; it affects and influences the way we think of our present; it loses its pastness and chimes with the breath of our everyday existence. This, thus, reinscribes our everyday discourse with the affect and pull of "presence."

Presence succeeds in introducing a tension in the way we perceive the limits of representability. The relationship that presence is seen to have with the past is problematized by the way we define the past in relation to the present. When the past is recorded and grounded in facts and has the sanction of historians and archaeologists, the ambiguities about our ways of representation are sparse. But since not all past is recorded history, the unrepresentability of the past encourages certain experiences and formations that the proper historian cannot be comfortable with. The language of representation changes as the historian is forced to enter the zone of speculative inferences; stepping across the line of certainty that scientific methodologies can provide, representation is often buttressed by imagination and the sublimity in historical experience is allowed to peek over its shoulder. To an extent, presence determines a historian's language, his choice of subjects, what he wants to represent, and what he cannot but leave unrepresented. On some occasions it has the misfortune of being the enemy of historical representation but on other occasions it is the strength and support in our understanding of things that rationality and reason traditionally expected of history cannot always explain. Do historical representations become typically more "present" than what they represent? Where does this "presence" come from if the represented, if reality itself, does not endow it with its credentials? Could there be anything that is more "real," and more present, than even reality itself? And, if so, what, then, is this "anything" and where should we locate it?[1] Presence is the "effectual" angel who can entice and also be the victim of its own enticement, for when historians fail to clip her wings the pseudo nonhistorians outrage her by manipulating her uniqueness to serve their own partisan ends. In fact, Hindu history is one such domain that teases us to think out the vicissitudes of presence's angelic flighty presence.

Presence conceived as the surfacing of the absent or of what is perceived to be absent, or of what has existed without stirring the consciousness, has influenced our understanding of Hindu history in many ways. Presence is complicit in the understanding of Hindu history and the unfolding ramifications of the contemporary essentialist and sectarian Hindu attitude toward the "other." How can we render a different dimension to the concept of the "presence" in relation to the shifts and turns of communal history? To what extent can it be appropriated to argue the current crisis in Hindu-Muslim relationships in India? How does "presence" render distinctness to the Indian concept of history and help explicate some areas in our understanding of religion, tradition, and historiography? What has presence managed to convey when meaning under the Western principles of historical understanding has failed to comprehend certain aspects of what Hindus understand and have argued as *itihasa*?

An Indian Approach to *Itihasa*

The charge, framed within a Western historiographical model, that Hindus lack a sense of history is both contentious and misleading. Narratives of the past in South Asia have too often been dismissed as "myth" simply because they did not conform to certain historiographic standards. V. S. Naipaul does not fail to note this alleged area of darkness: "Indian interpretations of their history are almost as painful as the history itself; and it is especially painful to see the earlier squalor being repeated today . . . people with a sense of history might have ordered matters differently . . . this is precisely the saddening element in Indian history; this absence of growth and development. It is a history whose only history is that life goes on. There is only a series of beginnings, no final creation."[2] Although this chapter does not intend to run a counterdiscourse against these allegations of achronicity and evinces no desire to reframe the categories of Indian historiography within the prescriptions and paradigms of the Western/Hegelian model of world history, it tries to draw attention to the ways in which history has been perceived by the Hindus, the frames and processes in which history has been practiced and understood. Rabindranath Tagore summarily dismisses all efforts to see history as tied to the dictates of world history as "superstition"; he believes that history cannot be practiced in the same way in every nation. One hears despairing sighs when inroads into archives fail to bless historians with sufficient resources to write about India; they would quip, "How can we find history here when there is no politics?" Tagore wisely notes:

"When one tries to search for brinjals [eggplants] in the rice field he is destined to meet with frustration and this disappointment makes him conclude that rice is not an agricultural crop."[3] If Hindus are endowed with a sense of history, what, then, is the nature of their historical sense-generation? How has the Hindu way of doing history provoked and made possible the emanation of "presence"? How has this distinctness allowed presence to run its own course and influence the ways in which Indians have staked out their tryst with history, their continual wrestling with the past?

An understanding of the distinct Indian approach to *itihasa* and historiography will, perhaps, give us a moderate clue as to the easy capitulation of most Hindus to the mythic and religious appropriation of the past. One may note that on most occasions religious faith for this community is usually independent of objective fact; rather, it is something that is attainable through mystical introspection. Religious consciousness is akin to a deeper spiritual reality where transrational faith and discursive intellect are not in dissonance with each other. More than deduction, differentiation, analysis, and integration, most Hindus are happy to remain embedded in subjective conditions and believe in advancement from one subjective state to another. One cannot ignore the luxuriance of popular imagination, the high emotional pitch in popular worship, and the intense connection between mythology and philosophy. Since the long history of such a civilization has resulted from many extraordinary processes, even a small mythological story or a folk tale (for instance, the story of the Indian epic *Ramayana* and the myth encircling Ayodhya) exhibits in a crystallized form all the vicissitudes of these periods. In general, the essence of old and new happenings is brought out by precisely such earthy, native traditions, which are specific to place and time. So, polarization of myth and history and secular distinctions between "facts" (and science) and "fiction" (and literature), which are the characteristic features of European modernity, are not integral to early Indian historiography. Much of traditional Indian history has, in fact, been embedded within cultural forms such as myths—forms in which historical consciousness awaits to be prized out—making, thereby, evident that the factors that have resulted in "modern historical consciousness" were not present in traditional India.

Dwelling on the "distinctness" of Indian historiography, N. A. Nikam writes, "What is history but a 'regressive' perspective of time; and, every culture has a sense of history; every culture has its 'golden age' and a memory of the deeds of its heroes, and has its tradition. But as a regress into the past is always possible so there is 'history' behind history, and so the paradox of history is that in human culture the beginnings of history are not in history but in 'pre-history', and pre-history merges into the myth. Indian culture, Hinduism in particular, is the forgotten memory of the beginninglessness of an undated tradition *sanatana dharma* [eternal law] alive to look back upon its own past in order to live in a changing time."[4] Hindus, in general, cannot avoid collapsing into ritual, fantasy, and myth, and have always cultivated an allegiance to *sanatana dharma,* deeming it as sacrosanct: Hindu ethos, thus, commands an unstinted fealty from all members of its community. At one level, "progress" for the Hindus means a movement toward achieving the heights of the "glorious past" (mythicized, for instance, in the notion of the *Ramrajya*, which is a utopic state of socio-economic condition commonly believed to have existed during the reign of Lord Rama) and at another level "there is always an attempt in modern India to interpret the present in terms of past and the past in terms of present."[5] Although Kalhana (in the mid-twelfth century) exclaimed that a "virtuous poet alone is worthy of praise who, free from love or hatred, ever restricts his language to the exposition of facts,"[6] Indian history plays a good deal looser with the notion of fact than that found in either Chinese or Western historiography. Unlike the Chinese, who have left behind for posterity well-attested historical treatises, Aryans are said to have left behind myths, and in several cases of transmutations we have history as a blend of fact and "imagination." Though the court of every important king in India is said to have been endowed with a chronicler (*Arthasastra* [a treatise on statecraft by Kautilya in the fourth century BCE] points out the existence of official records and the importance of officers responsible for maintaining them), and despite the fact that a strong oral, literary, and writing tradition in ancient India was somewhat informed with a sense of preservation, the unflinching commitment to the "factual" is nonexistent in the subcontinental culture. Hindus did not preserve records as diligently as the Chinese did; what the Hindus felt worth preserving was the meaning of events, not a record of when events took place. It is the particularity and meticulousness of historical details that do not bother Indians much. They care more for the truth of the experience or the soundness of doctrine than the circumstances that gave it birth.[7] They were more tradition-minded than history-minded, but this is the way they generated meaning out of their interface with the past.[8] In India, unlike in the West, neither philosophy nor religion has ever been considered in isolation. Indeed, the Indian concept of history can be seen as a combination of the two. Hence, a strong mythic structure undergirds the concept of history, and there is no denying that history for the Hindus is lived-in reality and Hindu culture has both a paleocentric and mythopoetic character.[9] This distinct sense of fact, in a certain indulgent frivolity with the strict terms of historical representation, and in a living conformity to tradition that is ritualistic and sacrosanct, makes "presence" a core constituent of Hindu historiography.

Hindus revere the past but not always in the religious sense; the past has come down to them as inspiration and prescription of social and personal conduct. Ancient Vedic literature, the later epics, and the medieval tales of the past (*Puranas*) illustrate through myth-making the essential relationships between humans and institutions. Whether in a family or a classroom, in politics or the workplace, ancient heroes and their deeds are recalled, and the present is compared with the past. Presence determines our ways of "recall"; presence throws its weight, at times unconsciously, behind what we choose from the past and how we make the past talk to us; having a hand at resurrections, it makes old myths change and gives birth to new ones. Unknown facts are filled in, and the accounts become richer as they pass from mouth to mouth and generation to generation. As every Indian would say, "Don't confuse me with facts; the ones I don't know, *I will make up*." Hindus "make up"; Hindus know the subtle art of mixing fact with myth, unlike their Western counterpart; Hindus choose to revel in diverse meanings and compose meaning out of their rather affective relations with the past. History is not sure of the character of baggage that presence puts on her back. Reconstructionism leaves enough room for "presences" to keep crawling in and debouch in ways that take the narrative by ideological twists, bias, and inventive bursts of historical interpretation.[10] The space that the Hindus have inherited in which to maneuver their past and to restructure and reinterpret forms of knowledge and items of history have given a certain pliancy to the rules of ethical and moral conduct. Old stories about ancestors are given new forms; stories gleaned and inherited from the past are adapted, molded, and welded to suit the needs of the present. Presence has futurized the past. Different versions of ancient texts exist, and different texts always tell slightly altered accounts of particular events. Such accomodationist tendencies and maneuverability challenge our understanding of the mental constructions of the Hindus; more important than the hard crust of facts are the emotions and ideas orbiting round myths that spring from the Hindu way of life, which knows little history and much philosophy and literature. These are the basis of the unique cultural formations that still dominate the nation's socioreligious consciousness.

Central to Indian historiography is the storytelling ability of the Hindus. In the act of storytelling the predominant role of "experience" is discounted, unlike in the long European tradition of storytelling. The immediacy of personal experience does not make up the story for *itihasa*. As Ranajit Guha ably argues:

> *Itihasa* as the repository of the tales told by tradition and bequeathed from one generation to the next since antiquity has little to do with the immediacy of experience. To the contrary, recursivity rules, as in the *Mahabharata*, the most outstanding example of the genre. Everything in this epic is an exercise in retelling. Even the very first narrator tells it as told by his guru, Vyasa. It is hard to improve on that as an instance of repetition. As for the audience, the stories they want to hear are stories they have already heard. In fact, there are numerous occasions when the storyteller is asked to follow up the shorter version of an episode immediately by a more elaborate one. And this is not a matter of any individual listener's caprice. Convention allows *itihasa* to be narrated in abridgement as well as at length, and one is as good as the other.[11]

The *charans*, or traditional minstrels, Brahminic *barots* and *bhats* (learned men/chroniclers) who composed eulogies of their royal employers reveled in the dialectic of history and story; they worked on the soil of facts with the ploughshares of imagination. The emergence of the *charans* expresses an attitude that "subordinates the historical reality of past individuals and individual events to the process of cultural continuity and cultural renewal."[12] The narratives of these Hindu storytellers have their own share of legends, fairy tales, and myths. It is a different way of conceiving history and its function: "In traditional Indian historiography, the data produced and the statistics used are often unique. A king is mentioned as having sixty thousand children, and the heavens are mentioned as being inhabited by three hundred thirty million gods, not only to make the point that the king is potent and gods are many, but also to wipe out what many would consider the real data, and obviate any possibility of verification or empirical treatment.... In other words, in this type of historiography data are important only so far as they relate to the overall logic and cultural symbols that must be communicated."[13] The ancient Indian view of history puts greater accent on the processes of thought and cultures than on the flow of events. The emergence of the concept of *yugas* [it is the name of an 'epoch' or 'era' within the cycle of four ages namely *Satya yuga*, *Treta yuga*, the *Dvapara yuga* and the *Kali yuga*] is one such dimension of the cultural process, for Indians found more interest in eternity than in temporal linearity. Referring to the *Puranas*, Ainslie Embree notes that "human existence must be seen against a background of an almost unimaginable duration of time." Compared to other civilizations that view history in term of thousands of years, the Indians—Buddhists, Jains, and Hindus—narrated it in terms of billions of years, and the historical process in its temporal manifestation becomes a part of a "vast cyclical movement."[14] Presence has come to nestle in such an unquantitative approach to history. Presence has also crept in through the fuzzy zones provided by the lack of sufficient evidence: cataclysmic dynastic clashes, waves of invasion, and marauding political bands destroyed important documents and other material, with the result that several junctures of Indian historiography have become unclear to us. This means that several strands of Indian history that would otherwise have been sufficiently chronicled suffer from factual inadequacy. This has rendered certain crucial events in Hindu history as "black holes," holes that serve as temptations for intrusive misadventures and are conducive to ultrareligious incursions.[15] Also, manuscripts in India have not been able to battle the climatic factor successfully (failing most often to survive anything more than five hundred years) except in the arid parts of western India. "Most of the Sanskrit books," writes Vincent Smith, "were composed by Brahmans, who certainly had not a taste for writing histories, their interest being engaged in other pursuits. But the Rajas were eager to preserve annals of their own doings, and took much pain to secure ample and permanent record of their achievements. They are not to blame for the melancholy fact that their efforts have had little success. The records, laboriously prepared and regularly maintained, have perished almost completely in consequence of the climate, including insect pests in that term, and of the innumerable political revolutions from which India has suffered."[16] The archival tradition also lost steam and fell prey not just to climatic changes or political violence but also perished on account of certain sudden changes of administrative centers that each dynasty created; preservation also suffered owing to the emergence of other local or regional powers who scarcely exhibited interest in archival preservation, preoccupied as they were with warfare.

Ayodhya and the Presence of Myth

A section of historians sees tradition as a decisive source of information in India because religion, they contend, holds a preponderant sway over the lives of most Indians. Tradition, it is argued, helps preserve historical information, and historical archaeology, at times, fails to hold its ground before the immovability and inviolability of tradition. Sites believed to be associated with religious heroes, related to sacred figures from the *Ramayana* and the *Mahabharata* and identified with incidents that have dropped anchors in public memory mostly through word of mouth, have crossed swords with the methodological enquiries of the archaeologists. What has come down through the years as lived tradition remains firm and deep, although on occasion it is dissonant with the historical findings endorsed by rational-scientific modes of investigation. In India, the ancient is never past; the ancient past is very much the present substance of India, demographically as well as culturally.[17] Myth is something that the nation or the civilization can never successfully objectify. The myth of Ayodhya is one such phenomenon. Ayodhya, the birthplace of Lord Rama and where Rama's kingdom is said to have thrived, has, I would like to argue, foregrounded the problem of "presence" and myth. Frank Ankersmit observes that "myth incarnates the parallel processes of civilizations, nations, and so forth, hence, and is the place where actions represented will continuously repeat themselves in the action of representation. 'Presence' is an appropriate term for referring to this stubborn persistence of the past in which it remains a presence in the present. In this way myth can also give meaning to 'presence,' that is to say, suggest where we may expect to find presence in a civilization's cultural repertoire."[18] Ayodhya is a part of "sacred history"; it exists as a reminder of what Hindus understand as *sanatana dharma* (the eternal law), which is symbolic of the religious sentiments about a sacramental past; it is timeless and instrumentalizes a synchronic unity. It is this distension of myth into history that makes

Ayodhya turn into a Hindu city that has its supposed "authentic" roots in the glorious past under Lord Rama's reign. Ayodhya's past, clarifies Julia Shaw, is "inscribed in a myriad of contradictory texts, literary, archaeological and countless others derived from oral sources, or from temporal spheres such as the dates upon which certain sites are supposed to be visited. Like all texts, none can be read in purely objective terms, especially since they are tied up with issues of invention and legitimation."[19] There is blurring of borders between archaeological and ritual time, space, and topography, which thus legitimizes the basis of invented biography. Even though archaeologists have not found anything of note that would have made them enthusiastic about any claims to the history of Ayodhya, the narratives of the *Ramayana* have grown on most Indians; there is no denying the temptation to see myth in an embrace with history that, most often, is an uneasy one. Ayodhya remains sacred in the heart of most Hindus; Lord Rama is invoked in various communal festivals with conviviality and religious ardor; idols of Rama find a revered place in the prayer room of most god-fearing Hindus. Rama and his kingdom in Ayodhya have a presence in the consciousness of most Hindus, evoking the benignity of a dharmic life that communicates the need for a peaceful neighborhood free from all forms of inhumanity. Secular historians have persistently demonstrated the preponderance of religious belief and consequently the etiolation of historical evidence in efforts that try to render a sacred status to the phenomenon of Ayodhya. Most Hindus have been happy to see Ayodhya in a shroud of myth. They are content to consider it as part of their unrecorded history: folklorish, oral, and hence unquantifiable, having a sublimity of its own. Nestled outside the claims of the scientific paradigms of historical investigation, Ayodhya enjoys a living presence both in Hindu consciousness and in India's unhistoricized and achronic past. It has an authenticity that "is clearly not the kind of authenticity that one attributes to a document from the past whose provenance one has verified. Rather, it is authenticity in the existential sense, deriving its force from the alleged fact that it emerges directly and immediately from the subject's encounter with the world."[20] Strangely, history in the Indian subcontinent is not authoritative enough to dictate a divorce from this slice of the Hindu past; quaintly, myth, too, is not formidable enough to have an undifferentiated existence of its own. For Indians presence links the two—presence has inspired Indians to both mythicize and historicize their encounters with the past; the midwifery of presence has compelled Indians to revel in a bemusement, and even the authority of consensus has most often failed to rescue them from this state.

Hindu fundamentalist leaders who juggle myth and history in their own astute ways lend a vicious spin on this discourse of presence. Religious maximalists and Hindutva historians argue that Indians have never bothered to question the space that myth and history should legitimately hold against each other in their engagement with Ayodhya. Taking advantage of how most Hindus get consumed by "moments of intensity"[21] and knowing how such moments fortify collective consciousness, which does not care much to rationalize its purposes, they have made presence serviceable to the ministration of the Hindu right. It is important to see how myth and history hide beneath the skin of each other in a pontificatory discourse that censors, suppresses, and mismaps events to domesticate a portion of the past to the service of the present.[22] Let me cite an instance to help us understand the nature of this discourse. This is how it runs: In 1528 AD the Muslim conqueror Babar came to Ayodhya (Aud) and halted for a week. He destroyed the ancient temple and on its site built a mosque, which is known as the Babri Masjid. In the long centuries before this destruction, around seventy-six battles had to be fought in the defence of the Janmabhumi, the birthplace of Rama. The first aggressor was the notorious king of Lanka, Ravana, who destroyed Ayodhya during the time of the ancestors of Shri Ram. The second attack came from the Greek king Milind or Menander; the third assault was commandeered by Salar Masud, a nephew of the much-maligned Muslim plunderer, Mahmud Ghaznavi. All this occurred till Babar arrived.

Such a description can certainly provoke the Hindus to put an ear out for an unknown part of the story of their civilization. But ironically this selective prodding does not inspire them to investigate the validity of these statements; the leisurely attitude of most Indians to the past prevents them from fussing about the "unrepresented." The politics of the "represented" is lost in moments of intensity, in a mythogenic construction that works on mechanisms of distortion. The charm and aura that presence knits around Ayodhya are lost when they are tailored to form a part of the stereotypes for ultra-religionists; the strategic carpentry of representation forces Ayodhya to lose all that it beatifically stood for; it is lost to the ruckus of nationalist blarney. Presence has indulgently allowed history to love and hate myth at the same time; it has made the domain of historical objectivity patient not to begrudge the footfalls of popular belief, legend, and folklore. But, caught in the loop of presence, communal historiography in India has become the victim of a concerted and consolidated historical practice that subordinates historical discourse to the behest and politics of myth. Myth undergirded with historical details is, thus, represented as historical knowledge and, in such representations, presence is seen to confound fact with fiction. It insidiously turns history, religion, and politics into a collective where each covertly gains out of the other's presence. It endows a collective with emotional and normative underpinning as well as a common language and set of understandings about how a particular society-community functions and how it ought to function. Ayodhya as a special segment of the viscous Hindu past is zealously privatized and politicized, spawning a feeling of *participation mystique*, and "presentified" with a heritage. Presence, thus harnessed and instrumentalized, is found to lend a specific identity to a community and in the process unfailingly empower a group of people who self-style themselves as moral custodians of an entire community's way of existence.

So presence in Indian historiography cannot avoid the stranglehold of Brahmin priests, *sadhus* (holy men), and the political scolds who, reveling as public intellectuals, labor hard on this festering nexus. As explicators of certain issues of Indian history to most of the poor and semiliterate Hindus, these people have been communicators of a particular set of messages to the youth. They establish their role as arbiters of the nation's fate; it is in their hands that the definition of Hinduism is modified and the concepts of the *Ramayana* and Ram undergo a paradigm shift. In fact, the centrality of Brahmins in the explication and legitimation of Indian history is all too well known to expatiate here. The influence of Brahmins and the elitist projection of the Sanskrit language (*devabhasa*, the language of the gods, as it was called) peripheralized several narratives and events in Indian history; it constructed an institutional power that helped inscribe the epistemological preference of the Brahmins into the mainstream discourse of Indian history. The sources, particularly those in Sanskrit, points out Romila Thapar, "were in the main the works of the Brahmans as keepers of the ancient classical tradition, and expressed the Brahminical Weltanschauung." Thapar cautions us by saying that "the reliance on 'pandits,' those learned in Sanskrit and supposedly the guardians of the ancient tradition, was not the most reliable—although undoubtedly the most convenient—access to ancient history. Many of the contemporary ideological prejudices of the pandits were often incorporated into what was believed to be the interpretation of the ancient tradition."[23] Evidence exists of Brahmans wielding political power in ancient India. However, it is conceivable that to a creative Brahminical mind, history—when accuracy predominates over imagination and fancy, and diligence over talent—proved to be less attractive than philosophy and literature; it, thus, provided ample scope for the display of creativity and merit. In fact, British orientalist scholarship availed itself of the services of learned Brahmans who would substantially accentuate both the concepts that were true to the Brahminical points of view and facts that were subservient to their sense of interpretation of the past. Several spaces of Indian pasts have been strategically exscinded; several discourses springing from non-Brahminical ways of perceiving the past have been silenced or at best are relegated to second-order knowledge. This is one potential way of encouraging the play of presences. Most often, it is in the strategic contemporanization of a discourse that "presence" makes it presence felt. The brahminization of Indian history is, to an appreciable extent, about presentification of the past, about "presencing"; it is about finding a character amid the chiaroscuro of historical understanding.

Presence as a Problematizing Catalyst

Presence has made it difficult for Indians to see history as a representational art, an art that is predominantly objective. The genesis of "presence" is in the limits of historical representation. It is the power that constructs the vestibule between what historical representation can convey and "what meaning cannot convey"; it is an experience, a generation of meaning that cannot always be strictly "material" or contingent, what Gumbrecht would call "materialities of communication." So history is pressed into service to work on the huge capital of mythic knowledge; presence, which so subtly demarcates the pulls and pushes of myth and history in the lives of Indians, is seen to catalyze this operation. Presence tantalizes most Indians with what they know and do not know, with what they know as truth and what they accept as truth because they are too complacent to investigate its validity. There exists a conspicuous indifference to what they see as history, the objective manifestation of historical investigation, as against what has remained with them for long as part of a received tradition. By way of its unrecorded, unstructured continuities with the "ancient past," the issue of Ayodhya compels the historian's attention. Perhaps there is more to history and myth in the ringing bells and aromatic *garbagriha* (shrines) of scores of temples that dot the landscape of this small and sleepy town. A typical Hindu concept of life places the ultimate reality and goal of life outside the pale of history and encompasses the mundane experiences of human beings.[24] But this attitude, coupled with the vile advantages that political scolds have drawn out of it, force Indians to confront the vulnerabilities and intangibilities of history in their lives. Presence problematizes the ethics of historical writing and representation.

Presence in history is the sense of "beyonding"; it is the provocation to unsettle what epistemic fossilization can do. It is the charm of interrogating a reified discourse, a temptation and, sometimes, an inspiration to probe into what one has come to accept as "mandir" (temple) and question what one has come to think of as the appropriate place to offer one's *namaz* (prayer). It is the temptation to know truths that the nation is fearful of making a clean breast of; presence can sometimes give the historian the handle to investigate hypostatized corridors of the past; it can arm the historian to unearth "hidden tubers" that have been tucked away in the cold storage of a nation's past. It becomes an abiding charm to tease history out with a thought and nibble at the strict disciplinary borders and epistemological fences. So presence is an imperceptible and aggregatory quadrant that the past never consciously records and whose emergence affects the way people negotiate with their present. It has an in-visible presence.

Has presence helped Indians to make a more varied sense of history? It is difficult to respond to this negatively. Fastened to the apron strings of British oriental historians, Indians have looked at their past acting on instructions from the other. But the history of the nation and its people solicit an internal position that urges Indians to look at their history in precisely the way they want. Views from without have long afflicted the nation; hermetic views that have made Indians see their own country through the eyes of the outsider blind them eventually to the abiding charm of the discontinuities and achronicities. Caught in the "waiting room of history," there has been some self-consciousness in countries like India, notes Amit Chaudhuri, "which asks to be judged and understood by universal standards. It isn't possible to begin to discuss that self-consciousness, or sense of identity, without discussing in what way that universalism both formed and circumscribed it."[25] If presence has provincialized the subcontinent, if being provincialized means vanquishment from the theater of world history, Indians need not mind.[26] What is important for Indians to realize is that presence has added an interesting dimension to the way in which they have conceptualized history, making claims to a form of indigeneity, a sort of nativism. Vinay Lal writes, "though modernised and civic minded Indians deplore the indifference of their countrymen and women to museums, historical monuments, and other relics of the 'national heritage,' the ahistoricism of the Indian sensibility remains one of the most attractive intellectual, spiritual, and cultural features of Indian civilization."[27] Rabindranath Tagore believed that historical knowledge could be imparted through *Katha* and *Jatra* (popular folk theatre forms) and that the role of imagination in the acquisition and dissemination of this knowledge could scarcely be ignored. Understanding the "past" does not emerge merely from a subservience to the dictates of "facts"; imagination, in its own peculiar and unenviable way, contributes to our pool of understanding. This combination of fact and imagination has never deserted the discourse of historical knowledge in India and, history, in its candid methodological unfoldment, has come to nestle close to the heart. Tagore writes, "My proposal is that it is through the modes of *Katha* and *Jatra* that history with its glowing description of places and events in time should get promoted."[28] It is myth that has encouraged a kind of open-endedness, an intrusive freedom, the lurid vice of "choice" to open up a portion of history. It provokes explanation, writes James Carse, where "explanation absorbs the unspeakable into the speakable, myth reintroduces the silence that makes original discourse possible."[29] It is through this silence that "presences" drop like paratroopers from the dark night sky.

It requires no hard debate to conclude that most Indians are not aware of the formal meaning of secularism, let alone its deeper implications. Complexities apart, what binds them together? The villages in India where most of her people reside do not need constitutional experts and social theorists to explain the art of peaceful and harmonious existence. There is something undefined, something uncategorized, something sublime, something outside the law that keeps various people believing in a variety of customs and belief systems together. "India's redemption," notes Arundhati Roy, with her characteristic irony, "lies in the inherent anarchy and factiousness of its people, and in the legendary inefficiency of the Indian state." This anarchy need not be mistaken as lawlessness; it is a way of life that denounces strict structuration and regimentation. Steeped in dissent, India cannot be expected to behave all the time in conformity with the principles and preferences of Western societies. Roy wisely observes that India is "too old and too clever to be made to jump through the hoops all over again." India is too diverse, too grand, too feral, and too democratic to be lobotomized into believing in one single idea.[30]

In 1990 the Bharatiya Janata Party (a Hindu nationalist party) leader Lal Krishna Advani triggered a ceremonious nationwide chariot march as a prelude to the construction of the Ram temple in Ayodhya. During the course of his journey through the Indian villages people flocked to take a look at the extravagantly decorated chariot and the garish entourage. It is highly unlikely that the poor tribals and village folks who thronged and cheered the march in droves shared the "sophisticated" reasons that goaded Advani to undertake the Rath Yatra (chariot march). Cutting across religious affiliations, people milled around to catch a glimpse of an extraordinary phenomenon. How much of history did these people know? What kind of history have they been indoctrinated with? What kind of historical consciousness binds these people together? It is perhaps what Eelco Runia would ascribe as the metonymic access to "common knowledge." It is an undifferentiated and uncritical convergence on a point in history; it is the power of "presence" that has been building up for a long time with the Indians that makes them asymmetrical, inconsistent, and idiosyncratic in their approach to history. Presence has lent a "fascination" to the character of Indian history; the subcontinent is ceaselessly, in the words of William Wordsworth, "disturbed with a presence." Presence agitates, it stimulates our sensations, it frustrates by being elusively indescribable, and it is compelling for it makes the present wrestle hard to subjugate it. So when the categories of understanding the past and the present become a "step careful" to define the premises of "presence," presence defeats their intent by making them a "step careless." Hindu history has this "step careless" streak temptingly on offer. Hindu history conveys sense when meaning fails to convey.

The Presence and Conceptualization of Contemporary Protesting Crowds

Suman Gupta

Conventionally, registering the physical presence of a crowd and conceptualizing it have been aspects of a single ontological engagement. Registering the presence of a crowd would consist in apprehending its density or shape, its occupancy of a place and time, the composition of its elements, its vociferousness and dynamism. The terms in which the materiality of a specifically located crowd is thus grasped would, in the selfsame move, lead into conceptualizing its broader place in the world: charting its psychological and political character, its historical agency and effect, its aesthetic resonance, the frames of representation it is amenable to; and so on. This unity of ontological engagement apropos the crowd is analogous to Alain Badiou's account of thinking about "multiple-being," where characterizing identifications and relations of beings in a locale occurs on the "site of these identifications and relations [which] we call the world."[1]

This chapter argues that contemporary crowd formations, especially those that gather to express political protest, often fracture the unity of the conventional ontological engagement. Registering the presence of a crowd (in a locale) is no longer necessarily coeval with conceptualizing it (placing it in the world) now. This is because the significances that are now attributed to a crowd are frequently no longer contained in or derivable from its discrete physical presence. These significances have to take in the relation of crowds, more or less simultaneously and immediately, across geopolitical and cultural boundaries. Doing so involves deploying media-based modes of representation that turn out to be removed from the physical presence of the crowds in question. Between registering the presence of a crowd and conceptualizing the cross-border or multilocation crowds through the prevailing mediascape there is a discontinuity. This discontinuity arguably has the effect of diluting the presence of the crowd, or of virtualizing crowds, in reckonings with them.

In the latter part of this chapter, I demonstrate how this fracture appears in mass media (news) reportage with regard to two kinds of contemporary manifestations of protesting crowds. The first I think of as *transnational massing*: the concurrent and programmatic appearance before the global eye of multitudinous crowds in many locations protesting against a single eventuality. My example here is the worldwide protests of February 15, 2003, against the impending invasion of Iraq. The second could be dubbed *contaminative crowding*: a speedy and cumulative appearance of crowds in multiple locations within a concentrated period, starting from an initial spark. The obvious example here is of the protests in North Africa and the Middle East, which started gathering momentum from December 2010. In both cases, I argue, the schism between registering and conceptualizing these protesting crowdings in the news (I cite primarily British news media by way of evidence) inserted ideologically motivated preconceptions that had little basis in the material manifestation of crowds.

To lead up to an examination of these two forms of contemporary crowd formations, in the initial part of this chapter I outline the conventional analytical field that has engaged with crowds. The outlined field exemplifies how the unitary ontological operation of registering and conceptualizing crowds has worked till recently, and is usually still applicable to specifically located crowds. At the same time, tracing some of the key strands across this field also shows that no break is a sudden break: the potential for dislocating the material presence from the worldly analysis of crowds has been implicit in the field. Numerous ideological and disciplinary fissures had already riven the field of crowd analysis, approaching crowds in binaristic ways as organically discrete and uncontainable, as creative and destructive, as antisocial and emancipative, as undifferentiable and segmented. Different disciplinary imperatives have exploited one or the other side of these binaristic accounts in ideologically-weighted ways—in sociology, social psychology, history, literature.

With this outline in view, it should become possible to gauge to what extent contemporary protesting crowds and their media representations derive or depart from or sit uneasily alongside conventional accounts. The implications of the break in ontological engagement with crowds vis-à-vis conventional approaches to the crowd are gestured toward in the conclusion, necessarily speculatively.

Ur-Crowd to Crowd

The crowd has conventionally been understood as a discrete organic presence in a specific space and time. The manner in which the presence of the crowd is described has generally been coeval with the manner in which it is conceptually approached. There is, in other words, usually a conceptual direction involved *within* descriptions of the discreteness and materiality of the crowd—one that starts from some sort of ur-crowd or precrowd element/condition and then proceeds toward outlining crowd formation and characterizing its presence. Typically, the outlining of this conceptual direction involves both continuity and certain breaks in realizing the crowd qua crowd.

Gustave Le Bon's classic *The Crowd* (1896) predetermined its understanding of the crowd as a discrete organic formation by focusing exclusively on the "organized crowd," or "that which acquires a collective presence as opposed to an individual one" and which "forms a single being, and is subjected to the law of mental unity of crowds."[2] This mutually defined opposition between individual person and collective crowd was held by the equivalence of their discrete singularities, and then mediated by establishing a path of definition from the individual mind to the crowd mind. The idea was that in the individual mind there is a balance of intellectual aptitudes (which enable individual differences) and subconscious human proclivities (which provides a common human base)—not dissimilar to Freud's later "das Ich" (ego) and "das Es" (id)—whereas in the crowd mind there is little individualizing intellectual aptitude and an overwhelming dominance of collectivizing subconscious proclivities: "In the collective mind the intellectual aptitudes of the individuals, and in consequence their individuality, are weakened. The heterogeneous is swamped by the homogeneous, and the unconscious qualities obtain the upper hand."[3] Thus, while a conceptually equivalent discreteness of individual and crowd was proposed in a mutually defined fashion, simultaneously a process *from* individual mind *to* crowd mind was also traced to define the crowd and elucidate its formation. After all, individuals form crowds, and individual minds are transformed into the crowd mind.

Another example of a similar conceptual direction from individual to crowd, differently framed, appears in Georg Simmel's "The Sociology of Space" (1903). The derivation of the crowd mind from the individual mind there is not according to an apportioning of intellectual aptitude and subconscious proclivity, but according to spatial occupancy:

> The often emphasized character of an assembled crowd—its impulsiveness, its enthusiasm, its susceptibility to manipulation—is certainly connected to some degree with the fact that the crowd is in the open, or at least in a very large space, compared with the spaces that its members normally occupy. The greater breathing space gives people a feeling of freedom of movement, of an ability to venture out into the unknown, of an indefinite ability to set broader goals—which would be decidedly more difficult to achieve in enclosed rooms. The fact that such rooms are indeed often relatively too narrow, that is, they are overcrowded, can only strengthen this psychological effect, namely the growth of individual psychological momentum beyond its usual limits: for it must raise that collective feeling which fuses the individual into a unity transcending his or her individuality, sweeping the individual along like a flood past their personal directions and responsibilities.[4]

There is a similar equivalence between the discreteness of the individual and the unity-transcending-individuality of the crowd, and a similar direction of realizing the crowd from the individual. But it is not the constitution of the human mind that's at stake from individual to collective presence, but the space that acts on the human mind when under conditions of individual and collective occupation.

The conceptual direction in these early social psychology accounts of the crowd draw a line from the individual to the collective, from the monad to the organic form. The ur-crowd is the individual itself, the constitutive element that is fused and transformed into the crowd. A somewhat different direction is sometimes tracked in later social psychology accounts of the crowd: not so much from the individual to the collective, as from everyday social existence (routinized, dispersed, of the moment) to the crowd (occasional, fused and dense, purposive). The individual is implicit in the former but as already collectivized, only differently from the collective of the crowd: this is a movement from the ur-crowd collective to the crowd collective. The notion of everyday social existence as an ur-crowd is a markedly urban notion, imbued with the modernity of the urban: people conduct their everyday lives in a large dense collective anyway, share and occupy spaces accordingly, negotiate the passages and routines of daily life with regard to others—that is, others not as individuals but as within a collective. But these are not crowds, not dense enough, purposive enough, or discrete enough. The idea is that the condition of crowd formation can be derived by close attention to the habits and habitus of dense everyday social life.

Elias Canetti's approach to the crowd in *Crowds and Power* (1960) is from the midst of everyday social life, from what he thinks of as the characterizing feature of dense everyday movements, "the fear of being touched": "The repugnance to being touched remains with us when we go about among people; the way we move in a busy street, in restaurants, trains and buses, is governed by it."[5] The impetus for crowd formation, by this account, is for overcoming that fear of being touched that underlies everyday social life: "As soon as a man has surrendered himself to the crowd, he ceases to fear its touch. Ideally, all are equal here; no distinctions count, not even that of sex. . . . Suddenly it is as though everything were happening in one and the same body."[6] And that's all Canetti says by way of realizing the crowd; his interest is primarily in the crowd that is realized and already there, so to speak, as a discrete, dense, organic beast. Canetti focuses mainly on the shapes and behaviors and categories of crowds, much as a zoologist might on an uncharted species. But there's that direction nevertheless, a direction of emotional response: from the fear that is constituted within Canetti's everyday social life to the overcoming of fear that becomes possible in Canetti's crowd. In Canetti's view, dense everyday social life is an anxiogenic element, but it is possible to have a friendly and comfortable sense of it, and quite possibly the concept of the crowd derived from that would be a somewhat different one. When everyday social life is regarded as an aggregate of performances, a grid of communicative acts, it has an at-home air about it; it's what we recognize as familiar. Here dense everyday social life could be an expansion of Erving Goffman's formulation of copresence in a "social situation," an "environment of mutual monitoring possibilities that lasts during the time two or more individuals find themselves in one another's immediate physical presence, and extends over the entire territory within which this mutual monitoring is possible."[7] Within this Goffmanian social life there is more mutual regarding and consideration than fear of touching, and if made dense the everyday social situation may become correspondingly mutually-regarding and considering in a more concentrated fashion. Michael Wolff, for instance, made a study of a particular aspect of dense everyday social life—the behavior of pedestrians on the streets of a metropolis—in a Goffmanian spirit, and found evidence of such concentration of mutual regard and considering, so that pedestrian flows are understood as a form of cooperation and communication:

> The most outstanding characteristics of pedestrians that have emerged from this study are the amount and degree of cooperative behavior on the streets of the city. While at an immediate and superficial level encounters on the street are hardly noticeable and devoid of pleasantry and warmth, pedestrians do, in fact, communicate and do take into account the qualities and predicaments of others regulating their behavior.[8]

The crowd that can be derived from this account of everyday social life would not be a crowd that is liberated from the fear of everyday social life but one that intensifies further the cohesions of everyday social life. This is a positively characterized crowd, which coheres not coldly and indifferently but purposively and collaboratively.

Crowd Control

What the above formulations mostly come to with their directions of approach from ur-crowd to crowd are delineations of the crowd as organic and discrete like an individual person. The presence of the crowd is registered much as that of a conscious individual being: solid, visceral, locatable, immediate, and with agency and movement. However, simultaneously the crowd is apprehended as uncontainable, unpredictable, threatening, overpowering—at least tendentiously and potentially—in a *constitutive* way unlike any individual. The individual presence is containable in society, containable within the structure of artificial spaces (architectural, administrative, institutional, organizational, communal, academic spaces). The crowd is, merely in being realized as such, a potentially subversive presence. It flows out of spaces, it could destroy spaces, it wills something, it tests the borders of law, of governance, of institutions. The ideology that is within these spaces, devoted to social stability and the status quo, cannot theorize the crowd in any way except as the "other" of the containable individual, the individual whose fear keeps him or her within the precincts of everyday social life; the crowd thus is the "other" of everyday social life. Apparently like an individual, the crowd can be ordered and rationalized (in a celebratory rally or for a ritualized event or performance), but more than any individual this crowd has the potential at the selfsame moment to break order and rationalized arrangements (the rally can turn into a riot, the ritual event into a mêlée) in unexpected ways. The presence of the crowd, however seemingly docile and organized, is inevitably registered with a touch of distrust or a frisson of danger.

In a way, the crowd seen thus—a presence that is as discrete as an individual but more forceful and larger and less containable—is the opposite of the capitalist corporation. The capitalist corporation, with its ordered and accountable incorporation of teams and organization, is also accounted as being discrete as an individual but larger and more forceful and expansive, but that is *within* legal and administrative and academic discourses. The corporation is the collective individual in abstract within establishment social formations. The crowd is the collective individual materialized as physically present—out there, so to speak; even if it forms to sanction or with the sanction of establishment social formations, it has in its very presence the potential to undermine them. The former needs merely to be regulated, while the latter has to be policed and controlled.

Social psychology has since (roughly since the 1960s) become more circumspect about the crowd. This caution is most effectively exercised through the linguistic register of social psychology: by employing an order of significations and linguistic relations that domesticates perceptions and potentialities that cannot be accounted within that order. It is effectively a jargon of ideological neutrality and emotional passivity that wrings the spirit of the crowd dry simply by resignifying and then talking about crowds in a particular way. But ideological polarities and anxieties continue to play under the surface of that listless register. So, the crowd appears hesitatingly in not quite *social* psychology but in *group* psychology. The more fluid concept of the "group" contains the crowd. It contains it as a metatheoretical category: there are all kinds of groups, of different quantities, variously organized, with normatively determined hierarchies and memberships or without such memberships, with identities, with aims and objectives and purposes, in relation to each other, and so on, and the crowd is a particular kind of group. The crowd now becomes conceptually small rather than conceptually overflowing, it is a small subset of a large set called "groups." This new register contains it as a "condition" subject to a clinical diagnosis rather than as an independent phenomenon:

> In the English language (and presumably in other languages, too) there are words which have an unpleasant or derogatory connotation.... The use of the word "regime" rather than "government" is always intended to suggest repression or illegality and "propaganda" tends not to be equated with "education." "Crowds" in contrast to "groups" is also one of these emotive terms. It suggests danger, uncontrollable violence, riots, vandalism, lynchings or other apparently irrational behaviours.[9]

The preferred term for "crowd" then is the "deindividuated group," drawing on social psychological experiments and their description and theoretical inferences in, particularly, Philip Zimbardo's work (1969).[10] Zimbardo is, it has sometimes been observed, Le Bon dressed up in clinical rhetoric, with an apparatus of experiments of doubtful credibility as scaffolding. The approach and direction is similar, the register and claims of validation different. The claims have been dispelled by his intellectual descendents, but the register retained. "Deindividuated groups" don't only replace "crowds" but also neutralize and fix them, in a perpetual emotive irrationality that is now conquered by a jargon of reason, not reason itself but reason imposed solely by terminology to fix the crowd as definitively irrational. As Andrew Adamatzky has recently put it, crowds are worth studying because

> the behavior of each person in a crowd can be reduced to a level of an abstract finite machine—due to the deindividuation process, and spatio-temporal dynamics of crowd global behavior. That is why a crowd psychology is sometimes attributed to "a science of the irrational."[11]

The rationale that is instantiated by jargon, and sustains itself in the overarching discipline of group psychology, has a corporate air about it. It is not that crowds disappear from social psychology, but that crowds can now only be related to the application of controls and containment in social psychology. Talking about crowds in this academic space means talking about violent disorder, street life and ethnicity (read race), policing, public disorder, and the peaceful crowd (an oxymoron)—not surprisingly, these are the titles of parts of a book on *The Crowd in Contemporary Britain*.[12]

But this is too ideologically definite, too definitively constricting, and of course not all social psychologists are so inclined. But the network of terms and phrases that mute the subversive and all too potent presence of the crowd has come to be recognized as the dominant register, productive of a tamed "deindividuated group." So, even when some social psychologists give a more upbeat and differentiated account of the crowd, it is as an argument *against* the dominant register (and occasionally by employing the terms of that register themselves). To reorient the ideological underpinnings of crowd studies is to take issue with the jargon and methodology associated with the "deindividuated group." Though beleaguered, the oppositional intent of such social psychological questioning of the dominant register is very much worth noting. Against the "deindividuated group" there is therefore the social psychology of the, so to speak, 'individuation' possible *within* crowds. This is available in numerous studies from, among others, Richard Berck, whose application of game theory led him to conclude that crowd participants "(1) exercise a substantial degree of rational decision-making, and (2) are not definedly less rational than in other contexts,"[13] to Clark McPhail, whose experiments persuaded him that "the majority of behaviors in which members of these crowds engaged are neither mutually inclusive nor extraordinary, let alone mad, and are therefore not even addressed by traditional theories."[14] Such individuation within the context of crowds, while ideologically at odds with the concept of "deindividuation," is also referred to in the latter's terminology and thus assumes its linguistic register. Sometimes this oppositional stance can be overly celebratory of the crowd, as when John Drury and Georgia Winter (2003–04) argue that crowds manifest positive virtues compared to individual debility at times.[15]

On the whole, however, amid the mutual bind that conceptually holds crowd and individual together, and the power of ordered register in representing crowds (its dominance reified even by opposition), the crowd is tamed by social psychology. The constitutive subversiveness and uncontainability of the crowd, the thrust of its presence, is lost. What's left is either a quiet collection of reasonable persons or a collective that needs to be subjected to control and containment.

The Opacity of Representation

Employing an ordered and ostensibly scientific language to, so to speak, register and tame the crowd is a particular kind of ideological move; it appears alongside other, differently oriented, discourses. The social *representation* (in the sense of re-presenting, imaging, evoking) of crowds—in literary, historical, artistic, media discourses—offer nuances and slants that are worth noting. Let me pick up a strand of representation that I have already mentioned above, via Canetti and Goffman: the relationship of the crowd to dense everyday spaces.

In Walter Benjamin's view, sifted from his essay "On Some Motifs in Baudelaire" (1939),[16] the dense everyday spaces of the city are already occupied by the crowd, the everyday city life is the life of the crowd, with those qualities of shock, power, physical presence, and organicity that defined earlier sociological approaches to the crowd. This sense of the crowd disorients, but in a way grounded in [or rooted in] the daily experience of dense city life itself rather than as a departure from or particular intensification within city life. If there is something like "deindividuation," some overwhelming tidal unity, some sort of blind purposiveness, that is the character of the densely populated spaces of the city anyway. For Benjamin, both an outsider's revulsion toward and the unity within the crowd (along lines mentioned earlier) is grounded in everyday metropolitan life—he refers to accounts by nineteenth-century writers (Victor Hugo, Friedrich Engels, Edgar Allan Poe, Charles Baudelaire) to suggest this. It is not so much the superlative density of a particular gathering (a specific crowd) that Benjamin notes but the manner in which people traverse densely populated city spaces, negotiate traffic, walk the streets, congregate and disperse and flow in a daily fashion. The discrete and yet enormously larger-than-individual unity of the crowd is within the everyday of the city in Benjamin's account, and is marked against different departures from notions of individuality and collectivity. As a departure from individuality, Benjamin's reading of Baudelaire's *flâneur*, that contemplative person walking in the city, is a standard point of reference now. The at-homeness of the *flâneur* in the dense everyday life of the city is expressed in Baudelaire's poetic sensibility, so immersed in the environment of the city that crowds don't even have to be mentioned, written as it were from *inside* the crowd of the city. But Benjamin observes, so to speak, from outside and effectively dislocates the *flâneur*, and when he does this he effectively hyperactivates the individual, makes the individual excessive, so as to capture the spirit of the crowd:

> Baudelaire saw fit to equate the man of the crowd, whom Poe's narrator follows through the length and breadth of nocturnal London, with the *flâneur*. It is hard to accept this view. The man of the crowd is no *flâneur*. In him, composure has given way to manic behavior. Hence he exemplifies, rather, what has become of the *flâneur* once he was deprived of the milieu to which he belonged.[17]

At the other end of the scale, Benjamin draws a hesitant analogy between the collectivization of the industrial complex, the "machine," and the everyday life of the city—not as an exact match of order and purpose but to convey an impact and a scale: "The shock experience which the passer-by has in the crowd corresponds to what the worker 'experiences' at his machine,"[18] Benjamin observes intriguingly, and then concedes that this analogy might not have meant much to Baudelaire or Poe.

More important than the rationale for constructing the crowd in (primarily literary) representation, Benjamin presents the crowd as implicit in the form of representation itself. To think of the crowd in Baudelaire's work is not to discern how Baudelaire *talks* about the crowd (he doesn't) but to recognize it (hidden) *within* the forms and figures of Baudelaire's writing: "it is the phantom crowd of the words, the fragments, the beginnings of lines from which the poet, in the deserted streets, wrests the poetic booty."[19] Thinking about crowds, for Benjamin, is a matter of thinking about how the crowd is represented, and that is less an analysis of the crowd and more a discernment of the form of crowd representation (in words, narratives, images, and so forth). Representation casts a screen between the crowd and its impact, and draws attention to itself as representation—an opacity that is imposed by the uncontainability of the crowd. Especially where there's a direct complicity between conceptualizing dense everyday life and the notion of the crowd, the screen of representation is wrapped closely over the experience and expression of the crowd, or perhaps (to mix up metaphors) representation is like the lens through which Baudelaire's *flâneur* peers at the densely populated spaces of Paris. Since the crowd appears (or flickers) through the discernment of a number of mutually reflective layers of representation, representation itself becomes opaque. Representing the crowd seems to become a test for its own forms; representation captures and yet fails to capture more than the eye or text can contain. And, thereby, the subversive quality of the crowd and the enormous organicity of the crowd are effectively conveyed. The form of representing crowds itself quickens the pulse, imbues with attraction and revulsion, brings up something momentous and disorienting and shocking, assaults moral sensitivities and (sometimes) portends a climax. The self-conscious literary (or artistic or media) form of crowd representation remains one of the few ways of registering the subversive presence of crowds, by characterizing, for instance, the national canons of literary formation accordingly—the crowd in American literary history,[20] the crowd in British literary history,[21] the crowd in the city, and so forth.

To be attentive to the crowd *within* forms of representation, *as* forms of representation, is also to be attentive to the slipperiness of ideology in representation. The registers, syntax, selections, arrangements, juxtapositions, gaps and silences, tones and textures, perspectives of representation consist in ideological orientations that mold the crowd through and as representation. The nuances of representation themselves shape the ideological apprehension of the crowd. Equally, forms of representation are tested and rendered opaque by presenting the crowd as they do, all the more so because the crowd is ineluctably uncontainable and subversive of boundaries—including the boundaries of forms of representation. If Baudelaire's *flâneur* as man in the crowd might be a bit of a subterfuge, if the very form and figure of Baudelaire's verse evokes the crowd, it is because Baudelaire's poetic form has instrumentalized and absorbed the crowd to express his aesthetic and ethical—his ideological—universe. If Benjamin's discernment and critical clarification of this questions the ostensible role of the *flâneur*, and finds in Baudelaire's shock of the crowd echoes of a nineteenth-century personification of the crowd as a sociopolitical entity and of man's relation to the industrial complex, then that too is an ideological tilt. Literary expression and critical discourse of the crowd slip through the possibilities of ideological persuasion and presentation, which the concept of the crowd neither accepts nor resists, but becomes available to and yet is never wholly subjugated by.

Looking Back

This is not just a matter of literary representation; as with literary stylistics and critique, so with historical narrative and historiographical presumptions—indeed more so. When George Rudé introduced his 1959 study of the crowd in the French Revolution,[22] he was conscious of making as much a historiographical as a historical intervention; he was aware that ideological battles are fought more in historiographical decisions—in the selections and narrative strategies and methods of presenting history—than in the evidenced recovery of the past. The crowd in the French Revolution had been presented as purely destructive and composed of antisocial elements (Edmund Burke, Hippolyte Taine), on the one hand, and as representing popular and Republican virtues (Jules Michelet), on the other, and Rudé's task was not so much to present new historical documents and facts as to present the revolutionary crowd through a new tilt, with "a more detached, or scientific, spirit" based on the understanding that

> new social patterns and problems of the twentieth century have prompted historians to seek answers to new questions and, as a result of these considerations, to view the history of the Revolution from a new angle. An important consequence of their inquiries has been that the popular element composing the *sans-culottes*—the peasants, craftsmen, journeymen, and labourers—have begun to appear as social groups with their own distinctive identity, interests, and aspirations, whose actions and attitudes can no longer be treated as mere echoes or reflections of the ideas, speeches and decrees of the journalists, lawyers, orators, and politicians established in the capital.[23]

He saw his history of the Revolutionary crowd as a "new conception of the Revolution—seen as it were from below." All this is at a level that surrounds rather than contributes to the documentation of the French Revolution itself, and quite a number of strategies of choice and rhetoric are at work here. First, the crowd has been selected or differentiated as a particular kind of crowd, specifically the revolutionary or protesting crowd; second, the crowd has been segmented into social groups (not organic wholes, not a large group of individuals) and taken as the sum total of constituent groups; third, there is the claim of rising above ideological partisanship, not subscribing to existing polarities but offering a "detached, or scientific, spirit"; fourth, at the same time there is the assertion of a salutary focus on the agency of the people rather than of rulers. These historiographical presumptions construct the crowd and give it form: by trimming away abstractions and narrowing down specificities, by differentiating the resulting narrative from other narratives, by making claims about the spirit of itself as history, by manipulating the gaze and attention of readers. But the fact that it is specifically the French Revolutionary crowd, the quintessential protesting crowd, which is thus chosen and framed does not mean that Rudé has lost sight of the crowd in general. It is, in a way, as if the protesting crowd is the sense in which the crowd is meaningful, or that is the frame where the subversive potency of the crowd in general finds its contextually and historically specific concretized character. That *the protesting crowd is the crowd* is a notion that has slipped constantly into the history of crowds ever since, and has become parcel with the historiographical assumptions that actuate such histories. In an interesting way, just as social psychology has seen a move toward (with occasional protests against) taming and undermining the agency of the crowd, the historiography of crowds has been a move toward (with occasional protests against) releasing the agency of the crowd.

How the agency of the crowd is accounted depends on the agency that the writing of history accords itself, or tries to instantiate. The conventional Marxist account that I have picked up here involved Rudé (1964) and E. P. Thompson (1971)[24] following up with more historiographically nuanced examinations of the protesting crowd in England and France, deliberately working against the sociological anxiety of crowds and social-psychological determination to discipline or tame them—against accounts of crowds as in "political demonstrations and to what sociologists have termed the 'aggressive mob' or the 'hostile outburst.'"[25] In such Marxist historiography, the crowd's agency derives naturally through a crystallization of class conflict, both the driver and the outcome of the progressive direction of history. This teleology is often overdetermined in retrospective reckonings with Marxism, and seems itself a prison of necessitarian discourse; actually, Marxist history and historiography constantly teetered paradoxically and unresolvably between predetermined inevitability and a determined need to force outcomes (take them in hand). The agency of the crowd could accordingly be regarded as merely a cog in a predetermined process or the superlative actor that takes charge of change. Other left-wing historiographies account the agency of crowds differently: as a spontaneous subaltern outburst, as an anticolonial drive, as an expression of identity-based solidarity and marginalization, and so on. Understandings of the crowd's agency in left-wing history are generally imbricated with the agency that the historian seeks to actuate by writing history, through the historian's ideological purpose.

Unsurprisingly, the momentum of left-wing histories of the crowd such as Rudé's and Thompson's, formulated as they are according to their historiographical thrust, lead to something like an inward turn—histories of crowds have come to be articulated in a mode of disciplinary reference, in a register of such disciplinary history (much as social psychology is caged by the jargon of "deindividuation"). The proliferation of histories of the crowd is actually a proliferation of histories of histories of the crowd, and more so critiques of the historiographical assumptions that have attached to crowds.[26] But even more than that, the historical narrative that relates to crowds is the field of a duel between social psychology/sociology and history itself, and therefore burrows deeper inward toward histories of social-psychological accounts of crowds, toward the historicization of these accounts themselves.[27] One of the most significant historiographical turns that has occurred in attending to the crowd is that its history has engaged and historicized and absorbed the social psychology of crowds into its own register.

In histories of the crowd the presence and impact and subversive agency of the crowd flickers through manifold historiographical screens, becoming ever more obsessed with the self-referentiality of the historical text. And yet, through that self-referentiality an impression of the presence, the uncontainability and subversiveness, of the physical crowd is conveyed. Analogous to literary representation, historical representation lets the power of the crowd, with all its intractability, seep through by turning upon the modus operandi of its own imperatives and purposes.

Where We Are

In their introduction to the volume arising from the Stanford Humanities Laboratory Crowds Project, editors Jeffrey Schnapp and Matthew Tiews present the assumptions of the project as follows:

1. The era of popular sovereignty, industrialization, and urbanization saw the rise of a constellation of new forms of mass assembly and collective social action that reached their apogee in the first half of the twentieth century.
2. These forms began to attenuate gradually in the second half of the century, particularly in the wake of the protest movements of the 1960s and 1970s, as a result of the proliferation and ever-increasing prevalence of virtual or media-based forms of "assembly" over physical assemblies in post-industrial societies, as well as long-term trends promoting economic decentralization, suburban sprawl, increased mobility, and political disengagement.
3. This shift, rather than abolishing the equation between crowds and modernity, has reshaped it, channeling experiences of crowding in postindustrial societies into certain limited domains of civic and electoral ritual, entertainment, and leisure, while assigning to large-scale mass political action a fallback function restricted to times of exception (war, acute social conflicts, and the like).[28]

The three assumptions present in a sequential fashion a fairly persuasive dominant conceptualization of the contemporary crowd. In effect, the three assumed steps demarcate a process of taming the crowd—of restraining its visceral, organic, subversive presence—not so much by dispersing crowds or by disregarding them, but actually by containing them. The modes of containment work at two levels. According to assumption 2 above, this has to do with "the proliferation and ever-increasing prevalence of virtual or media-based forms of 'assembly' over physical assemblies in post-industrial societies." In other words, the crowd becomes dematerialized into pure representation, manifested only *through* virtual assembly and media appearances, and *at the expense of* the materialization of a seething subversive physical presence. The either/or logic of this is worth noting: there is either the virtual/mediatized crowd, or there's the real thing; to realize the one is to undermine the other. According to assumption 3 the crowd is *contained* by "channeling . . . into certain limited domains," by "assigning . . . a fallback function [that is] restricted." Put otherwise, the spaces and contexts where the possibility of the materialization of the physical crowd is possible are determined from above, are structured in advance, with a view to taming its subversive potential. The entire process of engaging with the crowd that is summarized above culminates into this three-fold contemporary taming of the crowd: the very discourse of analysis and representation of the crowd is sucked into a dematerialization of the crowd into representation in-itself, and the potential subversiveness of boundaries that defined the crowd is converted to an assignation of boundaries to define the crowd.

What I called a break in ontological engagement with crowds at the beginning of this chapter is grounded in this prevailing mediascape. In exemplifying this below, in a limited way I pick specific instances of two sorts of crowd manifestations (both transcending geopolitical borders) and cite a small segment of global media (mainly news media available in Britain). These limitations are pragmatic; the conceptual implications, I suspect, are much wider nevertheless. At any rate, if the lines of conceptualizing crowds traced above clarify a unity of ontological engagement, these examples of a break therein reverberate through those at the broadest worldly level.

Transnational Massing: February 15, 2003

The worldwide coordinated marches of Saturday, February 15, 2003, protesting against the impending invasion and occupation of Iraq by a U.S.-U.K. led alignment, brought to awareness a new kind of phenomenon: *transnational massing* as protest. Reportedly, somewhere between eight and thirty million people (depending on which agency offered estimates) in approximately eight hundred cities across about sixty countries participated.[29] Other similar events may perhaps be cited, but the particular *awareness* of transnational massing as a distinctive form of protest evidenced here seems to me—and seemed to reporters at the time—as unprecedented. This awareness has to do with the scale of the February 15, 2003, marches: in the global eye, involving unprecedentedly dense and multitudinous and simultaneous crowd formations in many specific locations. This awareness has to do with the concentration of it: within that day, and somehow coordinated and conscious of the whole across a wide range of geopolitical boundaries. This awareness has to do with the media narratives of the demonstrations: anticipated, documented, and responded to immediately as a transnational massing event. This awareness also has to do with the pathos of it: the excitement and achievement and theatricality of its enactment, and the sense of futility that shadowed that enactment even as it unfolded, the pathos that comes from the contradictory passing of a grand yet failed gesture.

The unprecedented awareness of these simultaneous crowdings as transnational massing presented curious challenges to their news framing, which is the first line of assimilation in the prevailing mediascape. By its very multilocation appearance, any top-down management or assignment of an "appropriate" context for massing turned into nonsense. It doesn't matter how ordered and controlled and policed a specific crowd in a particular location was on February 15, 2003. As a transnational massing gesture it was nevertheless outside those measures, because the transnational is not an arena that is available to crowd control or crowd management. That is the paradoxical force of this gesture: it may consent to be peaceful and managed in specific locations, and yet by materializing and asserting its transnational scope it has already defeated the impulse of control and containment.

This sort of transnational massing as protest is evidenced as *transnational* purely through representation, despite being physically experienced and encountered worldwide as an all too material act of crowd forming. This is also paradoxical, and doesn't subscribe to the immiscibility of virtual assembly and physical crowding in Schnapp and Tiews's second assumption quoted above. There was undoubtedly a series of coordinated physical crowding events in various parts of the world on February 15, 2003, but the realization of these as a transnational gesture—the apprehension of the series of specific events as coalescing into a transnational event—was only possible through their representation in news media before or after the fact. The materialization of crowds in various locations as a gesture of protest is available as a transnational gesture only through their enactment as such on screens of media representation.

Under the circumstances, registering transnational massing and conceptualizing it diverged along three lines in news media. First, there were attempts to render the potency of transnational massing abstract by turning reportage and analysis on the methods and perceptions of quantification itself. The news was not so much about the crowds that composed the transnational mass and their demands; it was about the process of quantification— the abstraction of quantity perceived and registered, and the slippages therein. It became a matter of contending numerical claims, and the mechanics of numerical measurements and the interests that played in offering numbers. It was reported that the London rally of February 15, 2003, had 500,000 to 750,000 protesters according to police estimates, and between 1.5 to 2 million according to organizers' estimates; in Rome campaigners claimed three million people had converged, though police put the figure at 650,000; and so on.[30] Interest in how such numbers are generated or manipulated was widely evidenced. The focus on numbers and differences in numbers in the news was an appeal to the obvious symbolic function that numbers have in multiparty democracies. The very fact that obvious state functionaries like the police go for smaller estimates can be understood to be indicative of a desire to underplay democratic legitimacy. Similarly, the very fact that obviously oppositional parties like protest organizers offer large estimates can be interpreted as a claim of adequate democratic legitimacy. Numbers are used primarily for effect, much as numbers are counted up for determining election results in domestic democratic processes. Ultimately, however, the preoccupation with numbers drowned before the transnational scale of the massing; the difference of estimates (inevitably a localized matter) became immaterial against the absolute scale (however seen) of the transnational gesture, and sealed its perception as a transnational gesture. Under the circumstances, perhaps more effective were the strategies evident in political response to the *perception* of quantity. President George W. Bush's response to the "size of the protest" was that "you know, size of protest, it's like deciding, well, I'm going to decide policy based upon a focus group."[31] Prime Minister Tony Blair's response was less brusque and more demagogic: "But as you watch your TV pictures of the march, ponder this: If there are 500,000 on that march, this is still less than the number of people whose deaths Saddam has been responsible for. If there are one million, that is still less than the number of people who died in the wars he started."[32] The focus on quantity in such public statements had presumed and placed transnational massing as an abstract entity; they seemed ironic because, of course, it wasn't.

A second line of registering and conceptualizing transnational massing appeared through speculation on the underlying mechanisms of its formation. In a loose way, the importance of the Internet and mobile communication technologies were floated; the transnational nature of massing seemed a function or output of a transnational communications industry and technological system.[33] The idea was that the underlying structure of transnational massing reflected the decentered and yet linked structure of recent (within the last ten years) information technology developments (such as in the World Wide Web, e-mail, instant or text messaging). The decenteredness is important: what was involved in the use of the Internet, for instance, in building up toward the February 15, 2003, anti-invasion protests was not a concerted and centralized publicity drive; it was instead an accrual and growth of variously located and dispersed and linked and cross-connected efforts, which often occurred after the initiation, in process as it were. Much reportage was devoted to the use of these by some of the organizations that surfaced as key to the transnational massing event.

The third line of news about the February 15, 2003, protests, and possibly the most interesting, was in allocating the impetus for bringing it about to the "left." Though numerous reports identified the very diverse range of ideological alignments involved, the "left" became the fulcrum of transnational protest and the horizon against which the participation of other ideologically oriented groups could be located. In Britain, the *Guardian* carried analyses of the current position of the left and its relation to the growing anti-invasion protests. A feature entitled "Left Over?," published there on February 11, 2003, reflected on the apparent paradox of the post–September 11 unpopularity of left political positions and the increasing scale and diversity of the anti-invasion movement (which seemed willing to channel their protests through events organized by left alignments).[34] In the more conservative British mainstream press, primarily (somewhat gently) the *Times* and (more hardnosed) the *Daily Telegraph*, features struggled to cope with the diversity of factions. One derided Committee Men, Poshniks, Tricoteuses, Angry Young Muslims, Angry Old Lefties, and students,[35] and others accused the lot of being proterrorism and anti-Semitic.[36] With the marches of the 15 February 2003 in view, Nick Cohen's analysis in the *Guardian* complained that "The Left Isn't Listening";[37] a report in the *Times* of February

16, 2003, noted that "the appeal of the march went well beyond the left-wing activists who organised it";[38] and one in the *Telegraph* of February 17, 2003, averred, "Many 'hard-Left' groups dominated the front of the march. . . . There were, however, tens of thousands of 'moderate' protesters."[39] In the U.S. media some of the organizers were linked repeatedly, with increasing vehemence, to the dreaded "hard-left."[40] In the process, the signifier "left" was emptied of content, or supersignified to the extent of becoming meaningless. The "left" became a backdrop against which various kinds of expectations and anxieties could be projected, or a grid on which the complexity of transnational massing could be mapped.

But where were the crowds in all this, the material components of transnational massing? The materiality, the explosive potential, the uncontainability of crowds was comprehensively delinked from the media accounting of transnational massing. The pure presence of crowds across geopolitical boundaries in a concentrated moment, the thrust of transnational massing, was elided by the media abstractions through which transnational massing can be conceptualized. Transnational massing as realized in the news media became an abstract play of numbers, a manifestation of shadowy technological structures, and an expression of that empty supersignifier, the "left." Between registering the presence of the crowds and accounting (conceptualizing) transnational massing in the media there appeared an enormous schism—a fracture in ontological reckoning.

Contaminative Crowding: Middle East/North Africa since December 2010

Beginning with protests on December 18, 2010, in Tunisia, following the self-immolation of a street vendor in protest against ill-treatment by government officials, incidents of crowds gathering to demand regime change spread rapidly across cities and countries of North Africa and the Middle East. As this was written (April 2011), protests led to the removal of longstanding authoritarian leaders in Tunisia and Egypt, descended into civil war in Libya and Syria, and were ongoing in Algeria, Jordan, Bahrain, Yemen, Oman, and elsewhere. Naturally, each context has been focused and analyzed in the news media separately, and each context has distinctive alignments—ruling and oppositional—at work. But what the news media's coverage has also inevitably projected is the linkage between each context. Evidently, it was the spark in Tunisia that set off the growing wave of protests, each drawing inspiration from the others. As significantly, they simply appeared to be coherent: with protesting crowds in each context, appearing and accruing in quick succession, exerting the subversive organicity of their manifold presences, and apparently aware of their cumulative weight as a growing cross-boundary mass. Each protesting crowd in one place seems to spur into conglomeration other protesting crowds, so that a kind of contaminative movement develops, both contextually discrete and deliberately coherent across borders.

The news media's registering of the contaminative crowding phenomenon since December 2010 has been no more than a matter of reporting steps in its development. To that extent the registering has been as cumulative as the appearance of crowds across these regions have been, merely a shadowing of the process of social effervescence. Conceptualizing the contaminative crowding phenomenon, contemplating all the protesting crowds in their various contexts together (i.e., beyond the accounting within each context separately), has however unfolded in a more designed manner. As with the February 15, 2003, transnational massing, but through different strategies, this conceptualization has been at odds with registering crowds and has followed an autonomous logic. It seems to me that a reiteration of the break in ontological reckoning with contemporary crowds is under way.

The challenges to news media framing posed by the contaminative crowding phenomenon are somewhat different from those posed by transnational massing. The latter was unprecedented in its awareness of scale and simultaneity; the former has many structural analogues. Contaminative crowding has characterized numerous international movements from the 1848 revolutions to the 1960s student movements and the 1989 fall of Eastern Bloc regimes. The problem is that all these are powerfully associated with ideological polarizations, along the lines of class interests and left-wing (particularly Communist) alignments, which are far from clearly discerned in the Middle East and North Africa protests. In conceptualizing the latter contaminative crowding protests, the news media have therefore taken uneasy recourse to one of those past analogues, the most recent, the 1989 Eastern Bloc revolutions. This involves a series of extrapolations that have little to do either with the 1989 revolutions or the current manifestations of contaminative crowding protests. Given the prevailing global consensus on multiparty democratic and capitalist arrangements, the 1989 revolutions seem an apt marker of the moment when the polarized "other" ideology and its regimes fell and the currently dominant global order was consolidated. Powerful normative significance is consequently attached to 1989 in the currently dominant ideological dispensation, succinctly identified by Boris Buden as the myth of "an epochal victory of love that has finally reunited what Communist totalitarianism previously separated."[41] To evoke 1989 in relation to the Middle East and North Africa protests therefore provides a useful normative and ideological horizon against which to gauge them.

That has been repeatedly done in news coverage of these protests. Much of this started off as a perception of straightforward analogousness. On January 15, 2011, BBC Middle East editor Jeremy Bowen wondered on the *Today* program whether what is being witnessed is "the Arab world's Gdansk?";[42] and old Eastern Bloc watcher Timothy Garton Ash observed enigmatically on February 2 in the *Guardian* that "Europe's future is at stake this week on Cairo's Tahrir Square, as it was on Prague's Wenceslas Square in 1989"[43]—by February hardly any news feature or report on unfolding events in the region failed to make a connection to 1989. Even those who began to question this connection, to emphasize the difference rather than the similarity, reified the reference point of 1989 as the conceptual measure for the ongoing protests. In fact, marking the difference did become the principal way of maintaining the connection: in, among others, Harris Mylonas and Wilder Bullard's *Guardian* feature of February 8, "This Is No 1989 Moment for the Arab World";[44] in Peter Hallward's consideration of the analogy again in *The Guardian* on 22 February;[45] and in Kristian Coates Ulrichsen, David Held, and Alia Brahimi's extended February 11 *Open Democracy* article on the analogy, marking three similarities and one (overwhelming) difference.[46]

These direct considerations of the analogy apart, the ideological inclination that led to its evocation in the first place led also to an interesting rhetorical containment of the many crowds. They became subject to a register of comprehensive "deindividuation" in toto, across contexts, across the entire multinational zone of contaminative crowding. All these crowds became simply and homogeneously "the people" or "pro-democracy protesters" opposed to "dictators." It appeared that these crowds had no ideological investment apart from their uniform desire for democracy and the removal of dictators, formulated singularly in the abstract binary opposition of democracy and dictatorship. No representative of the protesters was interviewed except as a representative of "the people" and a seeker of normatively defined "democracy." In the 1989 revolutions the direction of change was clear: toward a replication of Western European regimes and abnegation of single-party governance and state-controlled economic arrangements. In the Middle East and North Africa the sought-after regimes needed, and must have been given, a *lot* more searching thought. Yet, none of those representing protests in any context for the media were asked what sort of regime change they contemplated: constitutional reform, secular arrangements, proportional representational or majoritarian or representative or consociational terms? There were no questions on what sort of economic and political relations they envisaged with Western Europe and the United States (a natural one to ask since many of the beleaguered regimes went hand in hand with the neocolonial policies of these "Western" regimes). The crowds were rendered as passive concretizations of the pure norm of democracy without political content. They were not presented in terms of the class, religious, political, or ethnic segments and factions within their fold. These were evidently seething, demanding, dynamic, explosive crowds that had been fixed by a simplistic binary between dictatorship and democracy by the news media—simply "pro-democracy protesters" without leadership and without variegation. Paradoxically, the conceptual inadequacy of this account merely accentuates the scale and intensity and complexity of the contaminative crowding that was registered.

What Next?

The accounting of contemporary cross-boundary crowds formed as transnational massing or contaminative crowding has only been very unevenly taken up in scholarly or creative efforts as of yet. The February 15, 2003, protests have attracted a smattering of sociological studies, political theorizations, and literary texts, but these are as yet too dispersed. And they have been overwhelmed by the enormous academic and creative attention paid to the larger conflict of the Iraq invasion itself that followed from March 2003. The unsuccessful, though grand, gesture of the February 15 transnational massing—and other protests thereafter—seemed to be snuffed out under the weight of that which it failed to prevent. The December 2010 onwards contaminative crowding phenomenon in the Middle East and North Africa is ongoing as this is written. Academic and creative efforts devoted to this are still to come.

So far, then, registering the presence of and conceptualizing these contemporary forms of crowding are primarily held on the screen of media representation. As I have observed above, this is in fact not simply a matter of these protests being too recent to have received any other kind of attention; by their very nature the relationship of the current mediascape and contemporary forms of crowding is an essential one. Since the latter are manifested across geopolitical and cultural contexts, their conceptualization as social phenomena is actually *enacted* on the screens of media representation; they are recognized as transnational massing or contaminative crowding because the media brings the many crowds together. That is already a first remove from registering the physical presence of the crowds qua crowds. That the media-based enactment of such cross-boundary forms of crowding also deploys inadequate, designedly abstract, and ideologically predetermined conceptual frames could be regarded as a second remove from the physical presence of the crowd. The twofold remove from that visceral, dynamic, uncontainable sense of the crowd in the conceptual articulation of its contemporary mediatized forms describes, in my view, precisely how conventional ontological reckoning with crowds are fractured now.

As this fracture comes to be examined in sociology, social psychology, history, and literature, the patterns of conventionally theorizing crowds outlined earlier will need to be reconsidered. This reconsideration will no doubt find that some of those patterns need to be modified, some dispensed with, and some could continue to apply as before. The kind of folding inward of literary representation or historiographical methodology in engaging with crowds noted above will, it seems likely, need to attend more carefully to the nuances of the prevailing mediascape and the *enactment* of contemporary cross-border crowds on its screen. Perhaps, along with layering literary representation, a layering of the literary dimensions of media representation has to take place in conceptualizing crowds. Or, the history of the history of the crowd will become increasingly a history of the history of media representation of crowds. The taming of the crowd in social psychology may seem, in some ways, more amenable to the media framing of cross-boundary crowd formations—which tame the on-the-ground presence of many crowds too. At the same time, the disconnection (twofold removal) between registering the physical crowds and their mediatized conceptualization could also seem to thrust forth their uncontainable and subversive potential anew. The inadequacy of the autonomous logic of mediatizing, the break of ontological coherence between registering the presence of and accounting for crowds, could reinforce the power and subversiveness and uncontainability of the crowd with renewed vigor.

Epilogue

Presence Continuous

Ranjan Ghosh

Is presence a "surplus"? A pregnant silence that is always betraying and betrayed, a silence in attendance on the "said," sparking a reverent intimacy with "saying"? The recital of a power, a project of thinking, that creates demands for more inventive modes of cultural and hermeneutic communication? An apparent reticence that is solicitous, stirring, and nontaciturn?

Art and literature have, most often, had their origin and exfoliation in "surplus." There is a certain joy in such engagements. Rabindranath Tagore points out that where "there is an element of the superfluous in our heart's relationship with the world, Art has its birth. In other words, where our personality feels its health it breaks out in display. What we devour for ourselves is totally spent. What overflows our need becomes articulate. The stage of pure utility is like the state of heat which is dark. When it surpasses itself, it becomes white heat and then it is expressive."[1] Presence can be argued to have its home in a surplus whose emanation and manifestation occur in a state of apparent nonutility. Presence can have its manifestation in the sublime;[2] it can also speak through surplus. It arrives when we are spent; it flows on occasions when one thought that all his needs were pragmatized. It emerges when literature or art has surpassed itself. There is an ineffability in the understanding and experience of literature and art, something that cannot be measured and, hence, cannot be defined. The visibility of presence is in the articulation of a hunger that literature and its transcultural understanding secretly harbor.[3] However, within the ambit of transcultural becoming, Bill Ashcroft's interesting observations in this book (chapter 7) inspire me to expand on a few issues.

In a transcultural reading of literature presence is about mediation, negotiation, and eventual transformation. Morphogenetically, there is a continuity of presence—the presence-continuous—that keeps aesthetic experiences "tense." We acknowledge the determinant and, most often, lose touch with the "constitutive," whose footsteps do not usually make any noise. There is nothing true-false about it; but, this invariably introduces a participation mystique. Presence presentifies both as a "surplus" and as an indefinable content that reshapes the product in its forming. The consciousness of presence renders it "present"; its unconscious ineliminability and irrevocability make it continue as presence. For me, presence is in the making and unmaking of the present, in flitting in and out of the chambers of the defined, formed, and constituted bounced off against the irrepressible, hard-to-define, and the ever-constituting. The threat that presence as "negativity" raises makes us essay a denial of its existence or its unperceived articulation in order to leave our established sense of understanding of things and the world undisturbed. Despite a conscious aversion to "absences," there are instances of submission to invisible inherent interferences that have a voice in the making of the future of a thing or a subject. Presence is present, projective, and proleptic. This is not to misconstrue presence as "mystic." Presence carries with it its own signifying practices. Repression, denial, determined relational contexts, and oversight are built into our discourses of thought. Our enabling discourses of meaning and order—whether it be the understanding of photographs, the politics of "borders," the crowd, as evidenced in some of the chapters of this book—are terrorized by the threat of deterritorialization generated through the unease that presence imports. Interestingly, onto-epistemologically, presence inhabits all our spaces of understanding and meaning and all moments of our sense-making and sense-generation—analogous to Husserl's emptied intentions. Presence is in "to be" and what was "not to be."

So presence is the "absent" in process. This is what transcultural ruminations evolve with. Understanding transcultural poetics then is putting the aesthetics of cross-border traffic always on trial. Correspondences among transcultural paradigms have an unsettling power whose strength lies in exceeding an understanding or literary reception hitherto thought as thetic. Literature appreciated within these versions of transcultural dialogism avoids repression of meaning and works up instead a circulation endowed by the motility of cultural semiosis, the gain derived from what we know as translational "lack" and the conceptual inflection and lubrication. Presence in transculturality is tantamount to holding and withholding subjectivity, desire, and a semiotic. Transcultural poetics, thus, is hinged on setting questions across cultural understanding of a text. But every question asked or raised is projected with another "question" which comes through as a possibility for attentive comportment. This possibility is cultivated imperceptively in a "presence" that is dispositional but scarcely volitional. In such possibilities and pervertibilities, in the flux of dispossession and "doing" that our transcultural experiences of literature are executed—the "subject-(non)work" is put in play. For instance, reading a poem across literary traditions, cultures, and conceptual domains is about encountering some meaning-deficit that becomes in Jacques Derrida's terms a "poison" to further crisis and "wandering." This builds around "love"—the love derived in the "taking-place" of the poem, the love of the poem in its unmaking, the love to demonstrate the "demon of the heart," which is a "passion," a sort of "wounding."[4] It is the "presence continuous," the subject-(non)work, that leaps forth and relates the poem to a complex array of intersections involving loss, anxiety, lack, excess, and perjury.

Transcultural poetics is premised in a revolt that, oedipally as it were, self-cancels itself for greater meaningful fulfilments. In trying to produce more meanings it has, as its hidden agenda, an inoperativity that, in its exposition, becomes a commitment to the death of meaning. The experience of reading a poem is not harmed by allowing it a "silence" studiously removed from prior or generic categories of understanding that, almost always, subsume the particular in the general. This leaves the aesthetic experience in the realm of feelings before concepts and frameworks of understanding emerge and invade to make the "tulip," as Kant has noted, beautiful. Approaching a poem then is also about being conscious of its singularity and the "presence" residing within it. Singularity as a poetic encounter is lost when the poem is read again with the intention to singularize it. The poem's singularity is not in being able to stay and survive as singular.

Poetic meaning has its "otherness" in an unmathematization that prospers in its failure; transcultural poetics, as I would like to interpret, is a transpolar (crossing over the poles in literary languages) and cross-national phenomenon—a phenomenon deeply invested in presences. The growth here is both vertical and horizontal—the survival and perpetuation of self in the possible exfoliation of the other. Transcultural poetics looks into this seeming "noiseless, motionless gap between inhaling and exhaling."[5] The silence disturbs poetic experience with a "presence," and this presence emerges from a transculturality that makes the poem deconstruct its received modes of "bearing witness." The silence of transcultural growth remains as a mute witness to the poem and thus, through silence, we reach for an interpretive noise that, again, in a negativity, preserves a silence, making for the horizontal poetic experience—each time overrunning the "economy of the discourse."[6] The poem shows itself as a fragment that is also fragmentary "in which," as Werner Hamacher notes, "the face of language passed behind or beyond it; a fragment would be the language in which something other than itself—nothing, for example—also spoke and, therefore, a language in which at least two languages always spoke—a broken language, the break of language."[7] It is the poem that, in its abilities to surprise the poet,[8] in its own poeticality, in its own self-generated poetic spaces, in being at once complete and incomplete, and in its silences and signatures makes meaning possible. Meaning is primarily about a prismatic other endorsed by cross-cultural points of inquiry and ingress. The poem without putting the poet into exile is not always the "learned cryptogram for experts" but is aimed for "members of a language community sharing a common world." The poem raises the question "who am I?" and silently quips "Who am I not?"; the cross-cultural other questions "Who are you?" and silently quips "Are you not what I think you are?"

What cultural logic and apperception make such poetic encounters across languages, cultures, and traditions possible? The poem *is* and yet *is not*; it becomes the property and propriety of both the self and the other—the apostrophic and prosopopeic. Jean-Luc Nancy notes that "to expose is to depart from a simple position, which is always also a deposition, a relinquishing of the contingence of a passing moment, a circumstance or a point of view. What is exposed is placed in the order of absolute, immutable and necessary presence. The word *poiesis* is derived from a word family that designates ordering arrangement, or disposition. Poetry disposes. Art is disposition. It disposes the thing according to the order of presence. It is the productive technique of presence."[9] So poetry, in this "disposing act," *presences* meanings where *poiesis* is *prae-est*. Under the transcultural import, poetry subtracts itself to add on to its life: a moving away from itself, its nature, to the act of foregrounding and the advancement of learning. Thus, from the "already no longer" to the "not yet" is a passage without pause, a road not taken, "neither disposed nor exposed, inexposable, only and ceaselessly deposing all things." Encounters across cultures and paradigms put poetry in a "conjunction of passing and presence, of fleeing and stasis," making meaning ahead of the present, of the existent, and ahead of the possible. Transcultural "access" to reading makes us agree with Nancy that "the sense of 'poetry' is a sense that is always still to be made."[10] It makes an access to the "poetic" and the conceptual striations that a genuine proper invocation of poetry perhaps does not often address. What identifies a text as poetry is lost to what was not thought poetry at all. The logarithm of poetry is deconstructed through an experience in "volume" that poetic foregrounding triggers. A poem becomes less poetry and more poetic; less verse, more verve; less method and more movement.

A poem has a meaning in time, in contexts, which produce graspable meaning and, hence, relevance of its limits. But the spaces that transculturality generates allow for subtraction in the rigid temporal existence of the poem—the poem self-generates itself through temporal decontextualization. So, in a chronomorphic *poiesy*, the evolving spaces distend time and "inexpose" itself. The disruption in chrono-structural patterns enjoins points of negativity (the beginning setting off with the ending) with successivity (generation emerging from termination) of meaning. The spaces, then, that the poem "puts forward" owes to a simultaneity that is both external and internal. Transcultural poetics, in a measured indiscretion, creates this ineludable clash of spaces—the "taking place." Poetry, in its eventhood, produces a creative hollow, an "ex-pos(t)ure" as Nancy has argued. Indeed, poetry exists in "taking-place"; it inhabits and appropriates spaces and yet continually configures itself; this is its "world-ing"; it occupies a place and yet cannot avoid dis*place*ment. Its address and its knownness become its own dislocation and its wilderness. This problematizes the notion of "access." Poetic encounters in transculturality see "access" as a difficulty that, in resisting "our efforts to make something of it," makes poetic experiences possible.

Presence and the Return of the Aesthetic

We can make reasonable affordances through a brief interpretive assignation with William Wordsworth's "Daffodils." The significance of "dance" in this poem (all its four stanzas have the word "dance") transculturally presences the word *lila* (this word is very difficult to translate without harming the depth and reach of its meaning; "play," at best, can be a loose translation) as derived from Sanskrit aesthetic theory and philosophy. This is the "interruption," the rupture in our horizon of understanding and the disruption in the chrono-conceptual continuity that a word or an idea brings with it. This "interruption" is the "poetic moment" that transculturality imports by creating in the present of the "self" (here the "dance," the meaning-effect) the space to accommodate the present of the "other" (the *lila*, the presence-effect). And most often, this happens through the dialectic of presences and absences. Poetry is seen as being caught in the dynamism of "selfing" and "othering," something that Derrida would call *teleiopoiesis*— the making from afar. The poem befriends the "arrivants" (the cross-cultural other and, in this context, it is the notion of *lila* that arrives both with pronounced and imperceptible footsteps) and withdraws too: a *retrait* in the sense of selfing with a consciousness of the other's "arriving"—the coming and arrival of the translated and the transformative other.[11] Poetry has this "true friendship" with the presencing/presenced other where "making friends" is an incompleteness accomplished in darkness. Transcultural poetics, in its "horizontality" and in its cultivation of the "mystery of encounter," addresses a "secret" (the experience of reading "Daffodils" becomes what it was not, a verse and *re*verse) and puts forth the question: "*Che-cos–è la poesia?*" (What [thing] is poetry?) However, in the matrices of transculturality we are not merely invested in horizontal reading and paradigm-meshing where networks of comparative investigation render a substance to the poem's existence; rather, alongside horizontality, we are invitingly "disoriented" by a verticality that aggravates the *difference* in the experience and manifestation of the poem. If verticality is about finding the poem's contextual propriety—its *substance* of being and emergence—horizontality is its *obstance*, a performative resistance that makes the poem what it *is not* and, at the same time, returns it to the grounds of what *it is*. Such a view of transcultural poetics would not allow the "self" and the "other" to remain as settled categories; "dance" as the self and *lila* as the other correspond in an iterability and progress by "mourning" over the normative settlement of communication. This approximates what Maurice Blanchot argues as the "work of the absence of (the) work"[12] that supplements the process, the *poiesis*, beyond the product.

What I mean is that the meaning of "dance" in the poem communicates differently once it "befriends" *lila* and it also presences something else by feeding into, for instance, the Chinese or Persian or Arabic poetics. This is the "interruption that the poem makes in its correspondence with transcultural investments: it does not make any claim to literary absolute, not Friedrich Schegel's hedgehog, which is isolated from the surrounding world and is deemed complete in itself.[13] Under transcultural dynamics, "dance" will have its internal *pharmakon*, a "demon" within, a counter law, an alterity to itself, and will hyphenate with its own ego. This is what I argue as the "presence-continuous." However, this extrapolates a different sense out of what Derrida proposes as setting "fire to the library of poetics."[14] This is about discrediting a well-beaten poetics to understand poetry, which Wittgenstein would prefer to term "torture"; poetics is about setting in motion and also about "resisting." The nonpropositional nature of "dance" is experienced in its cross-investments with *lila* but transculturality acknowledges the "indeterminacy in the port"[15] by making allowance for greater intrusions and infusions (*avenir*) through other perspectives of understanding—act(s) that "reiterate(s) in a murmur: never repeat."[16] So the subject (say, the "dance" in this instance) called and intervened in a transcultural location is irrevocably split and informed with a movement that repeats to announce itself with *difference*. Cultural translation brings transformation—the *becoming* and *between*—but not distortion and permanent displacement, something close to what Michel Deguy writes in the poem "Catachreses": "Turning outside to inside over and over, turning the inside out: what he is waiting for is not there—visibly; that which is not, neither the outside nor the inside."[17] This is one of the ways of arguing the horizontal and vertical collapse and, also, continuity that transcultural poetics performs and perpetuates, contributing to the possibility and the being of the "literary."

Transcultural poetics has an atypical career in certain moments of surplus, presence-continuous, which, to recall Derrida, is the poem's "singular impropriety"—"blessing *of the* poem."[18] And in such presence-continuity a poem is caught in a "white heat." Nancy perceptively questions: "What is making?" He observes: "To posit within being. There is nothing more to making than positing as its end. But the end that started out being a goal now turns into its end in the form of its negation, and making is unmade as it reaches perfection."[19] The "taking-place" of a poem is both making something and making itself. It posits but does not perfect; so "access is unmade as passage, process, aim, and path, as approach and approximation. It is posited as exactitude and as disposition, as presentation."[20] Rightly, "the poem is the thing made of making in itself."[21]

The poem, once written, starts writing itself, living a process of internal bleeding, as it were. It prospers in an internal power that challenges, as I pointed out, temporal segregation that determines its hermeneutical legitimacy under norms of evocritical receptions. A poem is "untruthful to itself" when it repeats itself reductively in a jejune self-mimesis through received semantics and the pragmatics of institutional ways of meaning. The "responsibility" of a poem lies in the ways in which it deconstructs its "witness" and "testimony" of meaning generation. This "bearing witness"—not to mire it in shallow dichotomies of "true" and "false" testimony—is about allowing a poem to create its own distances from itself and yet be indistinguishable from "absences" that put it on the point of its birth: its birth to presence. In this "play" that is the poem's "irrefutable witness" (the last words of Paul Celan's poem "Etched Away") and its singularity the meaning is no longer "solemn." Presence prevents solemnization of a poem. The desolemnization is what renders poetry "sacred." And the "sacred" is what initiates communication and transpolarity. Poetry encounters itself and bears witness to its "feigning"—a pretence to stasis coming from sacralization of meaning effects. In its auto-encounters, poetry turns the "gaze" on itself and the intentionalities that such gaze generates makes poetry distend its own "ego"—the ego of its "taking-place," a self-distantiation, acts of being "out of nature" that, thus, makes it "sacred." This "sacred" forms around what Nancy has identified as "depth, intensity, daring, feeling."[22] The sacred in poetry is "moving": both in the sense of its "taking-place" and changing frames of experience, affect, and presentification.

So poetry bears access to the excess, both in relation to itself and the other. Nancy writes that "when access occurs, it is clear that it had always been there, and that similarly it will always return. . . . the poem draws access from an immemorial past, which owes nothing to the reminiscence of some ideality, but is the exact existence, here and now, of the infinite, its eternal return."[23] This excess is the irreducible "secrecy" of poetic experience and understanding, bearing witness and testimony to what makes transcultural poetics "responsible." Such poetics bears responsible witness to cross-cultural "encounters" and consequently testimonizes meaning-formation without narcotizing the radical singularity of the event. This act does not foreclose the possibility of the poem where "it is silent, where it keeps its secret, all the while telling us that there is a secret, revealing the secret it is keeping as a secret, not revealing it, as it continues to bear witness that one cannot bear witness for the witness, who in the end remains alone and without witness."[24] Presence instils this secrecy and presentifies through the eros of the unmanifest. Presence makes poetry dwell in untrustworthiness.

Presence and the Postaesthetic

This untrustworthiness engenders the "hunger" in literature and provides a transitive career to the "literary." Presence is not just about producing meaning; it also communicates when meaning fails to convey. This is the zone of the postaesthetic. It is like looking into the "picture" and getting arrested by an uncertainty; it is about a failure to methodize the experience of "seeing"; it is a wrestle with an indefinable "secret" understanding, the nature of which is rarely in the loop of interpretive modes. My understanding of this secret is at the level of the ineffable and asymmetrical understanding of literary experience: the emotive, reflective, and the intangible. This is the inability to pinpoint hunger that literature evokes and invokes. It is also the ministration of presence. This is "for once, then, something":

Once, when trying with chin against a well-curb,
I discerned, as I thought, *beyond the picture*,
Through the picture, a something white, *uncertain*,
Something more of the depths—and then *I lost it*.

> Water came to rebuke the too clear water.
> One drop fell from a fern, and lo, a ripple
> *Shook whatever* it was lay there at bottom,
> *Blurred* it, *blotted* it out. What was that whiteness?
> Truth? A pebble of quartz? *For once, then, something.*[25]

I am tempted to see such experience and discernment as something close to Husserl's *epochē*, the suspension of existence, which leaves the object as existing independent of the perceiver, external to the domain of the universally presupposed interpretative factor. This experience is about the "transport" and the "delight" that certain conditions of understanding lend to the constitution of the self. This has a strange quality beyond the presuppositiveness of methodicity—an investiture that cannot decide between the "pebble" and the "quartz" and yet tenaciously delights in the "ripple" that blurs and blots; it is once something and then becomes something else—"I lost it." This experience inaugurates without a method—a flighty spontaneous emanation—and expires in a hint of a structure dourly loose at its ends and impermanent in nature. This is the presence-continuous at the level of the postaesthetic. What happens, for instance, when one reads the first two stanzas of Wordsworth's "By the Sea" with no knowledge of the poet and his aesthetics and also oblivious of all the conceptual parameters informing a tradition that can help figure the poem out methodologically? Expressions such as "The holy time is quiet as a nun" and "The gentleness of heaven is on the sea: / Listen! the mighty Being is awake" can put the whole economy of literature to test, igniting an experience that "moves" and defies all explanation conducted through the metaphorics of interpretive boundaries and conceptual structures. What kind of an experience am I talking about if I say "I don't know why it feels this way?" What happens when universes of discourse fail to "horizon" my literary experience? Here the hermeneutical and heuristically unutilized, rather, never-to-be-utilized energies become losses that write off a gain whose emergence is clearly out of step with conventional means of understanding and intellectual consumption. Literary worlds are also produced beyond what I have come to see as the (in)fusionized or presentified domain of literary experiences.[26] The tremble, the unperceived undulation of the text and the resonant volume that it silently mounts on us cannot exhaust the possibilities that the hunger of and for literature can verily and imperceptively offer.

If someone, instead of describing space as "the boundless, three-dimensional extent in which objects and events occur and have relative position and direction," writes that "space is a doubt," what kind of an experience does that project?[27] The words "space" and "doubt" ooze a thought, leaving behind a room for reflection that is unstructured, most often method-defying, and more in the nature of a provocation. This provocation does not prod one to work on theories of space but allows an experience that settles on our self and grows on us with a sense of confusion and ignorance we take delight in and very rarely feel embarrassed about. This is about "feeling" the thought out, and this implicates a difference that we make between the delight of the odor of a rose and a high fashion perfume with a label that declares its chemical composition. Our experience of literature is walking the fine line separating the knowing, the known, and the unknowable. Literature's internalized conventions—institutions, rules, and history—are deeply interlocked with possibilities of "freeing" up. Literature frees itself up in the postaesthetic when the trenchant rigor and regimes of "aestheticization" are discounted in favour of a pretheoretical state. The experience of the postaesthetic signifies a mobility that is beyond a given horizon of expectations: vectoring into a "surplus" that is, most often, difficult to discourse. This is the presence-effect.

This conjugality of presence and literature helps in forming the phenomenon I would like to term "becoming aesthetic." Presence works within the aesthetic and the postaesthetic of literature. Transculturally, beyond the compulsive duress of interpretation, our experiences of literature are brought home in a mix of unmethodicity and unacknowledged sociocultural influences that then work continuously and imperceptibly into our appreciation of the world or world-making. Transcultural understanding is not possible only in the domain of the method and structure but also in experiences that are inexplicable. I have always wondered what brought the smile on the faces of my Polish colleagues—unfamiliar with the Bengali language and Rabindranath Tagore's musical aesthetics—when I sang a Tagore number for them during my teaching stint at Wroclaw University. Such postinterpretive asymmetries and the inexplicability and the delightful imprecision of understanding are presence-induced. The postaesthetic has its phantom-presence, feeding on its own "uncanny" ability to salvage experiences beyond what methodological stridency and (in)fusionist's astuteness might allow. Here literature *moves* rather than constructs and signifies. Becoming aesthetic owes to literature's ability for "deviancy" that external competences in the form of "imposed aesthetic" inscribe in its making (the trained habits of aesthetic understanding that we bring to literature). Literature in its quotient of the "literary" makes itself "vulnerable"; but, vulnerability is also its fate in the postliterary. This is a provocation to make literature matter in postdiscursive ways.

The postaesthetic of hunger is the excess of energy that leaps beyond the interpreter's mortal and limiting abilities to submit to signification; it is the "useless" (beyond the ascribing and ascriptive domains of political economy) that literature exudes without the slightest aim to get noticed and inscribed. It is a hunger whose sovereignty is in a senseless loss, in being unremarkable to a *sensus communis* and to a certain collective reception. It emerges in response to an autonomous moment of readerly transaction without being obligated to surface in similar contours with the following reader or succeeding readerly intervention. Literature has its own unreserved expenditures in the sense of the prelogical and pretheoretical as distinguished from the preontological. The postaesthetic is built around a coyness with no apotheosization of meaning or determined identity. It is the experience that literature grows on us: an experience that, under a mild interrogation, invariably expires in a confused smile of helplessness. This is becoming-aesthetic-never-quite-and-yet-is. It is the presencing of a hunger whose constituents are ever so elusive and, at best, translucent. This is literature's unflappable presence-heritage.

Literature's strangeness is literature's informal and reflexive investment in presence. Literature grows on the everyday and everydayness inscribes literature; our transcultural experiences are part of our everyday, which we, most often, are not alert to. However, for me, presence presentifies not merely aesthetically but postaesthetically too in transformative events taking place in our culture, tradition, politics, and religion. It is just not the transitivity or beyonding or spillovers within the premises of art; its life of power performs by blurring the distinctions between art and nonart, bringing into its loop the sociocultural experience and heritage of the interacting participants. Presence is also the product of moments of history, historicality, and our lived everydayness. Presence has beetle-holed into our everydayness, and the conscious trappings and accoutrements of understanding literature, as distinguished from its everydayness, are fallacious. Literature's mystery is in rapporting with such everydayness and, by extension, with the inexorable and inscrutable aesthetics of presence. In a way, literature presentifies and is presenced simultaneously. When one knows that there is a "no" is when "yes" is born. When we have considered and conditioned a "no," "yes" infiltrates. The ill-said and ill-seen "yes" is presence. It is also yes-no. Both danger and saving grace, we are in the midst of the topology of Presence Continuous.

Notes

Prologue

1. Frank Ankersmit, *Sublime Historical Experience* (Stanford: Stanford University Press, 1993), 77. Here, too, the argument is presented in language that evokes an era of anxiety over the ability to determine friend from foe or right from wrong, as Ankersmit continues: "One could argue that in the days of logical positivism it was at least clear who was friend or foe. And we lost even this with Rorty, Derrida, and Gadamer."
2. Eelco Runia, "Presence," *History and Theory* 45, no. 1 (February 2006): 8; Eelco Runia, "Spots of Time," *History and Theory* 45, no. 3 (October 2006): 1; see also Hans Gumbrecht, *Production of Presence: What Meaning Cannot Convey* (Stanford: Stanford University Press, 2005), 47–49; Ankersmit, *Sublime Historical Experience*, 77–80.
3. Ankersmit, *Sublime Historical Experience*, 1.
4. Jean-Luc Nancy, *The Birth to Presence*, trans. Brian Holmes and others (Stanford: Stanford University Press, 1993).

Chapter 1

1. Charles Dickens, *A Christmas Carol and Other Stories* (New York: Modern Library, 1995), 5.
2. Ibid., 33.
3. Ibid., 80.
4. Ibid., 53.
5. Hans Ulrich Gumbrecht, *Production of Presence: What Meaning Cannot Convey* (Stanford: Stanford University Press, 2004), xv.
6. Eelco Runia, "Presence," *History and Theory* 45, no. 1 (February 2006): 5.
7. Eelco Runia, "Spots of Time," *History and Theory* 45, no. 3 (October 2006): 306.
8. See Ewa Domanska, "The Material Presence of the Past," *History and Theory* 45, no. 3 (October 2006); Gumbrecht, *Production of Presence*, xiii; Frank Ankersmit, *Sublime Historical Experience* (Stanford: Stanford University Press, 2005), 116.
9. Runia, "Presence," 5.
10. Gumbrecht, *Production of Presence*, 137.
11. I ask this not only in relation to the work of Ankersmit, Bentley, Domanska, Gumbrecht, and Runia but also in relation to the current prevalence of the use of "material culture," archeology (in the traditional, i.e., not Foucauldian, sense), oral testimony, as well as the categories of experience and subjectivity for the writing of history. See Ethan Kleinberg, "Haunting History: Deconstruction and the Spirit of Revision," *History and Theory* 46, no. 4 (December 2007): 142.
12. This emphasis on linguistics also came at the expense of the speculative philosophy of history. See Runia, "Presence," 2–3.
13. Hans Ulrich Gumbrecht, "Presence Achieved in Language," *History and Theory* 45, no. 3 (October 2006): 318.
14. Gumbrecht, *Production of Presence*, 7.
15. Runia, "Presence," 8; Runia, "Spots of Time," 2.
16. Ankersmit, *Sublime Historical Experience*, 1.
17. Ibid., 10, 2.
18. Gumbrecht, *Production of Presence*, 106.
19. Domanska, "Material Presence of the Past," 337.
20. See Kleinberg, "Haunting History."
21. Michel Foucault has largely been absolved of this criticism as the most recent accounts present his "latest" works as a return to agency and localized political engagement.
22. Ethan Kleinberg, "New Gods Swelling the Future Ocean," *History and Theory* 46, no. 3 (November 2007): 457.
23. See Kleinberg, "Haunting History," 136–41.
24. Runia, "Presence," 8; Runia, "Spots of Time," 307.
25. Ankersmit, *Sublime Historical Experience*, 77. Here too the argument is presented in language that evokes an era of anxiety over the ability to determine friend from foe or right from wrong as Ankersmit continues: "One could argue that in the days of logical positivism it was at least clear who was friend or foe. And we lost even this with Rorty, Derrida, and Gadamer."

26. Runia, "Presence," 8; Runia, "Spots of Time," 1; see also Gumbrecht, *Production of Presence*, 47–49; Ankersmit, *Sublime Historical Experience*, 77–80.
27. Runia, "Presence," 4–5.
28. Ibid., 5; on this point, see also Gumbrecht, *Production of Presence*, 107–11.
29. Runia, "Spots of Time," 306.
30. Runia, "Presence," 6. For a substantive investigation into the use of and problems with the trope of metonymy, see Anita Kasabova, "Memory, Memorials, and Commemoration," *History and Theory* 47, no. 3 (October 2008).
31. Runia, "Presence," 8.
32. Ibid.
33. Ibid., 8–9. This investigation into the surface seems akin to Foucault's archeological methodology best embodied in *Les mots et les choses* but as modified in service of his genealogical project to present a "history of the present" in *Discipline and Punishment*. This is certainly the case in Gumbrecht's presentation of presence: Gumbrecht, *Production of Presence*, 38–39.
34. Runia, "Presence," 9. Emphasis added.
35. Ibid., 20.
36. Ibid., 13.
37. Ankersmit, "'Presence' and Myth," 329.
38. Eelco Runia, "'Forget about It': 'Parallel Processing' in the Srebrenica Report," *History and Theory* 43, no. 3 (October 2004).
39. The term "presence" does appear in the article but in terms of the Dutch mandate to its battalions to "deter by acts of presence" (315–19). It would be equally interesting to explore the relation of Runia's 1999 book *Waterloo, Verdun, Auschwitz: Deliqidatie van hat verleden* (Amsterdam: Meulenhoff, 1999) in relation to the evolution of "presence" as a historical category. It is also of note that Ankersmit employs aspects of this work in his *Sublime Historical Experience*. See Ankersmit, *Sublime Historical Experience*, 143–44, 165–66.
40. Runia, "'Forget about It,'" 295.
41. LaCapra cited in Runia, "'Forget about It,'" 297; originally found in Dominick LaCapra, *Writing History, Writing Trauma* (Baltimore: Johns Hopkins University Press, 2001), 142. It is also worth noting Runia's indictment of "trauma studies" as the "busiest and liveliest speak-easy" of speculative philosophy of history, in Runia, "Presence," 4.
42. H. Gediman and F. Wolkenfeld, "The Parallelism Phenomenon in Psychoanalysis and Supervision: Its Reconsideration as a Triadic System," *Psychoanalytic Quarterly* no. 49 (1980): 234. Runia cites this article.
43. Runia, "'Forget about It,'" 299–300.
44. Ibid., 310.
45. Ethan Kleinberg, "Freud and Levinas: Talmud and Psychoanalysis before the Letter," in *Freud's Jewish World* (New York: McFarland, 2010).
46. Sigmund Freud, *Moses and Monotheism*, trans. Katherine Jones (New York: Vintage Books, 1967), 113; Richard Bernstein, *Freud and the Legacy of Moses* (Cambridge: Cambridge University Press, 1998), 40–41. Bernstein uses the James Strachey translation: "Fate had brought the great deed and misdeed of primeval

days, the killing of the father, closer to the Jewish people by causing them to repeat it on the person of Moses, an outstanding father figure."
47. Kleinberg, "Freud and Levinas." See also Brad S. Gregory, "The Other Confessional History: On Secular Bias in the Study of Religion," *History and Theory*, Theme Issue 45 (2006).
48. On this point, see Gumbrecht's discussion of "real presence" and transubstantiation in Gumbrecht, *Production of Presence*, 145; and Ankersmit's discussion of the "aura" in Ankersmit, *Sublime Historical Experience*, 115–16.
49. On this point, see Jacques Derrida, "*Ousia* and *Gramme*: Note on a Note from *Being and Time*," in Jacques Derrida, *Margins of Philosophy*, trans. Alan Bass (Chicago: University of Chicago Press, 1982); for a discussion of Derrida in relation to "presence," see B. Bevernage, "Time, Presence, and Historical Injustice," *History and Theory* 47, no. 2 (May 2008).
50. Sigmund Freud, "A Note upon the 'Mystic Writing-Pad,'" in Sigmund Freud, *The Standard Edition of the Complete Psychological Works of Sigmund Freud*, 24 vols., trans. and ed. James Strachey (London: Hogarth Press, 1953–74), vol. 19 (1923–25).
51. Ibid., 228–29.
52. Ibid., 229.
53. Ibid., 228.
54. Ibid., 230.
55. Ibid., 231. My emphasis.
56. Freud, "Beyond the Pleasure Principle," in Freud, *Standard Edition*, vol. 18 (1920–22), 28.
57. Jacques Derrida, "Freud and the Scene of Writing," in *Writing and Difference* (Chicago: University of Chicago Press, 1978), 215.
58. In response to this paper Dominick LaCapra suggests that what is common to Freud, Heidegger, and Derrida is the notion that past, present, and future mark one another and are mutually implicated. Thus it might make sense to relate the uncanny to the return of the repressed whereby the past returns to haunt the present without being reducible to a pure presence (although Heidegger does not have an explicit, worked-out notion of the unconscious). Furthermore, for Derrida space itself is not opposed to time but mutually implicated with it in the very process of spacing, which takes time.
59. It strikes me that this is probable given the way that Runia suggests that all of the past is literally accessible in the "storehouse of presence." On this point, see Kasabova, "Memory, Memorials and Commemoration."
60. Runia, "Presence," 9. My emphasis.
61. And where one finds the uncanny, the ghost is not far behind. Gediman and Wolkenfeld, "Parallelism Phenomenon in Psychoanalysis," 234–35.
62. Ibid., 237. My emphasis.
63. Ankersmit, *Sublime Historical Experience*, 115.
64. Runia, "Spots of Time," 308.
65. Dickens, *Christmas Carol*, 77.
66. Dickens, *Christmas Carol*, 78.

67. Runia, "Presence," 19.
68. Dickens, *Christmas Carol*, 6.
69. That is, except for the perverse notion that the only reason Hamlet's Father would do such a thing is "to literally to astonish his son's weak mind." That is, to drive him mad.
70. Emmanuel Levinas, *Existence and Existents*, trans. Alphoso Lingis (Pittsburgh: Duquesne University Press, 1988), 56. See Ethan Kleinberg, *Generation Existential: Heidegger's Philosophy in France, 1927–1961* (Ithaca: Cornell University Press, 2005), 245–58.
71. Levinas, *Existence and Existents*, 71.
72. Ibid., 80–81.
73. Gumbrecht, *Production of Presence*, 117.
74. Here one might consider that the appropriate model for Ankersmit's "historical kiss" (125) is not Romeo and Juliet but the Grand Inquisitor and Jesus in Fyodor Dostoevsky's *The Brothers Karamazov* because of the incommunicable nature of the gesture. Ankersmit, *Sublime Historical Experience*, 115–16, 121–28. Also, the review of Ankersmit by Michael S. Roth in *History and Theory* 46, no.1 (February 2007): 66–73.

Chapter 2

1. See George Edward Moore, *Principia Ethica* (Cambridge: Cambridge University Press, 1965), 27–36. As Aristotle put it, "In the case of all things which have several parts and in which the whole is not, as it were, a mere heap, but the totality is something besides the parts, there is a cause of unity" (*Metaphysics*, trans. W. D. Ross), in *The Complete Works of Aristotle,* 2 vols., ed. Jonathan Barnes (Princeton: Princeton University Press, 1984), 1045^a 8–10.
2. Heidegger had referred in a 1938 lecture to "the world-picture (*Weltbild*) of modernity" and in a subsequent essay to "the age of the world-picture," by which he meant primarily the era of Western technology since the Renaissance, which had so powerfully objectified and situated the world while establishing the centrality of the representing subject. But he also referred to the more contemporary appearance of the media, and especially to radio. See Martin Heidegger, "The Age of the World Picture" (1963), in *The Question concerning Technology and Other Essays*, trans. William Lovitt (New York: Harper and Row, 1977), 115–54.
3. Martin Heidegger, *Identity and Difference*, trans. Joan Stambaugh, with German text following English translation (Chicago: University of Chicago Press, 1969), 73.
4. Ibid., 73; German, 142.
5. See Jacques Derrida, "White Mythology: Metaphor in the Text of Philosophy," in Jacques Derrida, *Margins of Philosophy*, trans. Alan Bass (Chicago: University of Chicago Press, 1982), 207–71.
6. See Theodor W. Adorno, *Negative Dialectics*, trans. E. B. Ashton (New York: Continuum Publishing, 1983). One should note that the title of the German original (1966) is singular: *Negative Dialektik*.

7. Karl Marx, *The Eighteenth Brumaire of Louis Bonaparte,* trans. anon. (New York: International Publishers, 1963), 124.
8. Georg Lukács, *The Theory of the Novel,* trans. Anna Bostock (Cambridge: MIT Press, 1971), 29.
9. Ibid., 29.
10. See Jürgen Habermas, "The Entwinement of Myth and Enlightenment: Re-Reading *Dialectic of Enlightenment,*" *New German Critique* 26 (1982), 13–30; citation from 29.
11. For "Grand Hotel Abyss," see Lukács, *Theory of the Novel,* 22; for the original description, see Georg Lukács, *The Destruction of Reason,* trans. Peter Palmer (Atlantic Highlands, N.J.: Humanities Press, 1981), 242–43.
12. Ibid., 88.
13. Ibid., 92.
14. Theodor W. Adorno, *Ästhetische Theorie* (Frankfurt am Main: Suhrkamp, 1970), 86.
15. Ibid., 93.
16. Adorno, *Aesthetic Theory,* ed. Gretel Adorno and Rolf Tiedemann, trans. Robert Hullot-Kentor (Minneapolis: University of Minnesota Press, 1997), 143.
17. Walter Benjamin, "On the Mimetic Faculty," trans. Edmund Jephcott, in Walter Benjamin, *Selected Writings, Vol. 2: 1927–1934,* ed. Michael W. Jennings, Howard Eiland, and Gary Smith (Cambridge: Belknap Press of Harvard University, 1999), 720–22; citation from 720–21.
18. Ibid., 722.
19. Heidegger, *Identity and Difference,* 72–73; German, 141.
20. Martin Heidegger, "Building Dwelling Thinking," in Martin Heidegger, *Poetry, Language, Thought,* trans. Albert Hofstadter (New York: Harper Colophon Books, 1971), 145–59; citation from 150. For the German, see "Bauen Wohnen Denken," in Martin Heidegger, *Vorträge und Aufsätze* (Stuttgart: Klett-Cotta, 1954), 139–56; citation from 144. For A. J. Greimas's very influential account of the "semiotic square," see A. J. Greimas and François Rastier, "The Interaction of Semiotic Constraints," in A. J. Greimas, *On Meaning,* trans. Paul J. Perron and Frank H. Collins (Minneapolis: University of Minnesota Press, 1987), 48–62. Heidegger's *Geviert* would, in this account, be structured not so much by Greimas's vertical distinction between the meaningful and meaningless, or his horizontal distinction between the prescribed and the proscribed, but rather by a vertical distinction between the estranged or unseen (divinities—sky) along the upper axis, and the ready-to-hand (man—earth) along the lower; and by a horizontal distinction between Being (divinities—mortals) along the left hand axis and Place (sky—earth) along the right. The *Geviert* could thus be understood not as a system of logical or semantic contraries and contradictories that (à la Greimas) produce purposive meaning, or what I have been calling "representation," but rather as a nonoppositional, nonnegating structure of self-affirming difference. The basic elements of this nonsensuously mimetic structure (mortals, divinities, earth, and sky), whose authentic nature is normally concealed by the opaque (or false) transparency of the "world picture" provided by the logical identities and negations of representation, only

emerge into "unconcealedness" by means of activities (such as building, or dwelling, or thinking, or poetry) that, once having rent what Schopenhauer called the "veil of Maya," the veil of merely purposive significance, assume a purely mimetic (and hence authentic) character. For Schopenhauer's "veil of Maya," see Arthur Schopenhauer, *Die Welt als Wille und Vorstellung, Sämtliche Werke* (Wiesbaden: Eberhard Brockhaus, 1949), 1:447.

21. Heidegger, "Building Dwelling Thinking," 152; "Bauen Wohnen Denken," 146.
22. Heidegger, "Building Dwelling Thinking," 158; "Bauen Wohnen Denken," 153
23. Heidegger, "Bauen Wohnen Denken," 155 (my translation).
24. Martin Heidegger, "... Poetically Man Dwells...," in Martin Heidegger, *Poetry, Language Thought,* trans. Albert Hofstadter (New York: Harper Colophon Books, 1971), 213–29; citation from 228. For the German, see "'... dichterisch wohnet der Mensch...,'" in Martin Heidegger, *Vorträge und Aufsätze* (Stuttgart: Klett-Cotta, 1954), 181–98; citation from 197.
25. Benjamin, "On the Mimetic Faculty," 721.
26. Heidegger, "... Poetically Man Dwells...," 225–26; "'... dichterisch wohnet der Mensch...,'" 194–95.
27. Heidegger, "... Poetically Man Dwells...," 226; "'... dichterisch wohnet der Mensch...,'" 195.
28. Ibid.
29. Elaine Scarry, *On Beauty and Being Just* (Princeton: Princeton University Press, 1999), 3–5.
30. Scarry, *On Beauty,* 5, 16, 110; Walter Benjamin, "On the Mimetic Faculty," 720.
31. Scarry, *On Beauty*, 103–4.
32. Scarry is citing Bruce Russett, *Grasping the Democratic Peace: Principles for a Post–Cold War World* (Princeton: Princeton University Press, 1993), 59.
33. For a fairly thorough critique of the insubstantiality of Scarry's ideas of beauty and justice, see Denis Dutton, "Mad about Flowers," *Philosophy and Literature* 24, no. 1 (2000): 249–60. What Dutton misses, oddly enough in a journal with "philosophy" in its title, is just how indebted Scarry is to Heidegger, phenomenology, and the belief that one can "bracket" out historical context in favor of experience itself, not to mention the motif of mimetic reproduction that runs through her argument.
34. Hans Ulrich Gumbrecht, *Production of Presence: What Meaning Cannot Convey* (Stanford: Stanford University Press, 2004), 1–2.
35. Ibid., 118; my brackets.
36. Ibid., 117; emphasis in original.
37. Ibid., 145.
38. Ibid., 150.
39. Ibid., 150, 151.
40. Ibid., 151.
41. See Wallace Stevens, "The Idea of Order at Key West" (1935), and Archibald MacLeish, "Ars Poetica" (1926). For a polemical critique of such motifs in the postmodern—or rather, post–Cold War—period, see Walter Michaels, *The Shape of the Signifier: 1967 to the End of History* (Princeton: Princeton University Press, 2004).

For my response to Michaels, see "Words, Words, Mere Words, No Matter from the Heart...," *American Literary History* 19, no. 1 (2007): 232–50.
42. See the stories in James Joyce, *Dubliners*, ed. Robert Scholes and A. Walton Litz (Harmondsworth, England: Penguin Books, Viking Critical Edition, 1976); Marcel Proust, *Swann's Way*, trans. Lydia Davis (New York: Penguin Books, 2003), 45; Virginia Woolf, "A Sketch of the Past," in *Moments of Being*, ed. Jeanne Schulkind (Orlando, Fla.: Harcourt, Brace, 1985), 64–159, citation from 73; *Mrs. Dalloway* (Orlando, Fla.: Harcourt, 2005), 97.
43. James Joyce, *Finnegans Wake* (New York: Penguin Books, 1976), 182; Proust, *Swann's Way*, trans. Davis, 444; Virginia Woolf, *To the Lighthouse* (Orlando, Fla.: Harcourt, 2005), 66.
44. Walter Benjamin, "On the Concept of History," trans. Harry Zohn, in Walter Benjamin, *Selected Writings, Vol. 4: 1938–1940*, ed. Howard Eiland and Michael W. Jennings (Cambridge: Belknap Press of Harvard University, 2003), 389–400; citations from 397; Gumbrecht, *Production of Presence*, 113.

Chapter 3

1. Jacques Derrida, *Of Grammatology*, trans. G. Spivak (Baltimore: John Hopkins University Press, 1977), 163.
2. Jacques Derrida, *Margins of Philosophy*, trans. Alan Bass (Brighton, England: Harvester Press, 1982), 13.
3. Ferdinand de Saussure, *Course in General Linguistics*, ed. C. Bally and A. Sechehaye, trans. W. Baskin (New York: McGraw-Hill, 1966), 83–87.
4. Ibid., 117.
5. Derrida, *Of Grammatology*, 27–73.
6. Ibid., 266.
7. Saussure called on linguists to focus exclusively on *langue* because doing so would enable them to develop a science, not because he denied that we could have access to stable meanings. He explained that "in separating language from speaking we are at the same time separating (1) what is social from what is individual; and (2) what is essential from what is accessory" (14).
8. Jacques Derrida, *Writing and Difference*, trans. A. Bass (London: Routledge & Kegan Paul, 1978), 280.
9. Derrida, *Of Grammatology*, 50.
10. Derrida, *Margins of Philosophy*, 268.
11. Edmund Husserl, *Ideas: General Introduction to Pure Phenomenology*, trans. W. Gibson (London: George Allen & Unwin, 1931).
12. Edmund Husserl, *The Origin of Geometry*, published as an appendix to Derrida, *Edmund Husserl's "Origin of Geometry": An Introduction*, trans. J. Leavey Jr. (New York: Nicolas Hays, 1978).
13. Jacques Derrida, *Speech and Phenomena, and Other Essays on Husserl's Theory of Signs*, trans. D. Allison (Evanston: Northwestern University Press, 1973), 52.
14. Ibid., 40.

15. Derrida, *Edmund Husserl's "Origin of Geometry": An Introduction*.
16. Derrida, *Margins of Philosophy*, 268.
17. Mark Bevir, "Objectivity in History," *History and Theory* 33(3) (1994): 328–44.
18. See Nicholas Rescher, *Methodological Pragmatism* (Oxford: Basil Blackwell, 1977); Karl Popper, *Objective Knowledge: An Evolutionary Approach* (Oxford: Clarendon Press, 1972); Ludwig Wittgenstein, *On Certainty*, trans. D. Paul and G. Anscombe (Oxford: Basil Blackwell, 1974).
19. Ludwig Wittgenstein, *Philosophical Investigations*, trans. G. Anscombe (Oxford: Basil Blackwell, 1972).
20. Wittgenstein, *Philosophical Investigations*, 43, 126. Not all ordinary language philosophy exhibits these problems; much of Wittgenstein's work, and also that of many of his followers, conveys a view of philosophy very close to my account of a reconstituted phenomenology. See R. W. Newell, *The Concept of Philosophy* (London: Methuen, 1967).

Chapter 4

1. Consider yourself warned: I'm going to continue to make puns. Literary critics as diverse as William Empson and Jonathan Culler warned writers of what I already have experienced: that it's common to sneer at puns as the lowest form of humor, and that puns need to provide some excuse for being. Empson wrote, "Indeed, if the pun is producing *no* additional effect it has no function and is of no interest." William Empson, *Seven Types of Ambiguity: A Study of Its Effects in English Verse, Revised Edition* (London: Chatto and Windus, 1949), 102. But as Culler noted, puns are also "lively instances of lateral thinking, exploiting the fact that language has ideas of its own." Given the unstable circumstances of presence, puns seem appropriate; but readers must decide for themselves. See Jonathan Culler, "The Call of the Phoneme," in Culler, ed., *On Puns: The Foundation of Letters* (London: Basil Blackwell, 1988), 1–17; quote at 15. My thanks to Steven Minas for these references.
2. Michael Roth, "Photographic Ambivalence and Historical Consciousness," *History and Theory* Theme Issue 48 (December 2009): 82–94. This special issue of *History and Theory* is extraordinarily rich in essays dealing with how historians look at photographs.
3. Roland Barthes coined the term "punctum" to indicate a photograph's ability to strike its viewer as something significant: "a photograph's *punctum* is that accident which pricks me (but also bruises me, is poignant to me)." *Camera Lucida* (New York: Hill and Wang, 1981), 27; as presence, 87; for the "reality effect," see his "Historical Discourse," in *Structuralism: A Reader*, ed. Michael Lane (London: Jonathan Cape, 1970), 145–54. See also Roth, "Photographic Ambivalence," 87.
4. See Georges Didi-Huberman, *Confronting Images: Questioning the Ends of a Certain History of Art* (University Park: Pennsylvania State University Press, 2005).
5. Lloyd Kramer, "Searching for Something That Is Here and There and Also Gone," *History and Theory* 48, no. 1 (February 2009): 85–97.

6. Eelco Runia, "Presence," *History and Theory* 45, no.1 (February 2006): 1–29; quote at 1. Further references are given in the text.
7. Frank Ankersmit, *Sublime Historical Experience* (Stanford: Stanford University Press, 2005); Susan A. Crane, *Collecting and Historical Consciousness in Early Nineteenth Century Germany* (Ithaca: Cornell University Press, 2000), 1–37.
8. Kramer, "Searching," 86 and 92.
9. Ethan Kleinberg, "Presence *in Absentia*," *Storia della Storiografia* 55 (2009): 43–59; quote at 58.
10. Hans Ulricht Gumbrecht, *The Production of Presence: What Meaning Cannot Convey* (Stanford: Stanford University Press, 2004), 145.
11. Ibid., 4–7.
12. See Greg Dening, "Performing on the Beaches of the Mind," *History and Theory* 41, no.1 (February 2002): 1–24.
13. Of the many scholarly accounts of Ranke's vivid, sensual language in his descriptions of archival work, see the witty interpretation by Bonnie Smith in her book *The Gender of History: Men, Women, and Historical Practice* (Cambridge: Harvard University Press, 1998).
14. Julia Adeney Thomas, "The Evidence of Sight," *History and Theory* Theme Issue 48 (December 2009): 151–68; quote at 151.
15. Thomas, "Evidence," 157; see also Joan Scott, "The Evidence of Experience," *Critical Inquiry* 17 (Summer 1991), which Thomas also cites.
16. Jerome de Groot plays off the economics of consumption as much as the gastronomies of past cultures in reenactment festivals in his book, *Consuming History: Historians and Heritage in Contemporary Popular Culture* (London: Routledge, 2009).
17. Claudio Fogu, "Digitalizing Historical Consciousness," *History and Theory* Theme Issue 47 (May 2009): 103–21.
18. Gumbrecht, *Production*, 11.
19. William Dilthey, *Selected Writings* (Cambridge University Press, 1976), 209.
20. Ibid., 192.
21. Ibid,, 221.
22. Robin Kelsey, "Of Fish, Birds, Cats, Mice, Spiders, Flies, Pigs, and Chimpanzees: How Chance Casts the Historic Action Photograph into Doubt," *History and Theory* Theme Issue 48 (December 2009): 59–76.
23. Frank Ankersmit, "Statements, Texts and Pictures," in *New Philosophy of History*, ed. Frank Ankersmit and Hans Keller (London: Reaktion Books, 1995), 212–40.
24. J. D. Braw, "Vision as Revision," *History and Theory* 47, no.4 (December 2007): 48.
25. Ankersmit, "Statements," 239.
26. Walter Benjamin, "The Task of the Translator," in *Illuminations*, ed. Hannah Arendt (New York: Schocken, 1968); Paul De Man, "Conclusions: Walter Benjamin's 'The Task of the Translator,'" in De Man, *The Resistance to Theory* (Minneapolis: University of Minnesota Press, 1986). Further references are given in the text.
27. See Miriam Bratu Hansen, "America, Paris, the Alps: Kracauer (and Benjamin) on Cinema and Modernity," in *Cinema and the Invention of Modern Life*, ed. Leo Charney and Vanessa Schwartz (Berkeley: University of California Press, 1995).

Notes to Pages 73–80   209

28. Carol Jacobs, "The Monstrosity of Translation," *Modern Language Notes*, 90 (1975), 755–766; cited in De Man, 90–91.
29. Didi-Huberman, *Confronting Images*, 18.
30. Ibid., 28.
31. Cathy Card, *The Atrocity Paradigm: A Theory of Evil* (Cambridge: Cambridge University Press, 2002), 9–16.
32. See Susan A. Crane, "Choosing Not to Look: Representation, Repatriation, and Holocaust Atrocity Photography," *History and Theory* 47, no. 3 (October 2008): 309–30.
33. Jay Prosser, in his introduction to *Picturing Atrocity,* suggests that photography's ability to produce atrocity as spectacle is precisely one of the reasons that photography is now "in crisis." See Geoffrey Batchen, et al,. *Picturing Atrocity: Photography in Crisis* (London: Reaktion Books, 2012), 9.
34. See Elaine Scarry, *The Body in Pain: The Making and Unmaking of the World* (New York: Oxford University Press, 1985).
35. Omer Bartov, *Erased: Vanishing Traces of Jewish Galicia in Present-Day Ukraine* (Princeton: Princeton University Press, 2007).
36. See Paul Williams, *Memorial Museums: The Global Rush to Commemorate Atrocities* (New York: Berg Publishers, 2007), 72.
37. Ibid., 73.
38. I am grateful to David Gremling for this timely reminder.
39. Georges Didi-Huberman, *Images in Spite of All: Four Photographs from Auschwitz* (Chicago: University of Chicago Press, 2008).

Chapter 5

This article was written as part of the development of a book-length manuscript, *Curatorial Practice and the Pursuit of Social Justice: A Pedagogy of Witnessing,* forthcoming (Albany: State University of New York Press). The research informing this manuscript was funded by the Social Sciences and Humanities Research Council (Canada). Many thanks to members of the Testimony and Historical Memory Project at the University of Toronto for their comments on previous drafts. A special thanks to Laura Thrasher for her close reading and invaluable substantive suggestions.

1. Dora Apel, "On Looking," in *Imagery of Lynching: Black Men, White Women, and the Mob* (New Brunswick, N.J.: Rutgers University Press, 2004), 13–14.
2. The notion of "rendition" is precisely meant in its intertwined connotations of an action that gives forth, surrenders up, returns, and provides a visual representation.
3. Walter Benjamin, "On the Concept of History," in *Walter Benjamin: Selected Writings, Volume 4, 1938–1940* (Cambridge: Belknap Press of Harvard University Press, 2003), 390.
4. Robert Gibbs, "Messianic Epistemology: Thesis IV," in *Walter Benjamin and History*, ed. Andrew Benjamin (New York: Continuum Press, 2005), 197–214.
5. Photographs from the Allen and Littlefield collection appear in *Without Sanctuary: Lynching Photographs in America* (Santa Fe, N.M.: Twin Palms Press, 1999), as well as on the website http://www.withoutsanctuary.org.

6. Early in the twentieth century photographs of lynching began to appear in anti-lynching publications, particularly in the African American press. See Jacqueline Goldsby, *A Spectacular Secret: Lynching in American Life and Literature* (Chicago: University of Chicago Press, 2006). For an important discussion of the multivalent circulation of such photographs, see Shawn Michelle Smith, "The Evidence of Lynching Photographs," in Dora Apel and Shawn Michelle Smith, *Lynching Photographs* (Berkeley: University of California Press, 2007).
7. Dora Apel, introduction to *Imagery of Lynching*, 2
8. Ibid., 3.
9. Mark Reinhardt and Holly Edwards, "Traffic in Pain," in *Beautiful Suffering: Photography and the Traffic in Pain*, ed. Mark Reinhardt, Holly Edwards, and Erina Duganne (Chicago: University of Chicago Press, 2006), 8.
10. Mieke Bal, "The Pain of Images," in Reinhardt, Edwards, and Duganne, *Beautiful Suffering*, 96n3.
11. Ibid., 107.
12. Mark Simpson, "Archiving Hate: Lynching Postcards at the Limit of Social Circulation," *English Studies in Canada* 30, no. 1 (March 2004): 17–38, quote at 35.
13. See the notion of an image as dialectics at a standstill in Walter Benjamin, *The Arcades Project* (Cambridge: Belknap Press of Harvard University Press, 1999) [N2,3], 462.
14. Jill Bennett, *Empathic Vision: Affect, Trauma, and Contemporary Art* (Stanford: Stanford University Press, 2005), 36. In the context of his work on Marcel Proust, Gilles Deleuze argued for a dichotomy between signs grasped cognitively and those felt without perceived recognition. However, in regard to my discussion of the public exhibition of images of suffering, such dichotomization is unnecessary and unsustainable.
15. Gilles Deleuze, *Proust and Signs: The Complete Text*, trans. Richard Howard (London: Athlone Press, 2000), 95.
16. The exhibition logics of the various exhibitions of the Allen and Littlefield collection make evident divergent answers to questions such as how a photograph of a lynching is to be viewed and understood as a historical document, what it could mean to display it publicly, and what such a display would require. Exhibition logics not only refer to precise modes of displaying juxtapositions of selected texts, images, and sounds that structure preferred ways of viewing and comprehending what is shown, but also refer to the practice of consigning, bestowing, and bequeathing a difficult memory that attempts to set the terms on which it is to be inherited.
17. Research interview with exhibition development team, Chicago, October 10, 2005.
18. Research interview with Tom Sokolowski, Pittsburgh, May 23, 2006.
19. See, for example, "The Case of the Jena 6: Black High School Students Charged with Attempted Murder for a Schoolyard Fight after Nooses Are Hung from a Tree," http://www.democracynow.org/shows/2007/7/10.
20. Brian Massumi, ed., *A Shock to Thought: Expression after Deleuze and Guattari* (New York: Routledge, 2002).

21. Dora Apel, "Lynching Photographs and the Politics of Public Shaming," in Dora Apel and Shawn Michelle Smith, *Lynching Photographs* (Berkeley: University of California Press, 2007).
22. Georges Didi-Huberman, *Images Malgré Tout* (Paris: Les Éditions de Minuit, 2003), 217–23.
23. Apel, 14.
24. Jean-Luc Nancy, "Forbidden Representation," in *The Ground of the Image* (New York: Fordham University Press, 2005), 36
25. Bennett, *Emphatic Vision*, 36.
26. Stanley Cavell, "Knowing and Acknowledging," in *Must We Mean What We Say?* (Cambridge: Cambridge University Press, 2002), 238–66; Emmanuel Levinas, "Useless Suffering," in *Entre Nous: Thinking of the Other*, trans. Michael B. Smith and Barbara Harshav (New York: Columbia University Press 1998), 91–102. The felt responsibility to express one's nonindifference was evident in the numerous and extensive visitor comments written at both exhibitions. These will be discussed in depth in my forthcoming book, *Curatorial Practice and the Pursuit of Social Justice: A Pedagogy of Witnessing*.
27. Bennett, Emphatic Vision, 43.
28. Nancy, "Forbidden Representation," in *Ground of the Image*, 40.
29. Ibid., 38.
30. Goldsby, *Spectacular Secret*, 13–15. Goldsby's account is informed by citations from S. Burdett, "A Test of Lynch Law: An Exposé of Mob Violence and the Courts of Hell" (Seattle: n.p., 1904), in D. A. P. Murray Pamphlet Collection (microfilm), United States Library of Congress.
31. Bal, "Pain of Images," 102.
32. Nancy, "Forbidden Representation," in *Ground of the Image*, 38–39; quote at 39.
33. In a visual event constituted as a super-representation, the encounter with images is clearly traumatic and as such is unable to be processed as experience.
34. It is possible that the serial repetition of a large number of photographs side by side may have mitigated the affect force of the visual event. However, it is also conceivable that this visual abundance of difficult images drove viewers to concentrate on specific photographs in the series. See Jennifer Bonnell and Roger I. Simon, "Difficult Exhibitions and Intimate Encounters," *Museum and Society* 5, no. 2 (July 2007); http://www.le.ac.uk/ms/museumsociety.htm.
35. Michael Tymkiw, "Debunking the Myth of the *saubere Wehrmacht*," *Word and Image* 23, no. 4 (October–December 2007): 485–92.
36. Bernd Hüppauf, "Emptying the Gaze: Framing Violence through the Viewfinder," *New German Critique* no. 72 (Autumn 1997): 3–44.
37. Cited in ibid., 7.
38. Jan Phillip Reemtsma, "Two Exhibitions—A Review," posted spring 2004, Hamburger Institut für Sozialforschung, "*Verbrechen der Wehrmacht. Dimensionen des Vernichtungskrieges 1941–1944.*" Available at http://www.his-online.de/cms.asp?IDN=392&H='512'.
39. Theodor Adorno, "Cultural Criticism and Society," in *Can One Live after Auschwitz? A Philosophical Reader* (Stanford: Stanford University Press, 2003), 160.

Chapter 6

1. Hans Ulrich Gumbrecht, *Production of Presence: What Meaning Cannot Convey* (Stanford: Stanford University Press, 2004), xv.
2. Ibid., 53, 137.
3. Ibid., 138.
4. Ibid., 136.
5. Ibid., 66.
6. Ibid., 105, 133. See Jean-Luc Nancy, *The Birth to Presence*, trans. Brian Holmes and others (Stanford: Stanford University Press, 1993), 5.
7. Gumbrecht, *Production of Presence*, 139.
8. David Hume, *A Treatise of Human Nature,* 2nd ed., ed. L. A Selby-Bigge and P. H. Nidditch (Oxford: Clarendon Press, 1980), 319, 320.
9. Adam Smith, *Theory of Moral Sentiments*, ed. Knud Haakonssen (Cambridge: Cambridge University Press, 2002), 11–12.
10. See Talal Assad, "French Secularism and 'Islamic Veil Affair'," *Hedgehog Review: Critical Reflections on Contemporary Culture* (Spring and Summer 2006): 93–106; and Joan Wallach Scott, *The Politics of the Veil* (Princeton: Princeton University Press, 2007).
11. Harriet Beecher Stowe, *Uncle Tom's Cabin, or Life Among the Lowly*, intro. Darryl Pickney (New York: Signet, 1998), 480.
12. Ibid., 90.
13. Ibid., 99.
14. That Stowe's characters become caricatures and are not real people at all has too often been noted to require mention here except to add that there is no very easy way to distinguish the aesthetic effect of presence and the real presence of others. In all human dealings with the world, some element of schematization or caricature seems to play a part.
15. Paul Smith, *Primitive America: The Ideology of Capitalist Democracy* (Minneapolis: University of Minnesota Press, 2007), 1–27; Benjamin Franklin, *The Interests of Great Britain Considered with Regards to her Colonies . . . to which are added, Observations Concerning the Increase of Mankind, Peopling of Countries, etc.* (London and Boston: B. Mecom, 1760); Thomas Jefferson, *Notes on the State of Virginia*, ed. Frank Shuffleton (New York: Penguin Books, 1999), 91.
16. Even this, of course, was not wholly new in American discourse, which has associated various forms of civil strife and terrorist violence with immigrant groups including Irish workers, Italian anarchists, and an array of communist infiltrators from foreign lands.
17. Gumbrecht himself remarks that novels and films, even those usually thought of as debased, might create complex effects of "presentification" as notable as those in great art; Gumbrecht, *Production of Presence*, 123.
18. In much simpler terms than Nancy's, the opposition posed here relates to the distinction he makes in *The Creation of the World or Globalization* between globalization, as a discourse of the world as one finds it—a sophistry of policy, as Stowe might have put it—and mondialization, or the creation of the world meaning

"immediately, without delay, reopening each possible struggle for a world, that is, for what must form the contrary of a global injustice against the background of general equivalence" (54). In this particular work, Nancy equates this struggle with justice and meaning and I take his point here as my point of departure to consider what the struggle with or for justice might actually mean.
19. I refer, of course, to Agamben's widely influential analysis in *Homer Sacer: Sovereign Power and Bare Life*, trans. Daniel Heller-Roazen (Stanford: Stanford University Press, 1998) and *States of Exception*, trans. Kevin Attell (Chicago: University of Chicago Press, 2005). For a communitarian critique of liberal ideas of justice and the state, see Michael Sandel, *Liberalism and the Limits of Justice* (Cambridge: Cambridge University Press, 1982).
20. This work moves from philosophy and literature to the practical realm of jurisprudence. See, for example, Jennifer Gordon's lawyerly and activist attempt to conceptualize a citizenship not limited to national borders in "Transnational Labor Citizenship," *Southern California Law Review* 80 (2007): 503.

Chapter 7

1. Hans Ulrich Gumbrecht, *Production of Presence: What Meaning Cannot Convey* (Stanford: Stanford University Press, 2004), 3.
2. Amitav Ghosh, *The Shadow Lines* (New York: Mariner Books, Houghton and Mifflin, 1988), 228.
3. Michel Foucault, "Of Other Spaces," *Diacritics* 16 (Spring 1986): 24; originally published in 1967.
4. Mary Louise Pratt, *Imperial Eyes: Travel Writing and Transculturation*. (London: Routledge, 1992), 4. Ortiz, F. (1978) *Contrapunto Cubano (1947–1963)*, Caracas: Biblioteca Ayacucho, and Rama, Angel (1982), *Transculturacion narrativa en America Latin*, Mexico City: Siglo 21.
5. Mikhail Bakhtin, *The Dialogic Imagination: Four Essays*, ed. Michael Holquist, trans. Caryl Emerson and Michael Holquist (Austin: University of Texas Press, 1981), 330.
6. Ibid., 314–15.
7. Ibid., 272.
8. I first proposed this model in "Constitutive Graphonomy," *Kunapipi* 11, no. 1 (1989): 53–78, to address arguments about cultural "authenticity," but it is eminently adaptable to the question of transcultural negotiation. See an updated version in chapter 8, "How Books Talk," in *Caliban's Voice: The Transformation of English in Post-Colonial Literatures* (London: Routledge, 2008).
9. Gumbrecht, *Production of Presence*, 52.
10. Linton Kwesi Johnson, "Reggae Fi Dada," in *Tings and Times: Selected Poems* (Newcastle-on-Tyne: Bloodaxe Books, 1991).
11. Cited in Gumbrecht, *Production of Presence*, 66.
12. Ibid., 66.
13. James Berry, "Caribbean Proverb Poem 1," in *News for Babylon: The Chatto Book of Westindian-British Poetry*, ed. James Berry (London: Chatto and Windus, 1984).

14. Linton Kwesi Johnson, "Street 66," in *Dread Beat and Blood* (London: Bogle d'Overture, 1975).
15. Valerie Bloom, "Language barrier," in *Touch Mi, Tell Mi* (London: Bogle d'Overture, 1983).
16. Nissim Ezekiel, *Collected Poems 1952–1988* (Delhi: Oxford University Press, 1989), 268.
17. A. P. Elkin, *The Australian Aborigines* (Sydney: Angus and Robertson, 1974 [1946]), 78.
18. James Clifford, *Person and Myth: Maurice Leenhardt in the Melanesian World* (Berkeley: University of California Press, 1982), 172.
19. Chinua Achebe, *Arrow of God* (London: Heinemann, 1964), 12.
20. Martin Heidegger, "Conversation on a Country Path about Thinking," in Martin Heidegger, *Discourse on Thinking*, trans. John M. Anderson and E. Hans Freund (New York: Harper and Row, 1966), 56.
21. Ibid., 61.
22. Gumbrecht, *Production of Presence*, 128.
23. Ibid., 98.

Chapter 8

1. I thank Frank Ankersmit for letting me read his work on presence, historical experience, and representation. Also see chapter 8 ("Presence") of his *Meaning, Truth, and Reference in Historical Representation* (Ithaca: Cornell University Press, 2012).
2. V. S. Naipaul, *An Area of Darkness* (New York: Macmillan 1965), 213. Why should ahistorical features of Indian sensibility be seen as a "lack" and not as part of an "Indian" way of approaching and conceptualizing history?
3. Rabindranath Tagore, "Bharatbarsher Itihasa," in *Rabindra Rachanavali*, vol. 13 (Calcutta: Government of West Bengal, 1989), 123.
4. N. A. Nikam, *Some Concepts of Indian Culture: A Philosophical Interpretation* (Shimla: Indian Institute of Advanced Study, 1967), 10–11. The Vedic dharma signifies the teachings of the Vedas in regard to philosophy, rituals, and discipline in life. It is also known as the *sanatana dharma*, which is followed by the Hindus. It protects one from falling down or ruining oneself in any manner. It provides one with welfare, progress, and success, both spiritual and material, in life. It appears that *sanatana dharma* alone existed before the birth of other religions of the world, and still continues to exist. See Pranab Bandyopadhyay, *The Hindus: A Noble Race* (Calcutta: United Writers, 1993), 19–20.
5. Madhav Despande, "History, Change and Permanence: A Classical Indian Perspective," in *Contributions to South Asian Studies*, ed. Gopal Krishna (Delhi: Oxford University Press, 1979), 11.
6. Quoted from R. C. Mazumdar, "Sources of Indian History," in *The Vedic Age*, ed. R. C. Mazumdar (London: George Allen & Unwin, 1952), 49–50.
7. See D. S. Sarma, *Hinduism through the Ages* (Bombay: Bharatiya Vidya Bhavan, 1956), 1.
8. Troy Wilson Organ, *The Hindu Quest for the Perfection of Man* (Athens: Ohio University Press, 1970), 30–31.

9. Prakash N. Desai, *Health and Science in the Hindu Tradition: Continuity and Cohesion* (New York: Crossroads, 1989), 10.
10. Jawaharlal Nehru puts the matter in proper perspective: "This lack of historical sense did not affect the masses, for as elsewhere, and more so than elsewhere, they built up their view of the past from the traditional accounts and myth and story that were handed to them from generation to generation. This imagined history and mixture of fact and legend became widely known and gave to the people a strong and abiding cultural background. But the ignoring of history had evil consequences, which pursue us still. It produced a vagueness of outlook, a divorce from life, as it is, credulity, a woolliness of the mind where fact was concerned. That mind was not at all woolly in the far more difficult but inevitably vaguer and more indefinite realms of philosophy; it was both analytic and synthetic, often very critical, sometimes sceptical. But where fact was concerned, it was uncritical, perhaps it did not attach much importance to fact as such." See J. L. Nehru, *The Discovery of India* (New York: John Day Company, 1946), 93. This woolliness of the mind has confused history with presences and this messy ground has often been richly harvested by politicians in collusion with religious leaders.
11. Ranajit Guha, *History at the Limit of World-History* (New Delhi: Oxford University Press, 2003), 61.
12. See Ashis Nandy, *Alternative Sciences: Creativity and Authenticity in Two Indian Scientists*, in Nandy's *Return from Exile* (New Delhi: Oxford University Press, 1998), 5.
13. Ibid., 6.
14. Ainslie T. Embree, ed., *The Hindu Tradition* (New York: Random House, 1972), 220.
15. Zahiruddin Muhammad Babar founded the Mughal Empire in India after defeating Ibrahim Lodhi in the Battle of Panipat in 1526. His memoir survive as *Babarnama*, sustained narrative prose in Chagatai Turkish. Babar is believed to have destroyed a Hindu temple and in ruins of which he erected a masjid known as Babri Masjid.

A gust of breeze is reported to have blown away several pages of Babar's memoir. So contrary to what we know Babar as—the meticulous recorder of daily occurrences—the memoir provides a lacunae in the narrative (there is no account of what happened between April 2, 1528, and September 18, 1528). All historians agree on the fact that there is no way of finding out whether in the missing pages Babar had referred to either the Ram temple or the mosque in question. Questions remain as to the intent and politics behind the loss of pages: did Babar want to suppress the fact of his visit to Ayodhya for posterity so that he came through innocent of all charges related to the alleged demolition of the Ram temple? Why can't we accept the loss of papers as a mere accident? On the basis of the parallel drawn between the alleged demolition of the Ram temple, the building of the Babri mosque at the ruined site, and this particular lacuna in Babar's memoirs, can we assume that it is a mere coincidence of history? However, it is through such yawning holes in history that presence slithers in to rake up the cicada of controversy, teasing the past out with more stories that simmer and shimmer, stories which, most often, tantalize and avoid being dangled from the peg of hard, proven facts.

16. Vincent A Smith, *The Oxford History of India from the Earliest Times to the End of 1911* (Oxford: Clarendon Press, 1923), xviii–xix.
17. Gerald James Larson, *India's Agony over Religion* (Albany: State University of New York Press, 1995), 144.
18. Frank Ankersmit, "'Presence' and Myth," *History and Theory* 45(3), (October 2006): 335.
19. Julia Shaw, "Ayodhya's Sacred Landscape: Ritual, Memory, Politics and Archaeological 'Fact,'" *Antiquity* 74 (2000): 698.
20. Allan Megill, "History, Memory, Identity," *History of the Human Sciences* 11, no. 3 (1998): 47.
21. See Hans Ulrich Gumbrecht, *Production of Presence: What Meaning Cannot Convey* (Stanford: Stanford University Press, 2004), 96–99.
22. For an elaborate analysis of this aspect, see my "Memory, Narrative and the Doing of History," *Storia della Storiographia*, no. 54 (2008): 56–88.
23. Romila Thapar, *Ancient Indian Social History: Some Interpretations* (New Delhi: Orient Longman, 1978), 3–4.
24. D. K. Ganguly, *History and Historians in Ancient India* (New Delhi: Abhinav Publications, 1984), 7–8.
25. See Amit Chaudhuri, "In the Waiting-Room of History," *London Review of Books*, June 24, 2004, http://www.lrb.co.uk/v26/n12/chau01_.html.
26. In many ways it is difficult to explain what makes a religious festival for a particular community in India turn into a rendezvous for the rest and what makes our social fabric sustain itself within a hugely fragile communal network. Perhaps it explains to an extent the nature of Indian civilization in general outside the methodological entrapments of rationalist historiography. Even with the pogrom in Gujarat in 2002 where a minority community (predominantly the Muslim community) was put to the sword, the fires of communal animosity did not spread beyond the borders of this state. This cannot be fully explained as administrative efficiency. An indeterminate factor kept people elsewhere united.
27. Vinay Lal, "Gandhi, the Civilizational Crucible, and the Future of Dissent," *Futures* 31 (1999): 210.
28. See Rabindranath Tagore, "Itihasakatha," in *Rabindra Rachanavali*, vol. 14 (Calcutta: Government of West Bengal, 1989), 453–54.
29. James P. Carse, *Finite and Infinite Games: A Vision of Life as Play and Possibility* (New York: Ballantine Books, 1986), 165.
30. Arundhati Roy, *Power Politics* (Cambridge, Mass.: South End Press, 2001), 31.

Chapter 9

1. Alain Badiou, *Theoretical Writings*, ed. and trans. Ray Brassier and Alberto Toscano (London: Continuum, 2004), 191–92.
2. Gustave Le Bon, *The Crowd: A Study of the Popular Mind* (Kitchener: Batoshe Books, 2001), 13.
3. Ibid., 17.

4. Georg Simmel, "The Sociology of Space," *Simmel on Culture*, ed. David Frisby and Mike Featherstone (London: Sage, 1997), 145.
5. Elias Canetti, *Crowds and Power*, trans. Carol Stewart (Harmondsworth, England: Penguin, 1962), 15.
6. Ibid., 16.
7. Erving Goffman, "Where the Action Is," *Interaction Ritual* (New York: Pantheon, 1967), 167.
8. Michael Wolff, "Notes on the Behavior of Pedestrians," in *People in Places: The Sociology of the Familiar*, ed. Arnold Birenbaum and Edward Sagarin (London: Nelson, 1973), 48.
9. Hedy Brown, *People, Groups and Society* (Milton Keynes, England: Open University Press, 1985), 126.
10. Philip G. Zimbardo, *The Human Choice: Individuation, Reason, and Order versus Deindividuation, Impulse, and Chaos*, in *Nebraska Symposium on Motivation*, ed. W. J. Arnold and D. Levine (Lincoln: University of Nebraska Press, 1969).
11. Andrew Adamatzky, *Dynamics of Crowd-Minds: Patterns of Irrationality in Emotions, Beliefs, and Actions* (New York: World Scientific, 2005), 5.
12. Georg Gaskell and Robert Benewick, eds., *The Crowd in Contemporary Britain* (London: Sage, 1987).
13. Richard Berck, "A Gaming Approach to Crowd Behavior," *American Sociological Review* 39 (June 1974): 365.
14. Clark McPhail, *The Myth of the Madding Crowd* (Piscataway, N.J.: Aldine Transactions, 1991), xxii.
15. John Drury and Georgia Winter, "Social Identity as a Source of Strength in Mass Emergencies and Other Crowd Events," *International Journal of Mental Illness* 32 (2003–2004): 77–93.
16. Walter Benjamin, "On Some Motifs in Baudelaire," *Illuminations*, trans. Harry Zohn (London: Fontana, 1968).
17. Ibid., 168.
18. Ibid., 173.
19. Ibid., 162.
20. See Mary Esteve, *The Aesthetics and Politics of the Crowd in American Literature* (Cambridge: Cambridge University Press, 2003), and Nicolaus Mills, *The Crowd in American Literature* (Baton Rouge: Louisiana State University Press, 1986).
21. For example, John Plotz, *The Crowd: British Literature and Public Politics* (Berkeley: University of California Press, 2000).
22. George E. E. Rudé, *The Crowd in the French Revolution* (Oxford: Oxford University Press, 1959).
23. Ibid., 5.
24. George E. E. Rudé, *The Crowd in History: A Study of Popular Disturbances in France and England, 1730–1848* (London: Lawrence and Wishart, 1981 [1964]); E. P. Thompson, "The Moral Economy of the English Crowd in the Eighteenth Century," *Past and Present* 50 (February 1971): 76–136.
25. Rudé, *Crowd in History* , 4.

26. As a good example of this, see Mark Harrison, *Crowds and History: Mass Phenomena in English Towns, 1790–1835* (Cambridge: Cambridge University Press, 1988).
27. Numerous examples can be cited: Robert A. Nye, *The Origins of Crowd Psychology: Gustave Le Bon and the Crisis of Mass Democracy in the Third Republic* (London: Sage, 1975); Susanna Barrows, *Distorting Mirrors: Visions of the Crowd in Late Nineteenth Century France* (New Haven: Yale University Press, 1981); Serge Moscovici, *The Age of the Crowd: A Historical Treatise on Mass Psychology*, trans. J. C. Whitehouse (Cambridge: Cambridge University Press, 1985); Clark McPhail, *The Myth of the Madding Crowd* (Piscataway, N.J.: Aldine Transaction, 1991); Jaap van Ginneken, *Crowds, Psychology, and Politics, 1871–1899* (Cambridge: Cambridge University Press, 1992).
28. Jeffrey T. Schnapp and Matthew Tiews, introduction to *Crowds*, ed. Schnapp and Tiews (Stanford: Stanford University Press, 2006), x–xi.
29. Angelique Chrisafis et al., "Millions Worldwide Rally for Peace: Huge Turnout at 600 Marches from Berlin to Baghdad," *Guardian* (February 17, 2003). Writing in the *Sunday Times* on February 16, 2003 (page 2), Peter Conradi in "Demos Follow Sun around the Globe," for instance, offers "over 5 million" as a conservative estimate of numbers participating in "600 demonstrations around the globe."
30. Chrisafis et al., "Millions Worldwide Rally for Peace."
31. Press conference after the new Securities and Exchanges Commission chairman, Bill Donaldson, was sworn in at the White House on February 18, 2003. See http://www.npr.org/programs/atc/transcripts/2003/feb/030218.gonyea.html.
32. Blair's speech of February 15, 2003, at Labour's Local Government, Women's, and Youth conferences in Glasgow. See http://news.bbc.co.uk/1/hi/2765763.stm.
33. See, for instance, Lynette Clemetson, "Protest Groups Using Updated Tactics to Spread Antiwar Message," *New York Times* (January 15, 2003); Dominic Kennedy and Ben Hoyle, "Protesters Use Internet as Weapon to Stop a War," *Times* (February 14, 2003), 13; AP, "Anti-war Protesters Use Technology to Organize," *Sunday Morning Herald* (April 1, 2003).
34. Gary Younge, "Left Over? The Left in America Was Once a Powerful Force That Fought for Civil Rights and Helped to End the Vietnam War. But Today, with the US Poised to Attack Iraq, Where Are the Voices of Dissent?" *Guardian* (February 11, 2003).
35. Robbie Millen, "March for Anything, Anywhere," *Times* (February 12, 2003), 22.
36. Mark Steyn, "Marching for Terror," *Daily Telegraph* (February 15, 2003); Barbara Amiel, "If This Was a Peace March, Why Did Saddam Get No Stick?" *Daily Telegraph* (February 17, 2003).
37. Nick Cohen, "The Left Isn't Listening: The Stop the War Coalition Is the Greatest Threat to Any Hope for a Democratic Iraq," *Guardian* (February 15, 2003).
38. Scott Millar and Dearbhail McDonald, "Generations March against Iraq War," *Sunday Times* (February 16, 2003), 3.
39. Rajeev Syalm, Andrew Alderson, and Catherine Milner, "One Million March against War," *Daily Telegraph* (February 16, 2003).
40. Reports such as the following offered links between organizations such as International ANSWER and Not in Our Name to the "hard-left" and 1960s New Left:

Byron York, "Follow the Money: The Antiwar Money, That Is (Finance of the Antiwar Group Not in Our Name)," *National Review* (February 24, 2003); Dan Springer, "Anti-War Protests Have Big Price Tags," *Fox News* (March 18, 2003); Michael J. Waller, "Who's Paying for It All?" *Insight Magazine* (March 4, 2003).
41. Boris Buden, "The Revolution of 1989: The Past of Yet Another Illusion," in *The Manifesta Decade: Debates on Contemporary Art Exhibitions and Biennials in Post-Wall Europe*, ed. Barbara Vanderlinden and Elena Filipovic (Cambridge, Mass.: Roomade and MIT Press, 2005), 115.
42. Interview with Jeremy Bowen, "Today Programme: Arab World's Gdansk," *BBC News* (January 15, 2011). See http://news.bbc.co.uk/today/hi/today/newsid_9362000/9362677.stm.
43. Timothy Garton Ash, "If This Is Young Arab's 1989, Europe Must Be Ready with a Bold Response," *Guardian* (February 2, 2011).
44. Harris Mylonas and Wilder Bullard, "This Is No 1989 Moment for the Arab World," *Guardian* (February 8, 2011).
45. Peter Hallward, "Arab Uprisings Mark a Turning Point for the Taking," *Guardian* (February 22, 2011).
46. Kristian Coates Ulrichsen, David Held, and Alia Brahimi, "The Arab 1989?" *Open Democracy* (February 11, 2011). See http://www.opendemocracy.net/kristian-coates-ulrichsen-david-held-alia-brahimi/arab-1989.

Epilogue

1. Rabindranath Tagore, "What Is Art?," in *Personality* (London: Macmillan and Co., 1945), 29–30.
2. See Frank Ankersmit, *Meaning, Truth, and Reference in Historical Representation* (Ithaca: Cornell University Press, 2012).
3. See my "Aesthetics of Hunger: (In)fusion Approach, Literature, and the Other," *Symploke* 19, no. 1 (2011): 11–25.
4. "*Checos–è la poesia?*," in *A Derrida Reader: Between the Blinds*, ed. and trans. Peggy Kamuf (London: Harvester Wheatsheaf, 1991), 233.
5. See Fred Dallymyr, *Beyond Orientalism* (New Delhi: Rawat Publications, 2001), 42.
6. See Jacques Derrida, *Shibboleth: Pour Paul Celan*, trans. Joshua Wilner, in *Midrash and Literature*, ed. Geoffrey Hartman and Sanford Budick (New Haven: Yale University Press, 1986), 339.
7. Werner Hamacher, *Premises: Essays on Philosophy and Literature from Kant to Celan*, trans. Peter Fenves (Stanford: Stanford University Press, 1996), 225.
8. Gadamer notes that "the poetic text . . . does not refer back either to an original utterance nor to the intention of the speaker but is something that seems to originate in itself, so that in the fortune and felicity of its success, a poem surprises and overwhelms even the poet." Hans-Georg Gadamer, "Text and Interpretation," in *Dialogue and Deconstruction: The Gadamer-Derrida Encounter*, ed. Diane P. Michelfelder and Richard E. Palmer, trans. Dennis J. Schmidt and Richard E. Palmer (New York: State University of New York Press, 1989), 41–42.

9. Jean-Luc Nancy, "The Technique of the Present," http://www.usc.edu/dept/comp-lit/tympanum/4/nancy.html.
10. Jean Luc-Nancy, *The Multiple Arts: The Muses II*, ed. Simon Sparks (Stanford: Stanford University Press, 2006), 4.
11. See Jacques Derrida, *Politics of Friendship*, trans. George Collins (London: Verso, 1997).
12. Maurice Blanchot, *The Infinite Conversation*, trans. Susan Hanson (Minneapolis: University of Minnesota Press, 1993), 353.
13. Friedrich Schlegel, *"Athenäum* Fragments," in *Lucinde and the Fragments*, trans. Peter Firchow (Minneapolis: University of Minnesota Press, 1971), 206. Schlegel notes: 'a fragment like a miniature work of art, has to be entirely isolated from the surrounding world and be complete in itself like a hedgehog' (206).
14. Jacques Derrida, *"Checos–è la poesia?,"* in *A Derrida Reader: Between the Blinds*, ed. and trans. Peggy Kamuf (New York: Harvester Wheatsheaf, 1991), 233.
15. Ibid., 227.
16. Ibid., 233.
17. See Michel Deguy, *Recumbants: Poems*, trans. Wilson Baldridge (Middletown, Conn.: Wesleyan University Press, 2005), 84.
18. See Jacques Derrida, "Uninterrupted Dialogue: Between Two Infinities, the Poem," *Research in Phenomenology* 34 (2004): 12.
19. Nancy, *Multiple Arts: The Muses II*, 7.
20. Ibid., 8.
21. Ibid.
22. Ibid., 3.
23. Ibid., 7.
24. Jacques Derrida, "Poetics and Politics of Witnessing" (2000), trans. Rachel Bowlby, in *Sovereignties in Question: The Poetics of Paul Celan* ed. Th. Dutoit and O. Pasanen (New York: Fordham University Press, 2005): 95–96.
25. "For Once, Then, Something," Mark Richardson and Richard Poirier, eds., *Frost: Collected Poems, Prose and Plays* (Washington, D.C.: Library of America, 1995).
26. See my "Making Sense of Interpretation: Yes-ing and the (In)fusion Approach," *parallax* 16, no. 3 (2010): 107–17, and "Institutionalised Theory, (In)fusion, Desivad," *Oxford Literary Review* 28 (2006): 25–36.
27. Lisa Robertson, "The Present," in *R's Boat* (Berkeley: University of California Press, 2010).

Contributors

Bill Ashcroft is Professor of English at the University of New South Wales. A founding exponent of postcolonial theory, he was the coauthor of *The Empire Writes Back*, the first text to examine systematically a field that is now referred to as "postcolonial studies." He is author and coauthor of sixteen books including *Post-colonial Transformation* (Routledge, 2001), *On Post-colonial Futures* (Continuum, 2001), *Caliban's Voice* (Routledge, 2008), and over 120 chapters and papers.

Mark Bevir is Professor in the Department of Political Science, University of California, Berkeley. He is the author of *The Logic of the History of Ideas* (1999), *New Labour: A Critique* (2005), and *Key Concepts of Governance* (2009), and coauthor of *Interpreting British Governance* (2003) and *Governance Stories* (2006). His research interests include the philosophy of the human sciences, modern intellectual history, and governance.

Susan A. Crane is Associate Professor of Modern European History at the University of Arizona. Her research focuses on thematic issues of collective memory, historical consciousness, and Romanticism, particularly in modern German history. She is the author of *Collecting and Historical Consciousness in Early 19th-Century Germany* (Cornell University Press, 2000) and *Museums and Memory* (Stanford University Press, 2000). She is widely published in *History and Theory, Journal of Modern History, Criticism, American Historical Review, History and Memory, Storia della Storiographia*, and others.

Contributors

Ranjan Ghosh teaches in the department of English at the University of North Bengal. He was an Alexander von Humboldt Fellow in Germany and European Research Fellow in London. He has published in journals such as *diacritics*, *Oxford Literary Review*, *History and Theory*, *Parallax*, *Nineteenth Century Prose*, *Rethinking History*, *Storia della Storiografia*, *Angelaki*, and others. His many books include *(In)fusion Approach: Theory, Contestation, Limits* (2006), *Globalizing Dissent* (Routledge, 2009), *Edward Said, the Literary, Social and the Political World* (Routledge, 2009), and *Lover's Quarrel with the Past: Romance, Representation and Reading* (Berghahn Books, 2012).

Suman Gupta is Professor of Literature and Cultural History at the Open University UK, and Honorary Senior Research Fellow at Roehampton University. He is the author of, recently, *The Theory and Reality of Democracy: A Case Study in Iraq* (Continuum, 2006), *Social Constructionist Identity Politics and Literary Studies* (Palgrave Macmillan, 2007), *Literature and Globalization* (Polity, 2008), and *Imagining Iraq: Literature in English and the Iraq Invasion* (Palgrave-Macmillan, 2011).

Ethan Kleinberg is Professor of History and Letters at Wesleyan University and Executive Editor of *History and Theory*. He is the author of *Generation Existential: Heidegger's Philosophy in France, 1927–1961* (Cornell University Press). His research focuses on modern intellectual history and philosophy and theory of history. He is finishing a book-length manuscript on Emmanuel Levinas's Talmudic lectures in Paris after World War II and beginning work on a book about deconstruction and the writing of history.

John Michael is Professor of English and Visual and Cultural Studies at the University of Rochester and Chair of the English Department. He has published many articles on American literature, contemporary cultural studies, and critical theory. He is the author of *Emerson and Skepticism: The Cipher of the World* (Johns Hopkins University Press, 1988); *Anxious Intellects: Academic Professionals, Enlightenment Values, and Democratic Politics* (Duke University Press, 2000); and, most recently, *Identity and the Failure of America from Thomas Jefferson to the War on Terror* (University of Minnesota Press, 2008). He is working on a book called *Modern American Poetry in the Nineteenth Century: Poe, Whitman, Dickinson and the Figure of Death*.

Vincent P. Pecora is the Gordon B. Hinckley Professor of British Literature and Culture at the University of Utah. He is the author, most recently, of *Secularization and Cultural Criticism: Religion, Nation, and Modernity* (University of Chicago Press, 2006). He has just completed a book manuscript titled *Secularization without End: Beckett, Mann, and Coetzee,* and is working on a new book to be called *Anyone Is As Their Land Is: Autochthonous Modernism*.

Roger I. Simon was a Professor in the Department of Sociology and Equity Studies, Ontario Institute for Studies in Education at the University of Toronto. Over four decades he wrote extensively on culture, pedagogy, ethics, and social memory. His recent work addressed issues concerning the exhibition of material relating to mass violence, the implications of remembrance as a public pedagogy, and the ethics and impact of "difficult" images. His forthcoming book (in press) is entitled *Curatorial Practice and the Pursuit of Social Justice: A Pedagogy of Witnessing,* Albany: The State University of New York Press. Roger passed away on Rosh Hashanah of 2012.